jason shawn alexander
creator_writer_artist

luis nct
colorist

sherard jackson
lettering_book design

darragh savage
story editor

———

dedicated to
rheya alexander_windell middlebrooks

———

with story contributions by
christopher a taylor

additional story contributions by
dinora walcott

special thanks
gina walcott_brad r sohn

empty zone™

conversations with the dead

0001 00100000 01101111 01100110 0010

D1303463

IMAGE COMICS, INC.
Robert Kirkman – Chief Operating Officer
Erik Larsen – Chief Financial Officer
Todd McFarlane – President
Marc Silvestri – Chief Executive Officer
Jim Valentino – Vice-President

Eric Stephenson – Publisher
Corey Murphy – Director of Sales
Jeff Boison – Director of Publishing Planning & Book Trade Sales
Jeremy Sullivan – Director of Digital Sales
Kat Salazar – Director of PR & Marketing
Emily Miller – Director of Operations
Branwyn Bigglestone – Senior Accounts Manager
Sarah Mello – Accounts Manager
Drew Gill – Art Director
Jonathan Chan – Production Manager
Meredith Wallace – Print Manager
Briah Skelly – Publicity Assistant
Randy Okamura – Marketing Production Designer
David Brothers – Branding Manager
Ally Power – Content Manager
Addison Duke – Production Artist
Vincent Kukua – Production Artist
Sasha Head – Production Artist
Tricia Ramos – Production Artist
Jeff Stang – Direct Market Sales Representative
Emilio Bautista – Digital Sales Associate
Chloe Ramos-Peterson – Administrative Assistant
IMAGECOMICS.COM

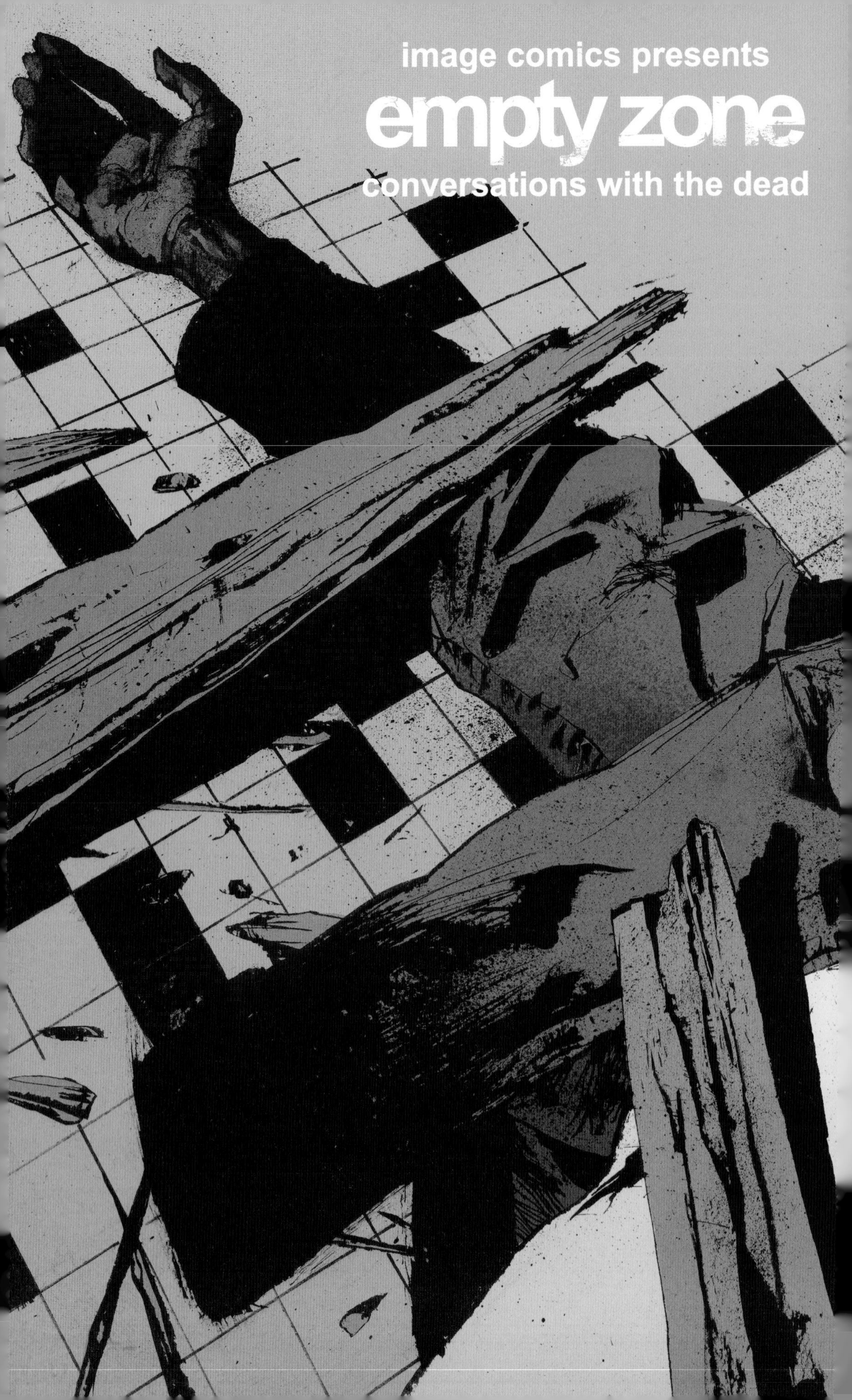
image comics presents
empty zone
conversations with the dead

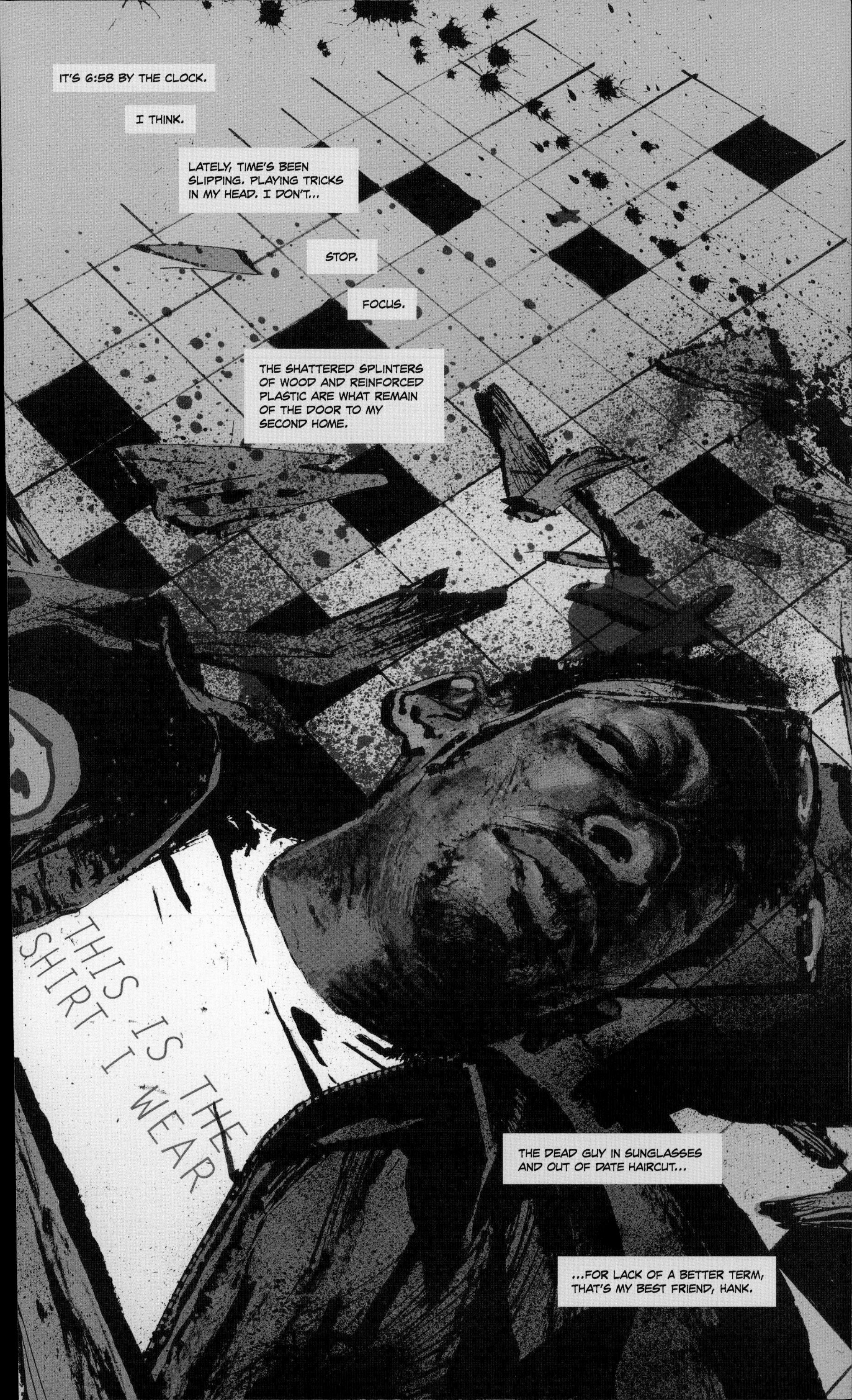
IT'S 6:58 BY THE CLOCK.
I THINK.
LATELY, TIME'S BEEN SLIPPING. PLAYING TRICKS IN MY HEAD. I DON'T...
STOP.
FOCUS.
THE SHATTERED SPLINTERS OF WOOD AND REINFORCED PLASTIC ARE WHAT REMAIN OF THE DOOR TO MY SECOND HOME.
THIS IS THE SHIRT I WEAR
THE DEAD GUY IN SUNGLASSES AND OUT OF DATE HAIRCUT...
...FOR LACK OF A BETTER TERM, THAT'S MY BEST FRIEND, HANK.

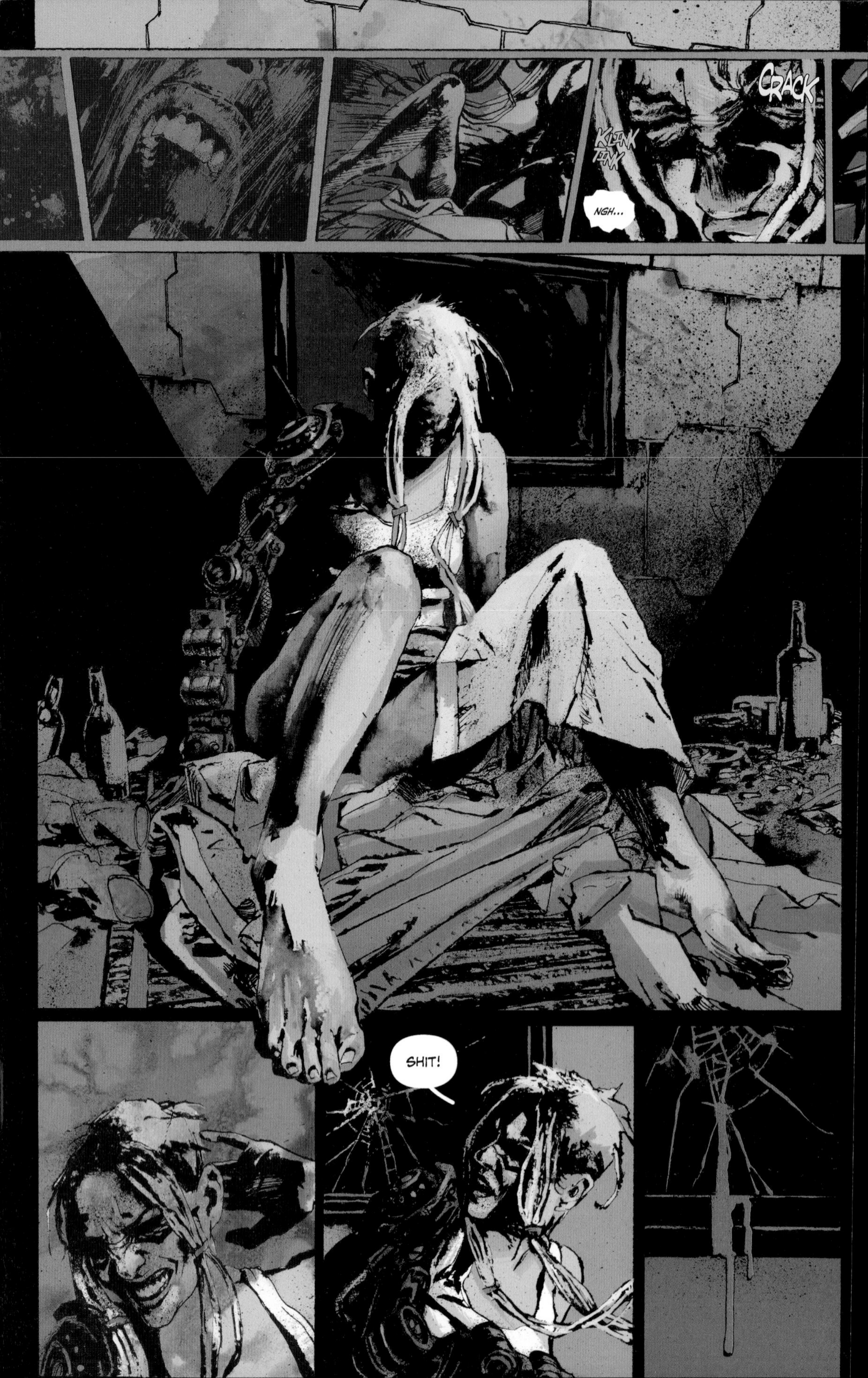
CRACK
KLINK
TINK
NGH...
SHIT!

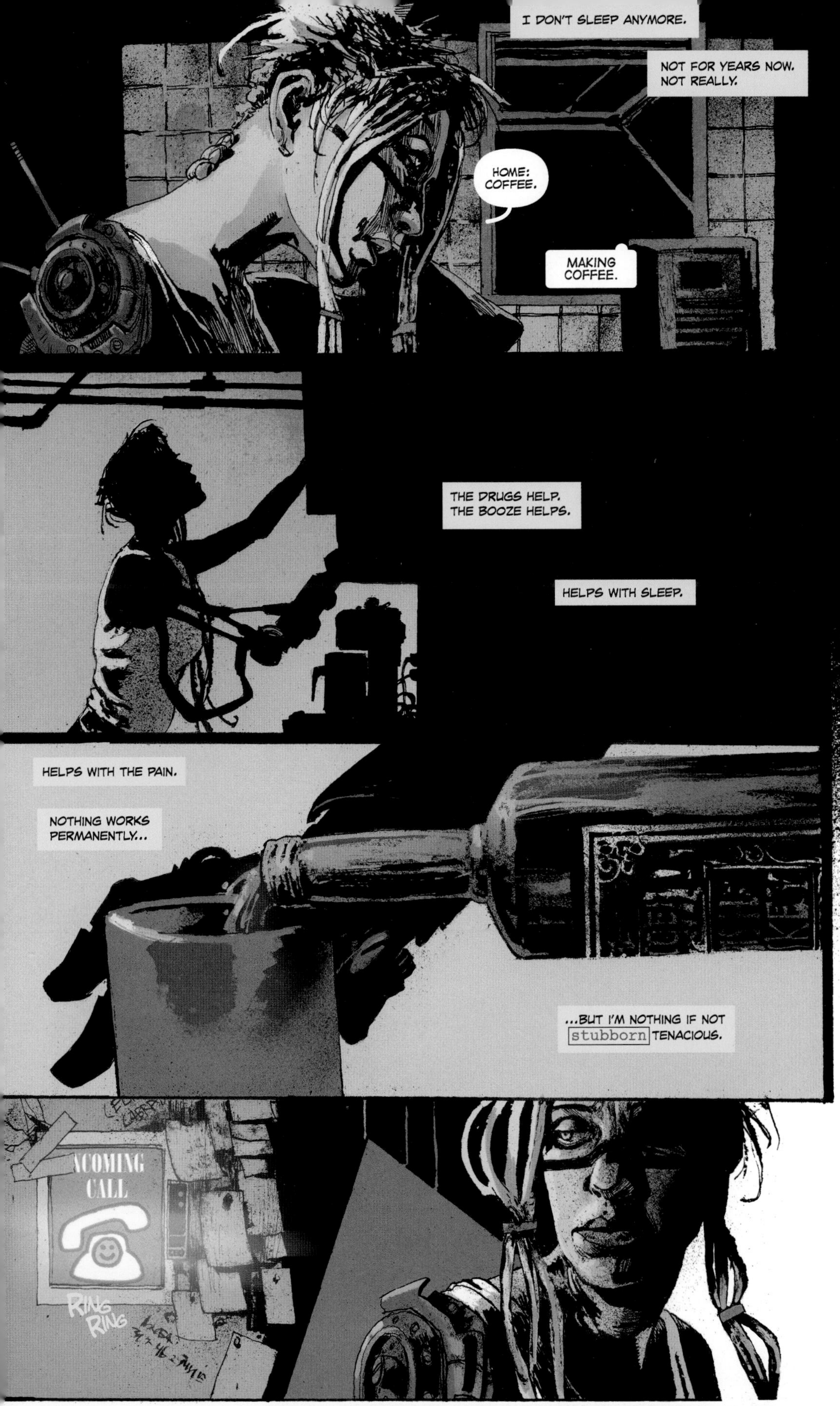
I DON'T SLEEP ANYMORE.
NOT FOR YEARS NOW. NOT REALLY.
HOME: COFFEE.
MAKING COFFEE.
THE DRUGS HELP. THE BOOZE HELPS.
HELPS WITH SLEEP.
HELPS WITH THE PAIN.
NOTHING WORKS PERMANENTLY...
...BUT I'M NOTHING IF NOT stubborn TENACIOUS.
NCOMING CALL
RING RING

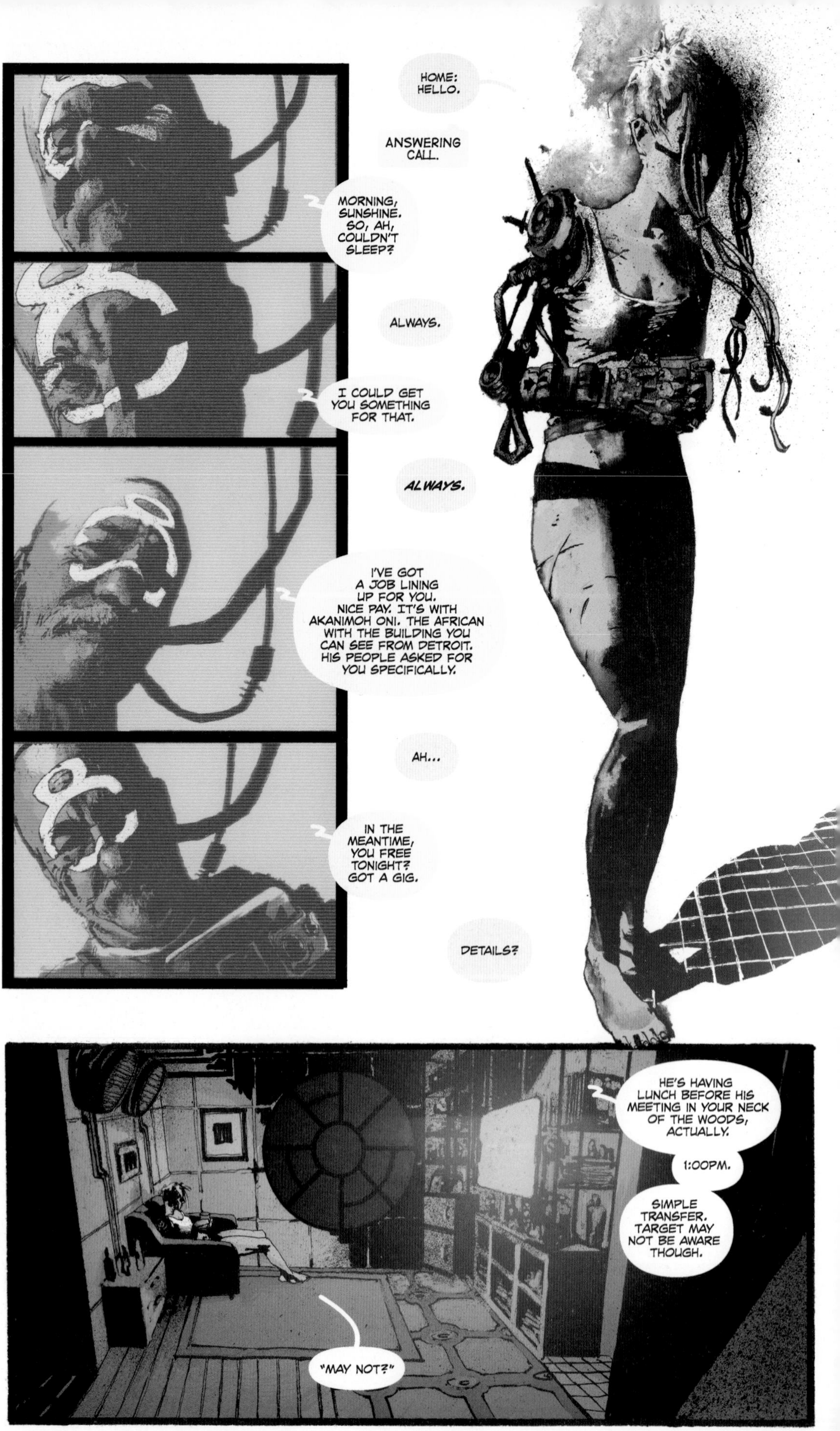
HOME: HELLO.
ANSWERING CALL.
MORNING, SUNSHINE. SO, AH, COULDN'T SLEEP?
ALWAYS.
I COULD GET YOU SOMETHING FOR THAT.
ALWAYS.
I'VE GOT A JOB LINING UP FOR YOU. NICE PAY. IT'S WITH AKANIMOH ONI. THE AFRICAN WITH THE BUILDING YOU CAN SEE FROM DETROIT. HIS PEOPLE ASKED FOR YOU SPECIFICALLY.
AH...
IN THE MEANTIME, YOU FREE TONIGHT? GOT A GIG.
DETAILS?
HE'S HAVING LUNCH BEFORE HIS MEETING IN YOUR NECK OF THE WOODS, ACTUALLY.
1:00PM.
SIMPLE TRANSFER. TARGET MAY NOT BE AWARE THOUGH.
"MAY NOT?"

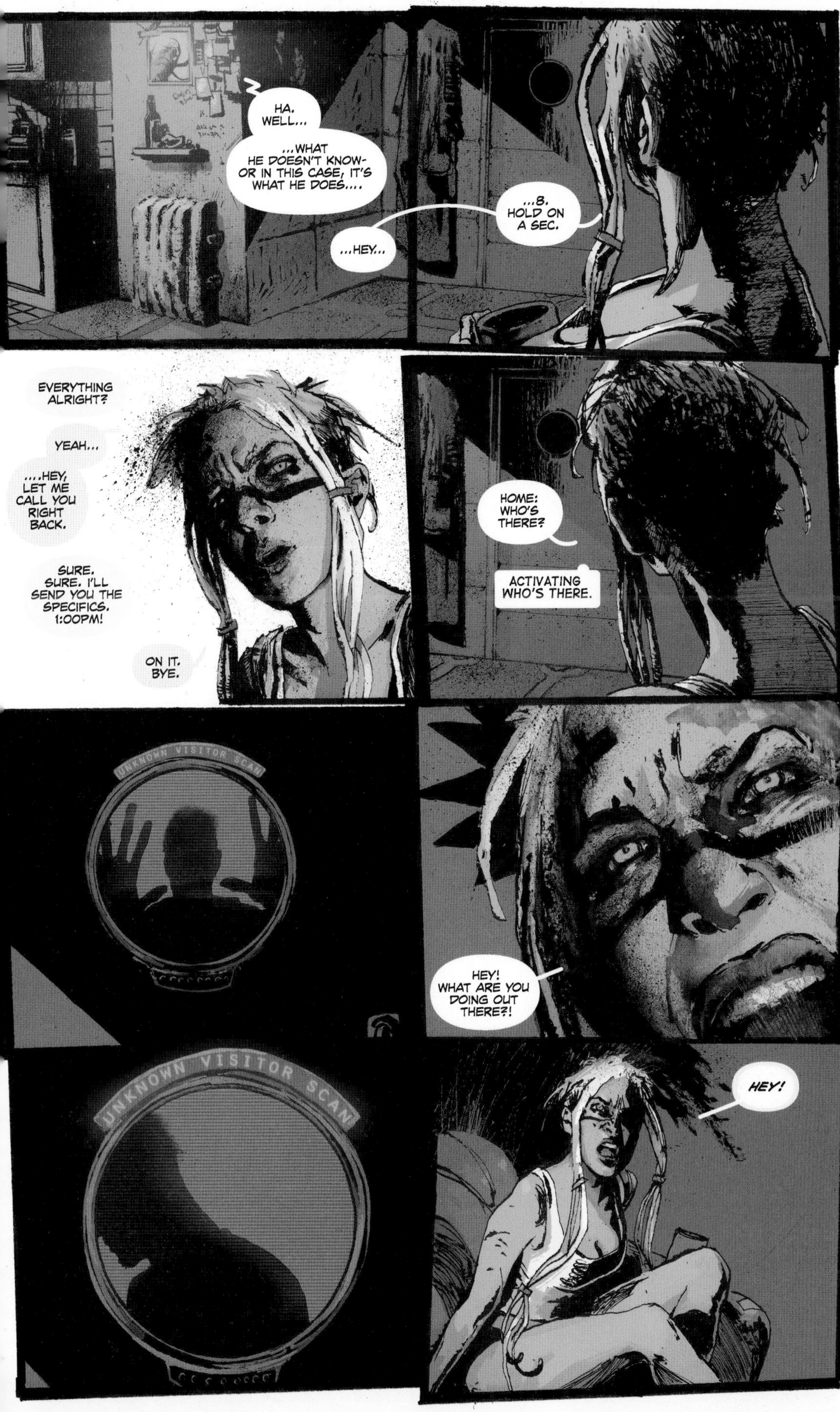

HA. WELL...
...WHAT HE DOESN'T KNOW- OR IN THIS CASE, IT'S WHAT HE DOES....
...HEY...
...8. HOLD ON A SEC.
EVERYTHING ALRIGHT?
YEAH...
....HEY, LET ME CALL YOU RIGHT BACK.
SURE. SURE. I'LL SEND YOU THE SPECIFICS. 1:00PM!
ON IT. BYE.
HOME: WHO'S THERE?
ACTIVATING WHO'S THERE.
UNKNOWN VISITOR SCAN
HEY! WHAT ARE YOU DOING OUT THERE?!
UNKNOWN VISITOR SCAN
HEY!

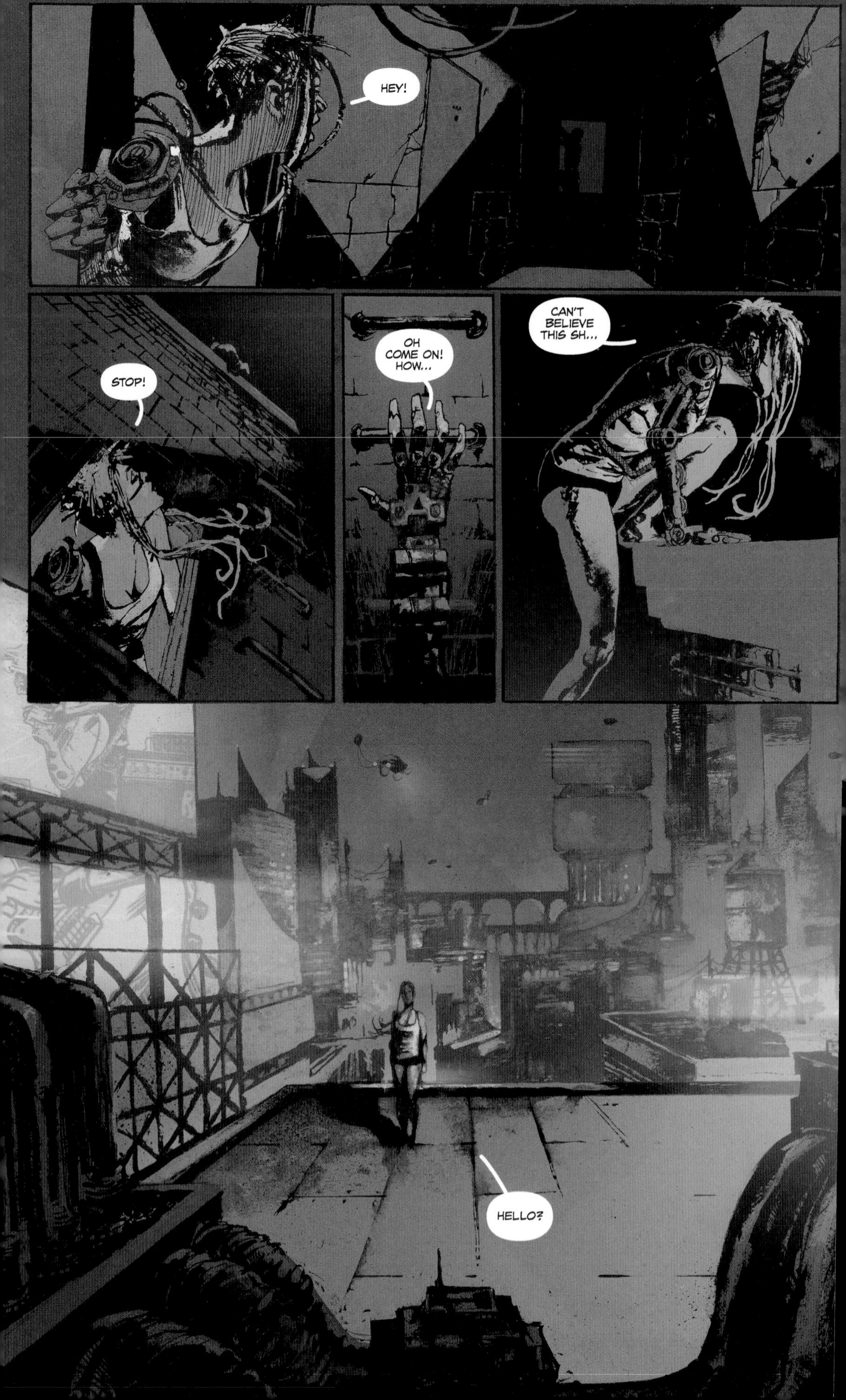
HEY!
STOP!
OH COME ON! HOW...
CAN'T BELIEVE THIS SH...
HELLO?

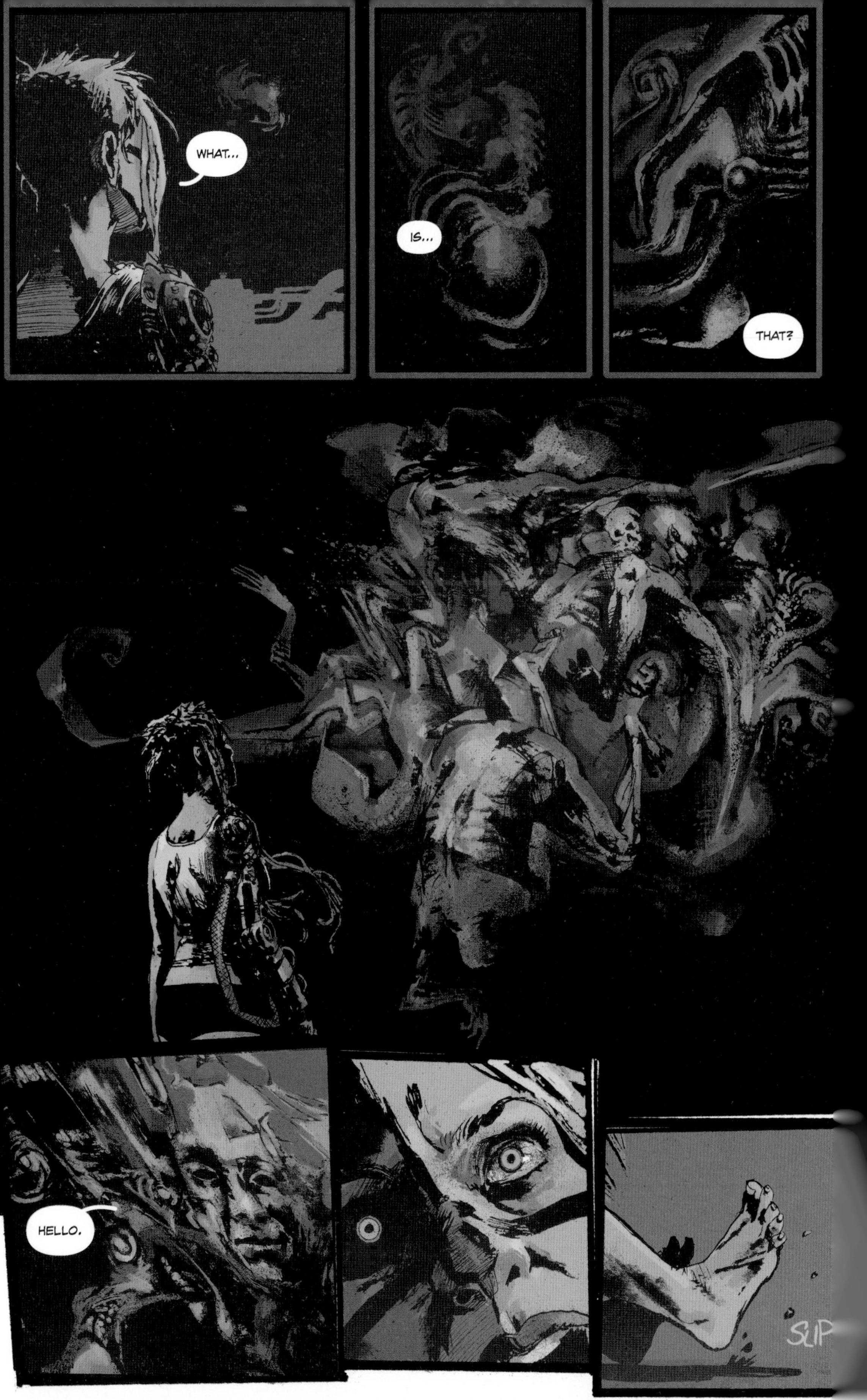
WHAT...
IS...
THAT?
HELLO.
SLIP

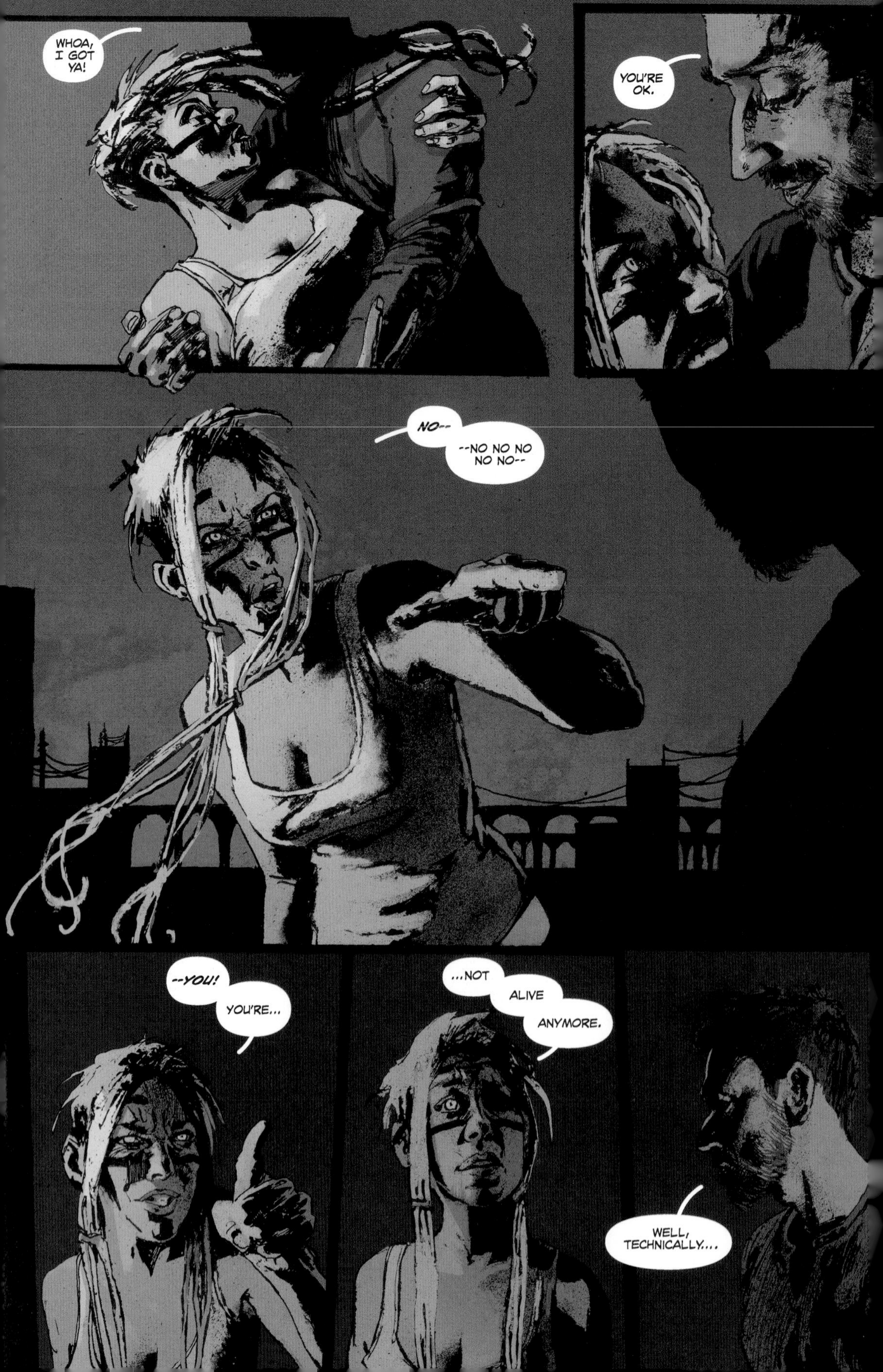
WHOA, I GOT YA!
YOU'RE OK.
NO--
--NO NO NO NO NO--
--YOU!
YOU'RE...
...NOT
ALIVE
ANYMORE.
WELL, TECHNICALLY....

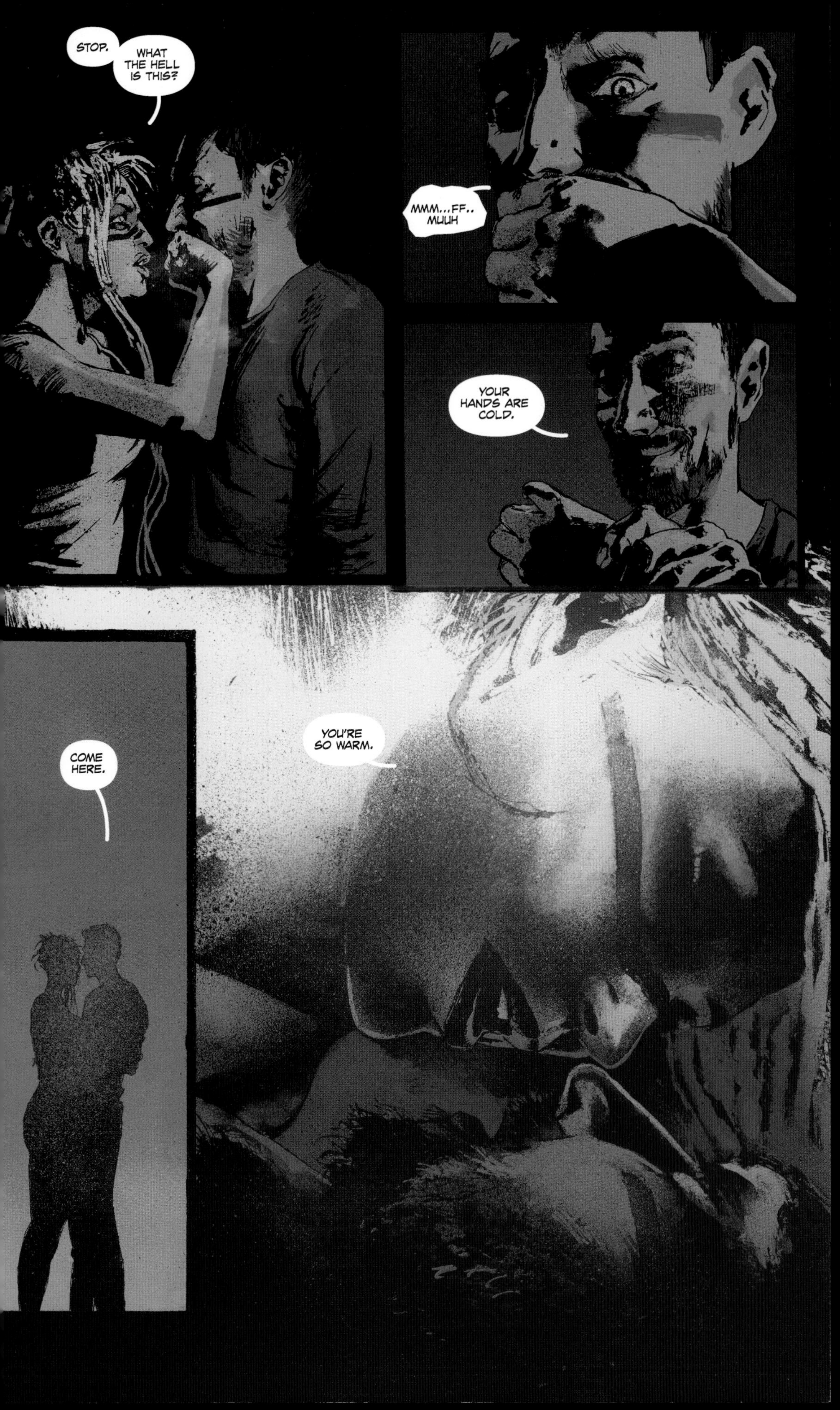
STOP.
WHAT THE HELL IS THIS?
MMM...FF.. MUUH
YOUR HANDS ARE COLD.
COME HERE.
YOU'RE SO WARM.

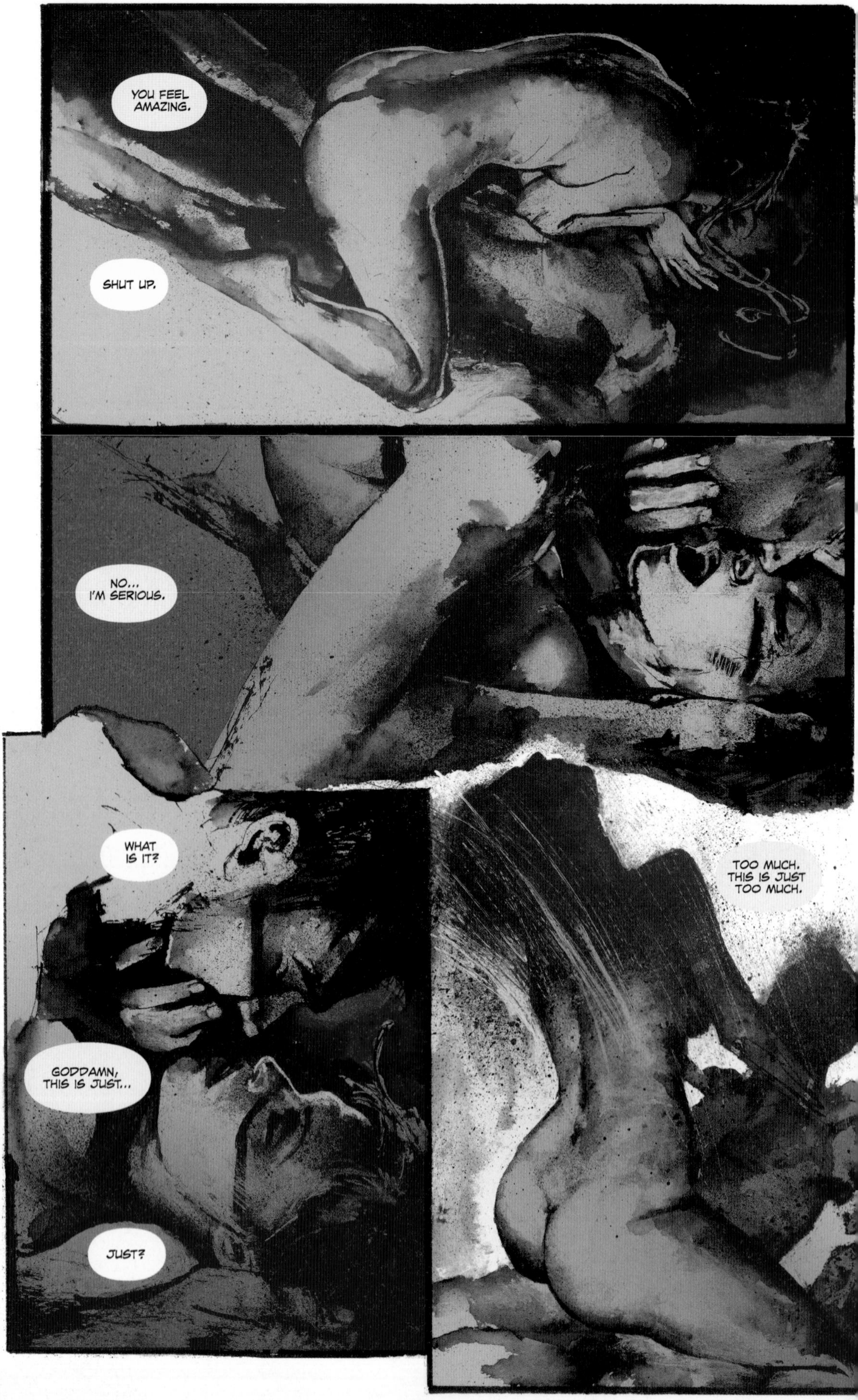
YOU FEEL AMAZING.
SHUT UP.
NO... I'M SERIOUS.
WHAT IS IT?
TOO MUCH. THIS IS JUST TOO MUCH.
GODDAMN, THIS IS JUST...
JUST?

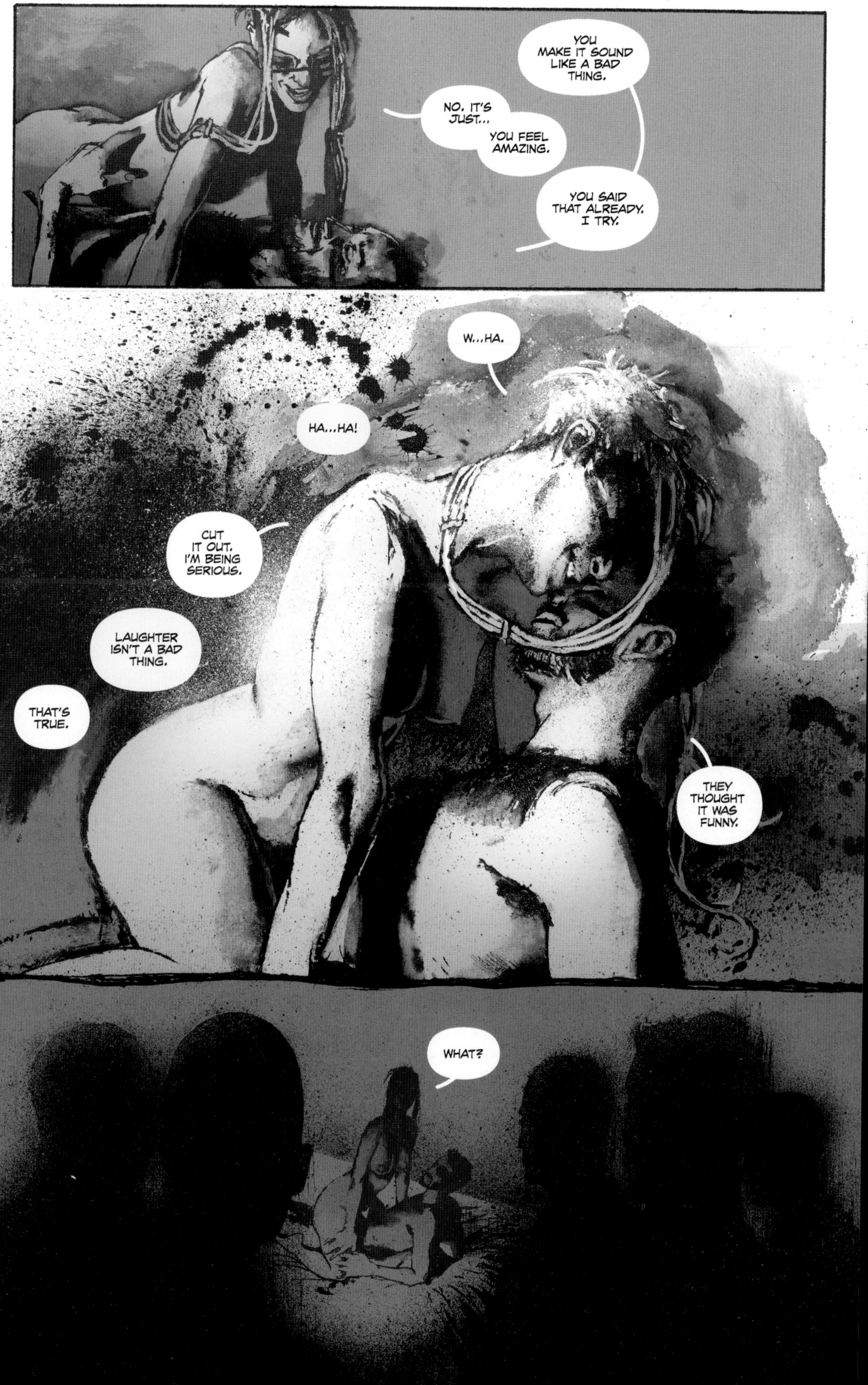
YOU MAKE IT SOUND LIKE A BAD THING.
NO. IT'S JUST...
YOU FEEL AMAZING.
YOU SAID THAT ALREADY. I TRY.
W...HA.
HA...HA!
CUT IT OUT. I'M BEING SERIOUS.
LAUGHTER ISN'T A BAD THING.
THAT'S TRUE.
THEY THOUGHT IT WAS FUNNY.
WHAT?

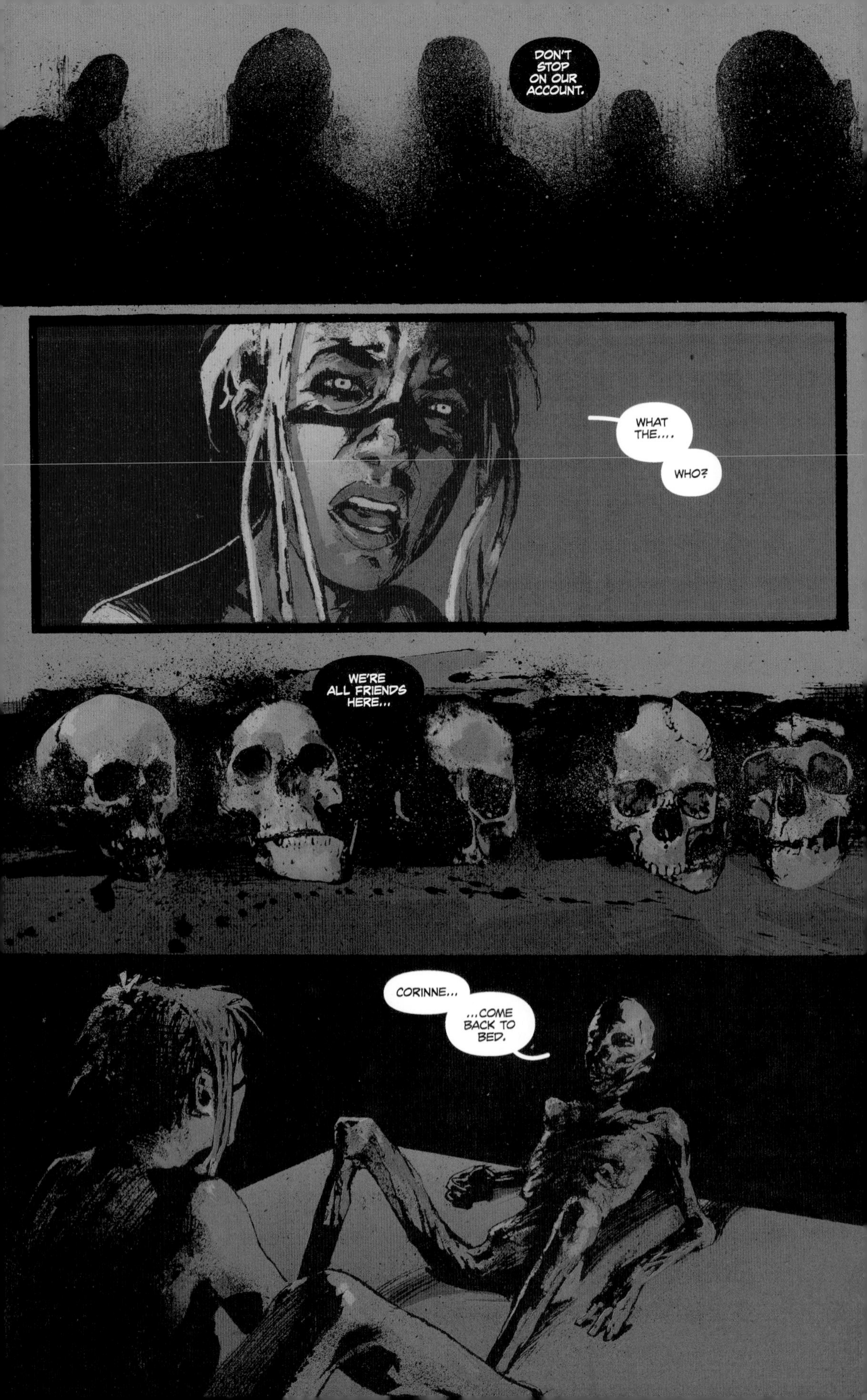
DON'T STOP ON OUR ACCOUNT.
WHAT THE....
WHO?
WE'RE ALL FRIENDS HERE...
CORINNE...
...COME BACK TO BED.

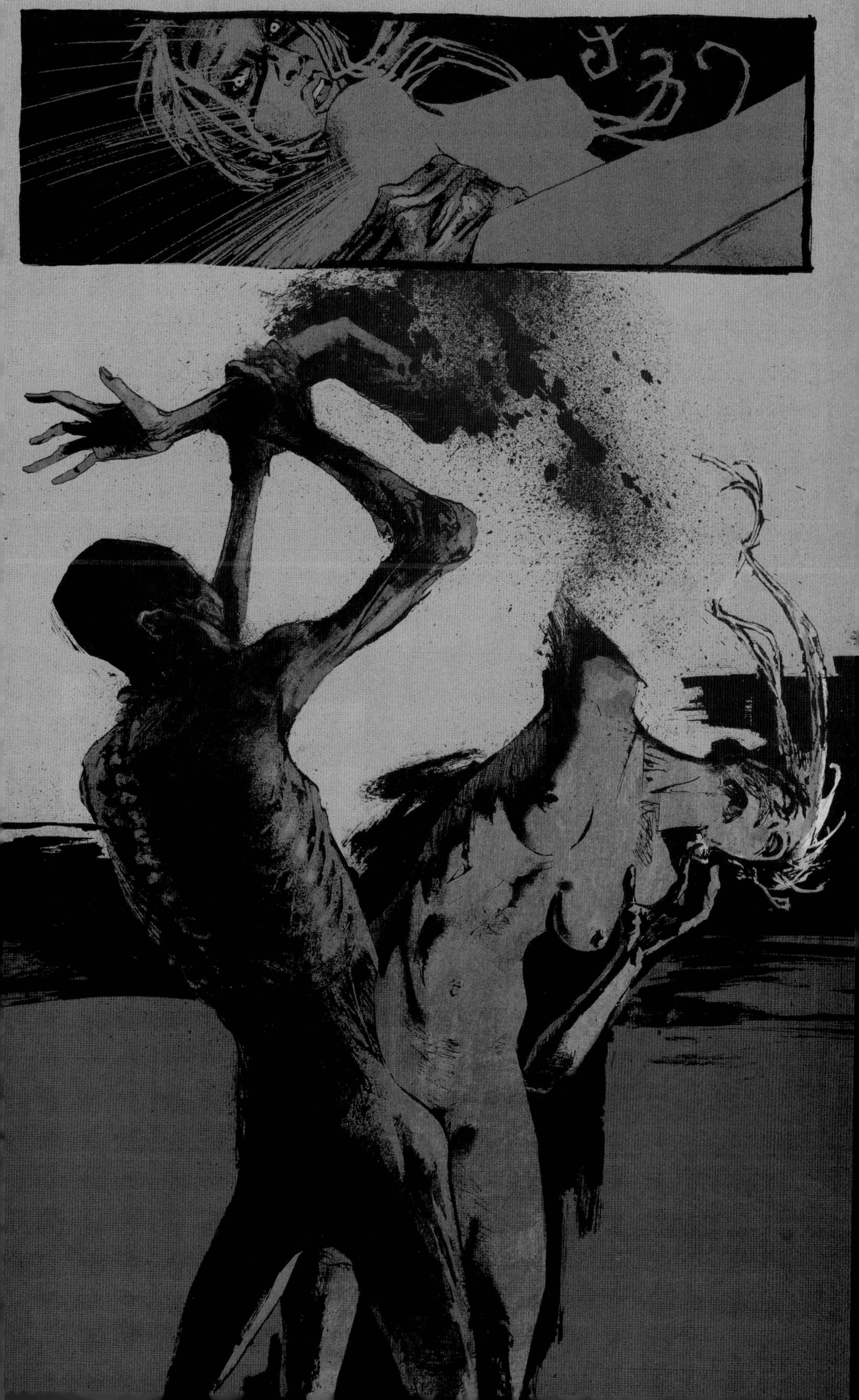

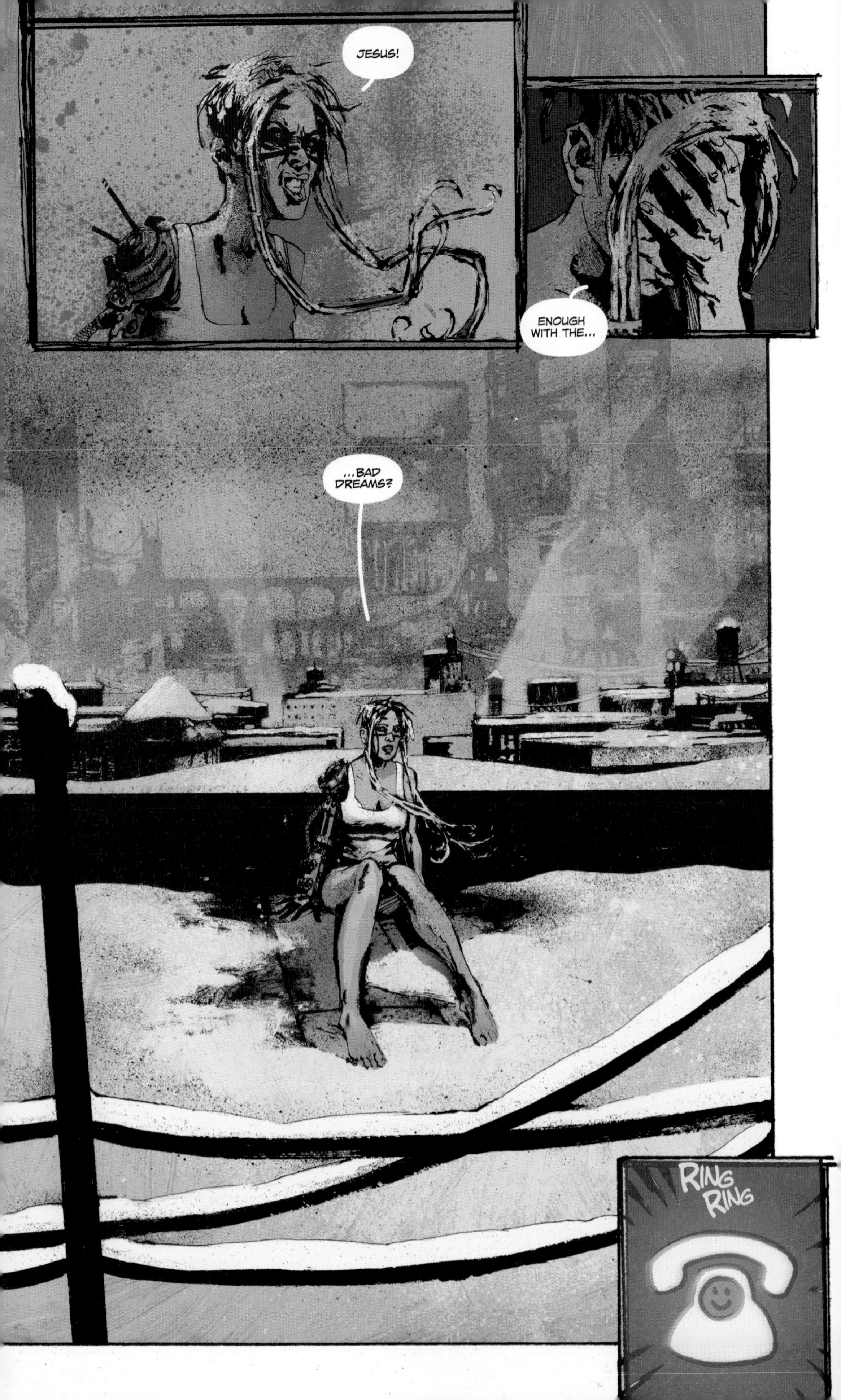
JESUS!
ENOUGH WITH THE...
...BAD DREAMS?
RING RING

HOME: HELLO.

ANSWERING CALL.

CORINNE!

HEY 8.

DEFINITELY GOING TO NEED THAT THING TO HELP ME SLEEP...

WHAT'S UP?

WHERE HAVE YOU BEEN?!

RELAX. I'LL BE THERE BY 1:00. MAYBE 1:30.

CORINNE, IT'S 4:00PM.

WHERE HAVE YOU BEEN FOR THE LAST 10 HOURS? DON'T ANSWER.

WHAT?

LUCKILY HIS MEET GOT POSTPONED. I JUST GOT WORD HE'S WALKED INTO THE BITWIZE.

HE'S STILL THERE. LEAVE NOW AND YOU CAN CATCH HIM.

10 HOURS.

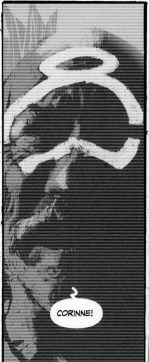

CORINNE!

YEAH. ONNIT.

THE TEMPERATURE OF THE WATER IS JUST SOUTH OF SCALDING.

THE HEAT WARMS MY HALF-FROZEN BODY AND THE PAIN BRINGS EVERYTHING BACK INTO FOCUS.

HOW MUCH OF THAT WAS A DREAM?

10 hours.

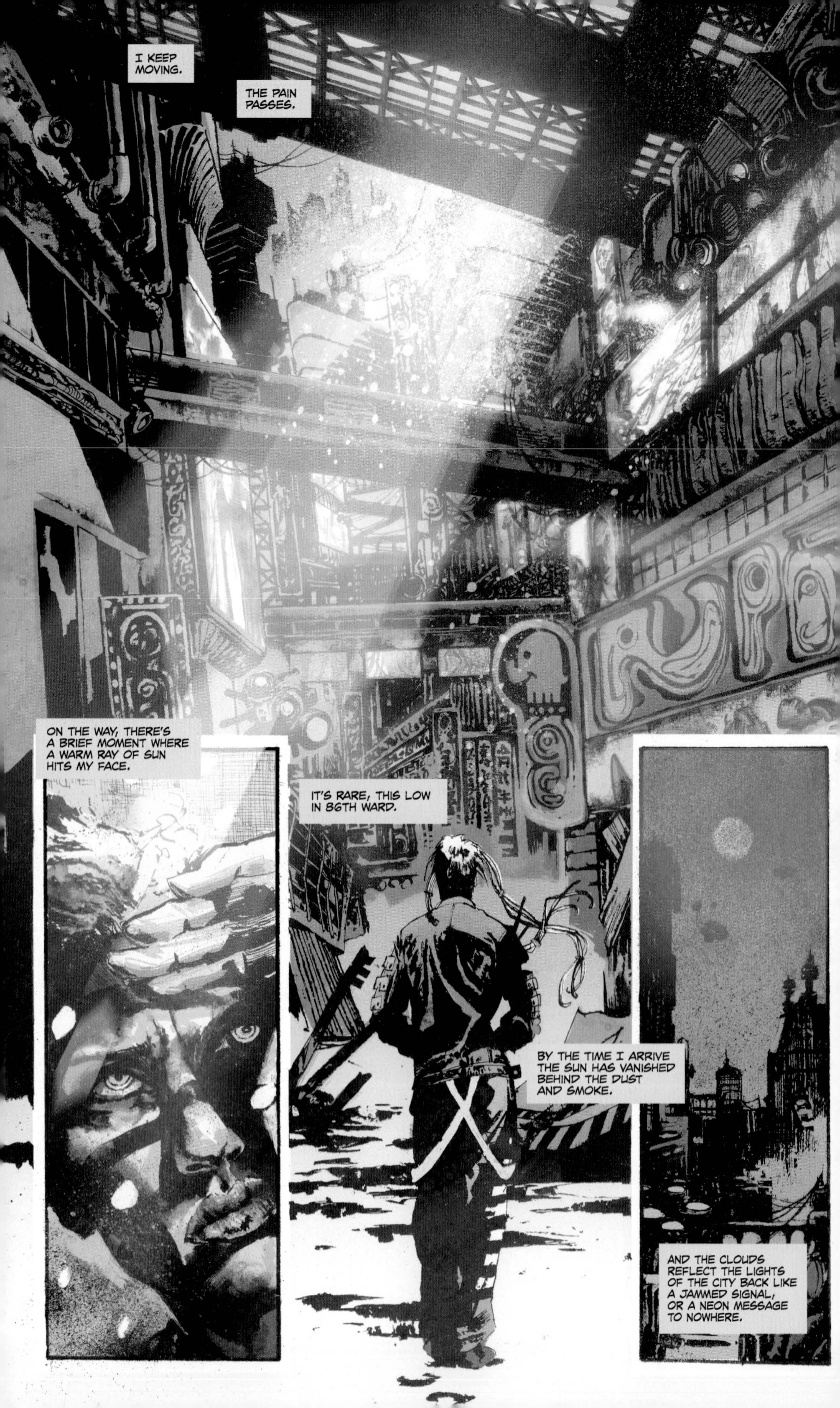

I KEEP MOVING.
THE PAIN PASSES.
ON THE WAY, THERE'S A BRIEF MOMENT WHERE A WARM RAY OF SUN HITS MY FACE.
IT'S RARE, THIS LOW IN 86TH WARD.
BY THE TIME I ARRIVE THE SUN HAS VANISHED BEHIND THE DUST AND SMOKE.
AND THE CLOUDS REFLECT THE LIGHTS OF THE CITY BACK LIKE A JAMMED SIGNAL, OR A NEON MESSAGE TO NOWHERE.

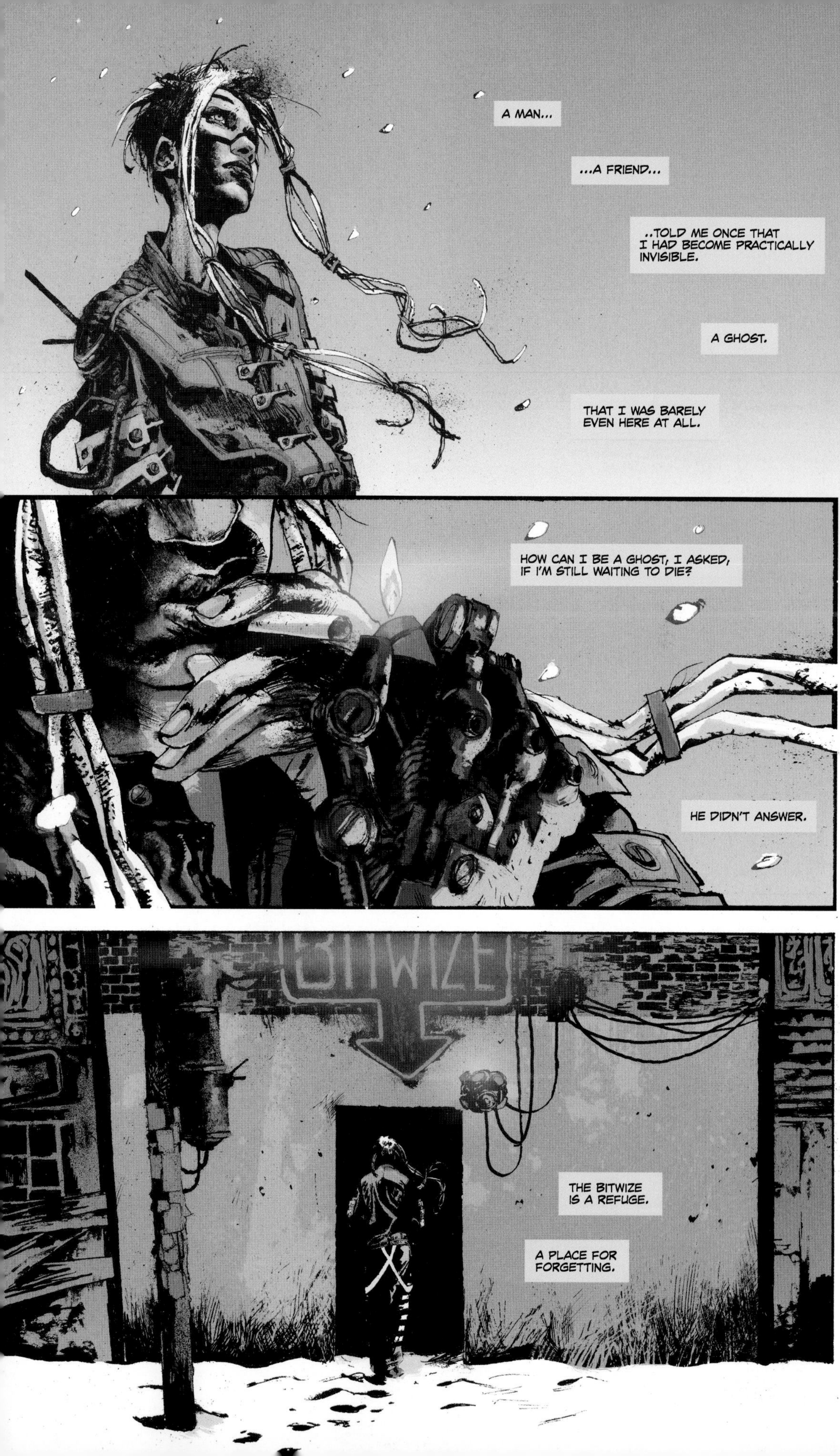
A MAN...
...A FRIEND...
..TOLD ME ONCE THAT I HAD BECOME PRACTICALLY INVISIBLE.
A GHOST.
THAT I WAS BARELY EVEN HERE AT ALL.
HOW CAN I BE A GHOST, I ASKED, IF I'M STILL WAITING TO DIE?
HE DIDN'T ANSWER.
BITWIZE
THE BITWIZE IS A REFUGE.
A PLACE FOR FORGETTING.

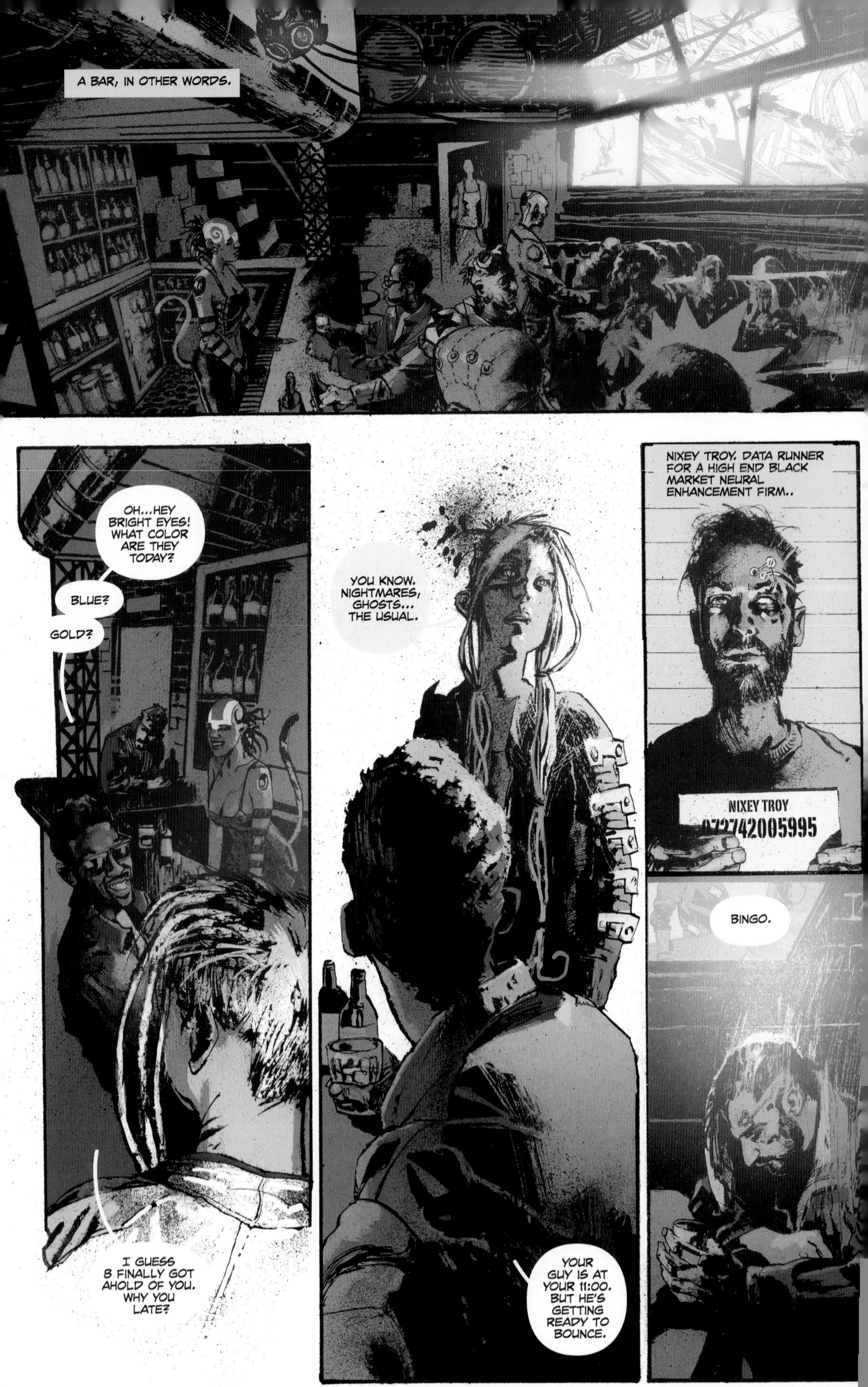

A BAR, IN OTHER WORDS.
OH...HEY BRIGHT EYES! WHAT COLOR ARE THEY TODAY?
BLUE?
GOLD?
I GUESS 8 FINALLY GOT AHOLD OF YOU. WHY YOU LATE?
YOU KNOW. NIGHTMARES, GHOSTS... THE USUAL.
YOUR GUY IS AT YOUR 11:00. BUT HE'S GETTING READY TO BOUNCE.
NIXEY TROY. DATA RUNNER FOR A HIGH END BLACK MARKET NEURAL ENHANCEMENT FIRM..
NIXEY TROY
BINGO.

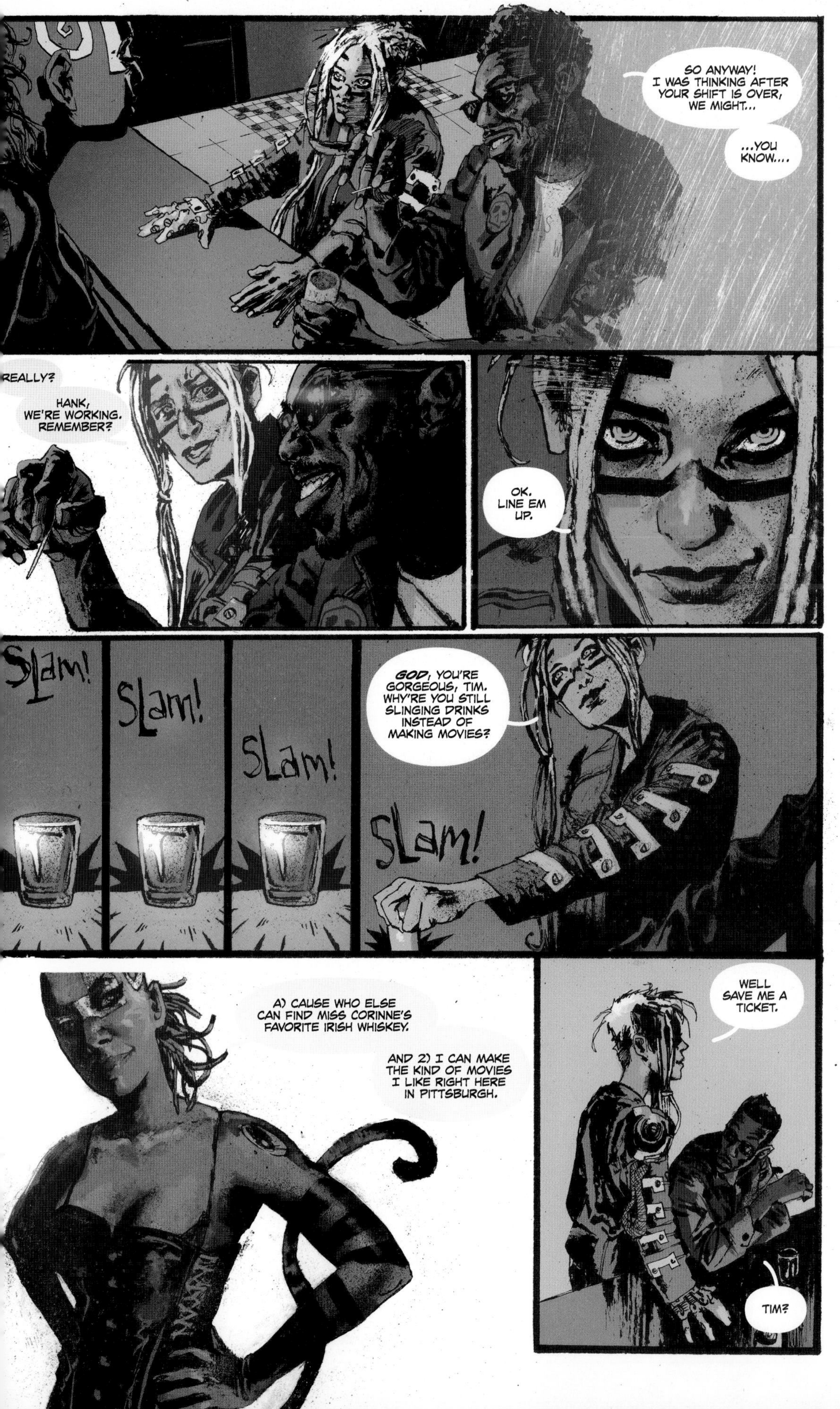

SO ANYWAY! I WAS THINKING AFTER YOUR SHIFT IS OVER, WE MIGHT...
...YOU KNOW....
REALLY?
HANK, WE'RE WORKING. REMEMBER?
OK. LINE EM UP.
SLam!
SLam!
SLam!
GOD, YOU'RE GORGEOUS, TIM. WHY'RE YOU STILL SLINGING DRINKS INSTEAD OF MAKING MOVIES?
SLam!
A) CAUSE WHO ELSE CAN FIND MISS CORINNE'S FAVORITE IRISH WHISKEY.
AND 2) I CAN MAKE THE KIND OF MOVIES I LIKE RIGHT HERE IN PITTSBURGH.
WELL SAVE ME A TICKET.
TIM?

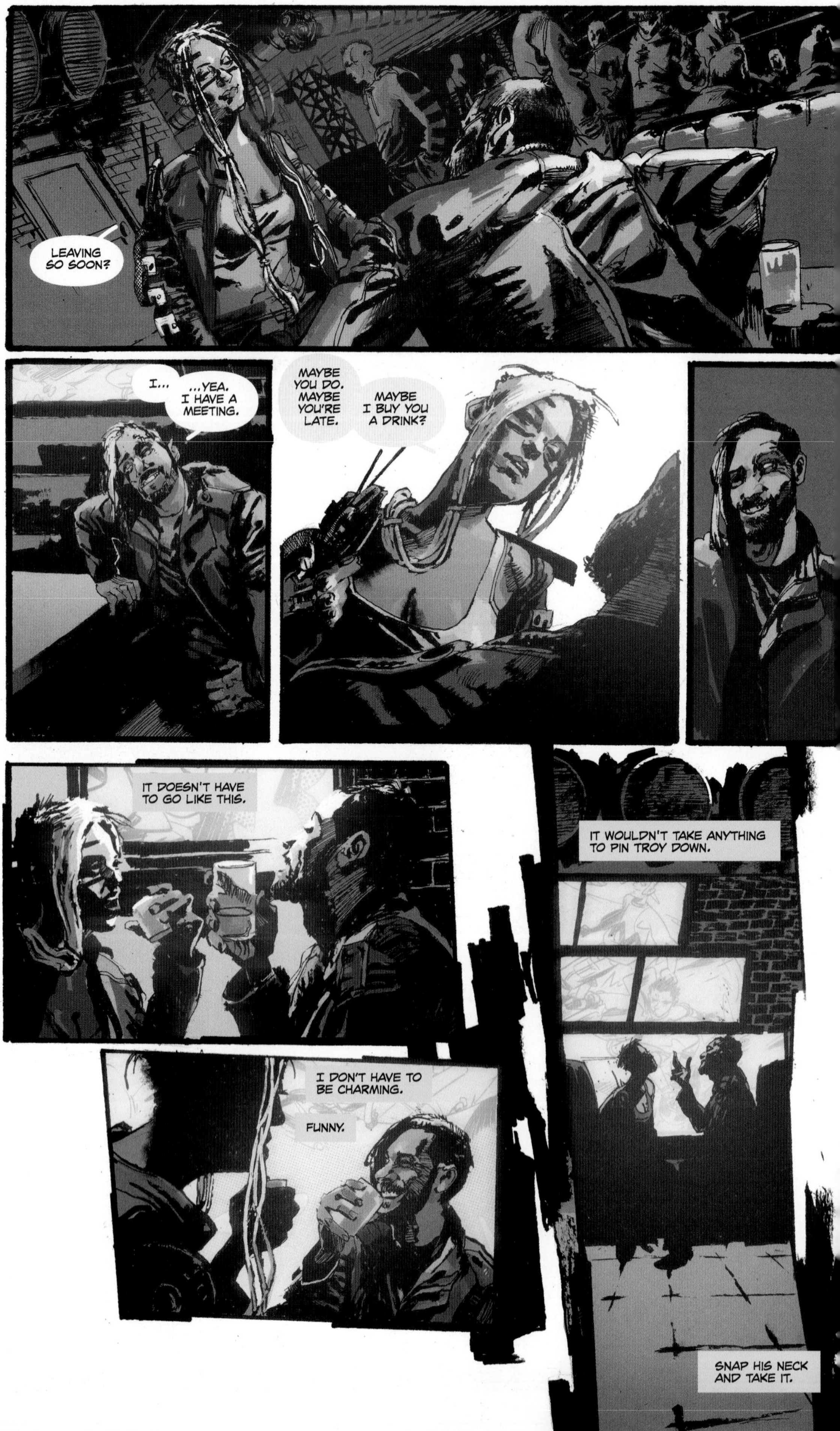

LEAVING SO SOON?
I...
...YEA. I HAVE A MEETING.
MAYBE YOU DO. MAYBE YOU'RE LATE.
MAYBE I BUY YOU A DRINK?
IT DOESN'T HAVE TO GO LIKE THIS.
I DON'T HAVE TO BE CHARMING.
FUNNY.
IT WOULDN'T TAKE ANYTHING TO PIN TROY DOWN.
SNAP HIS NECK AND TAKE IT.

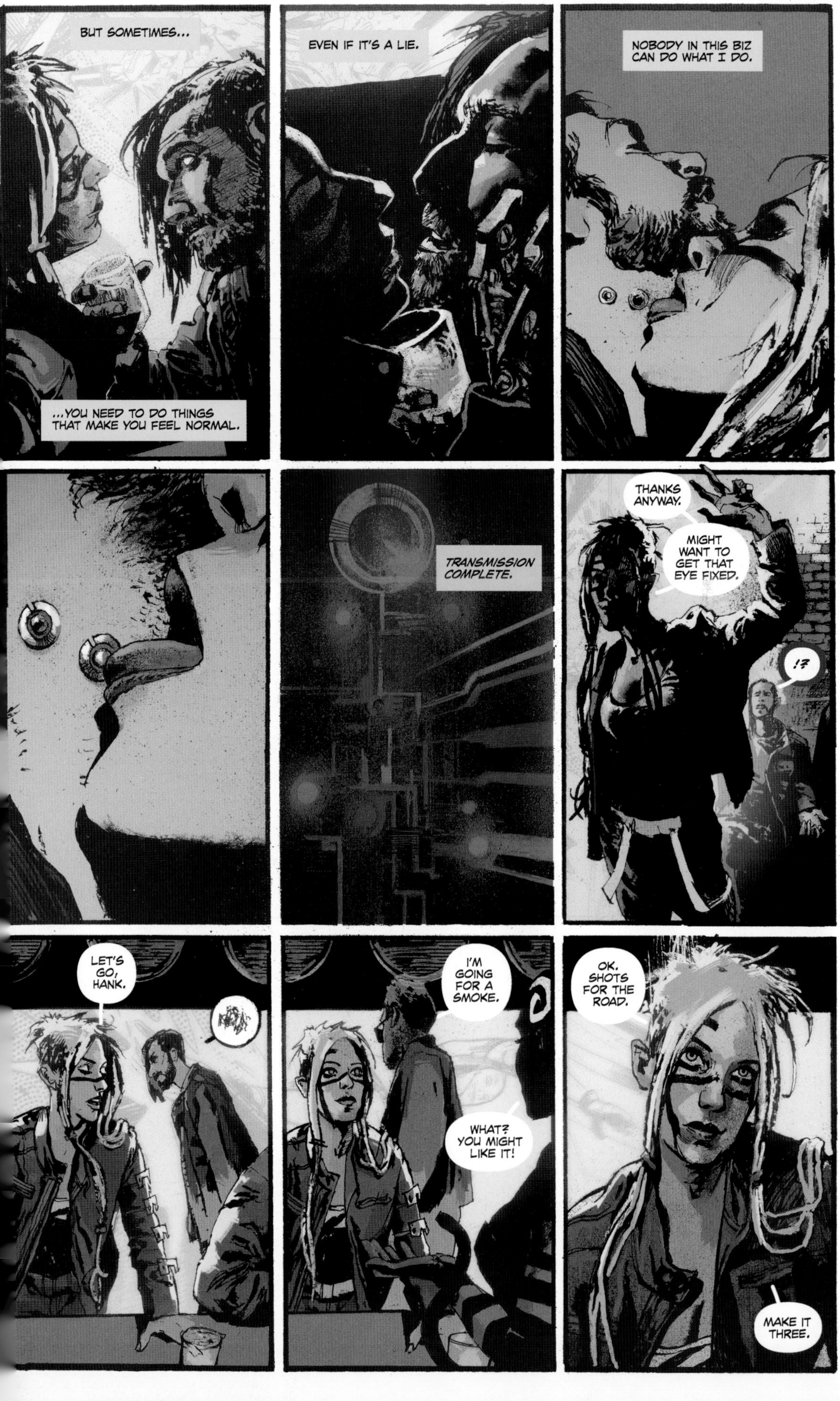
BUT SOMETIMES...
...YOU NEED TO DO THINGS THAT MAKE YOU FEEL NORMAL.
EVEN IF IT'S A LIE.
NOBODY IN THIS BIZ CAN DO WHAT I DO.
TRANSMISSION COMPLETE.
THANKS ANYWAY.
MIGHT WANT TO GET THAT EYE FIXED.
!?
LET'S GO, HANK.
I'M GOING FOR A SMOKE.
WHAT? YOU MIGHT LIKE IT!
OK. SHOTS FOR THE ROAD.
MAKE IT THREE.

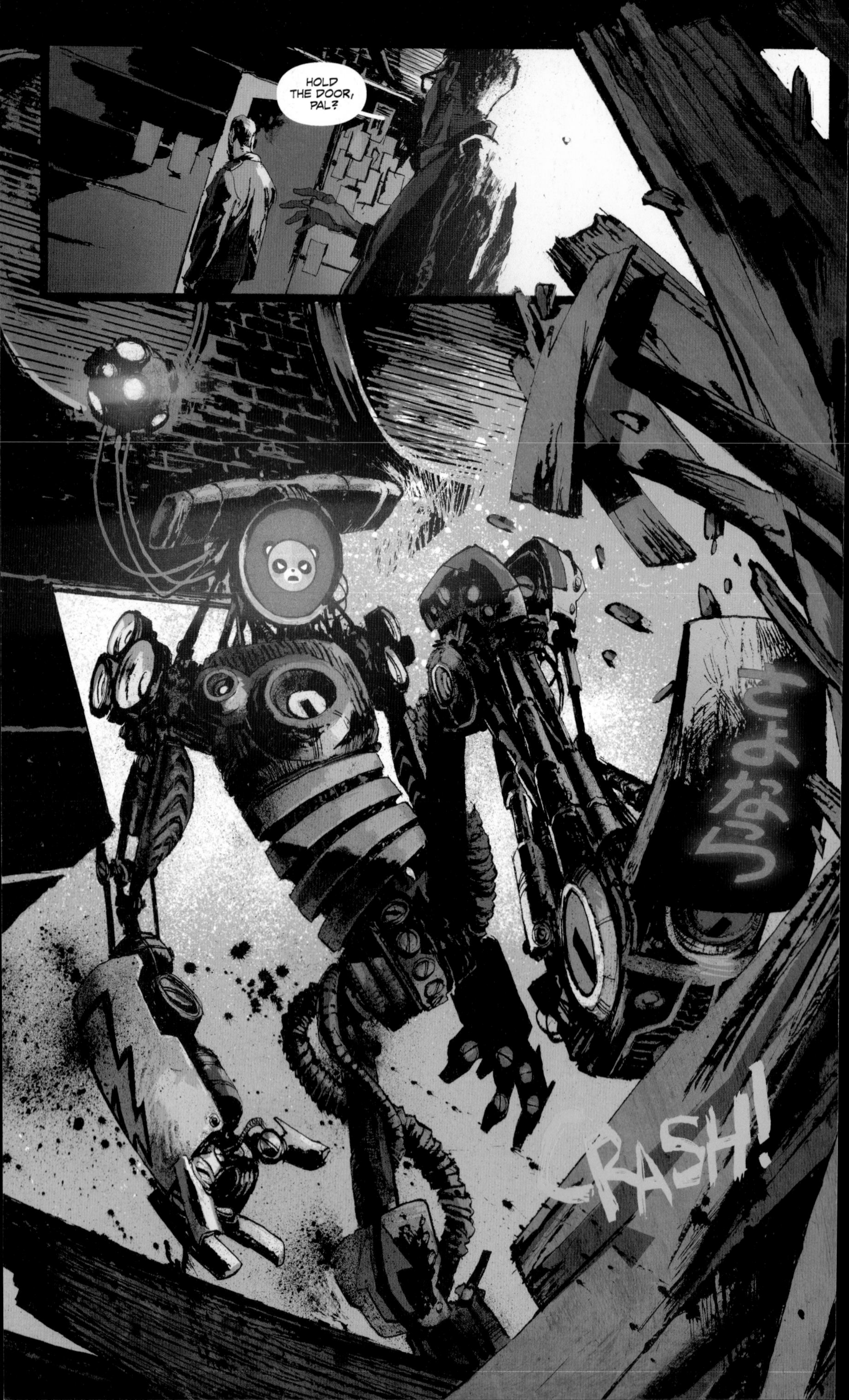
HOLD THE DOOR, PAL?
さよなら
CRASH!

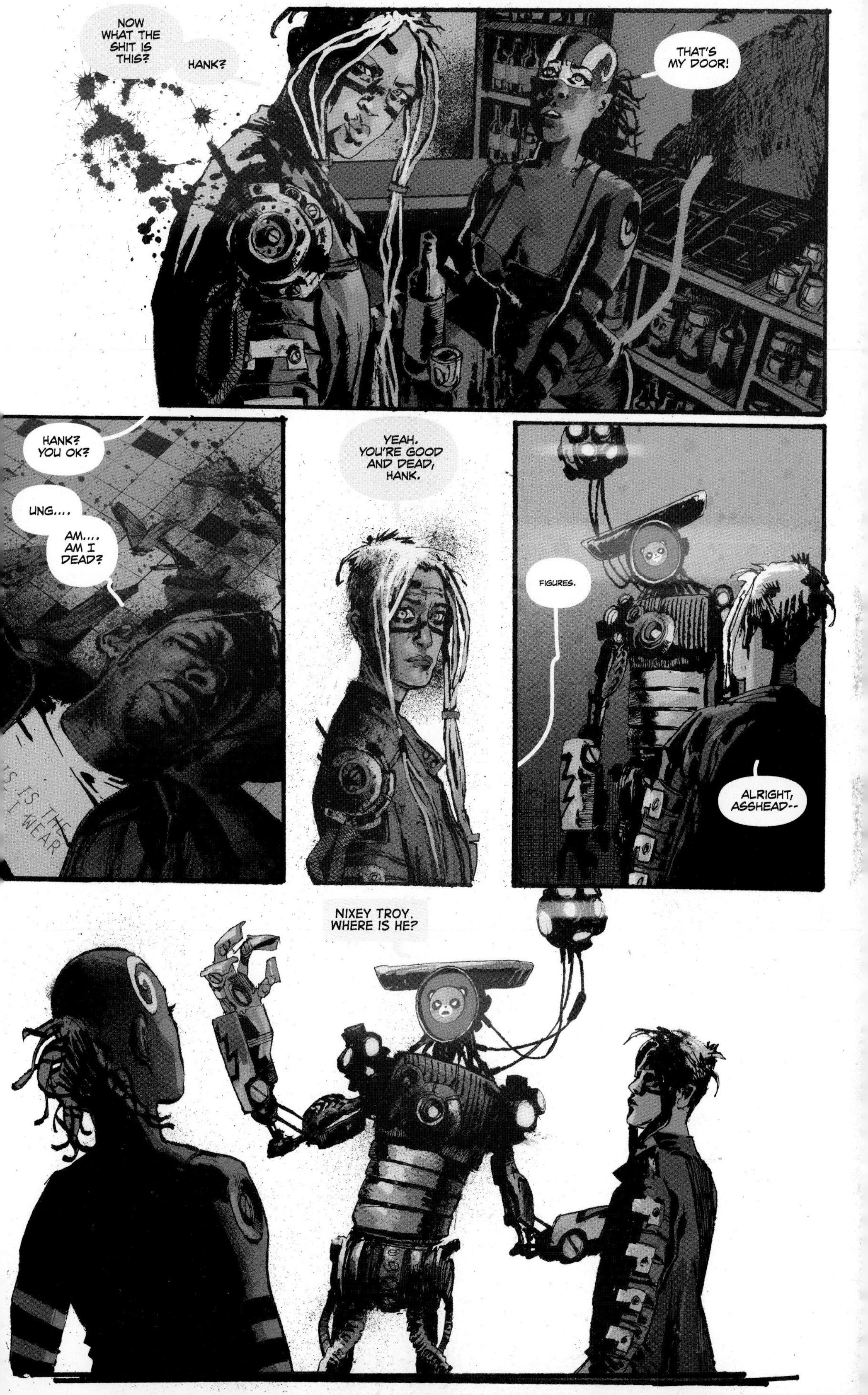
NOW WHAT THE SHIT IS THIS?
HANK?
THAT'S MY DOOR!
HANK? YOU OK?
UNG....
AM.... AM I DEAD?
YEAH. YOU'RE GOOD AND DEAD, HANK.
FIGURES.
ALRIGHT, ASSHEAD--
NIXEY TROY. WHERE IS HE?

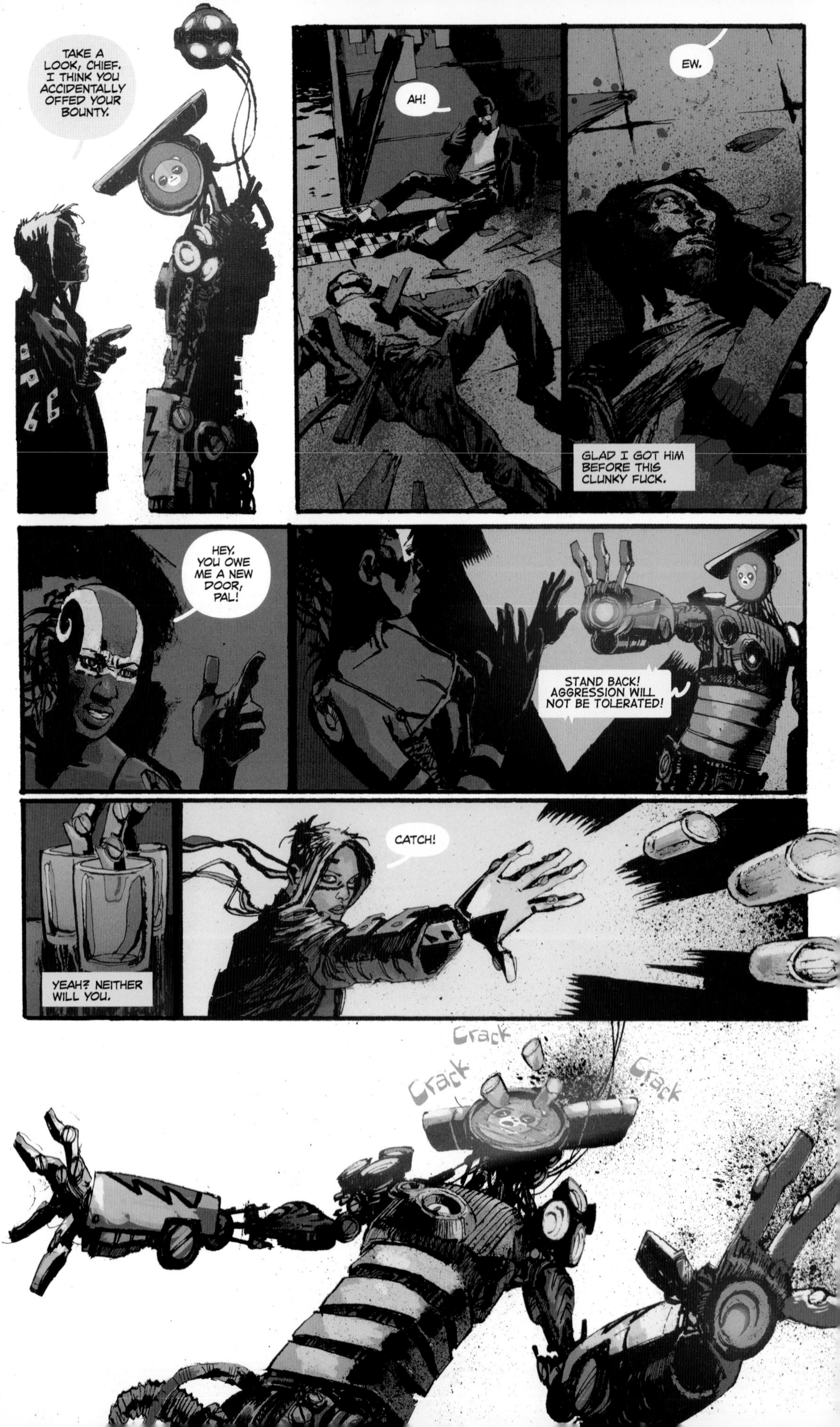
TAKE A LOOK, CHIEF. I THINK YOU ACCIDENTALLY OFFED YOUR BOUNTY.
AH!
EW.
GLAD I GOT HIM BEFORE THIS CLUNKY FUCK.
HEY. YOU OWE ME A NEW DOOR, PAL!
STAND BACK! AGGRESSION WILL NOT BE TOLERATED!
YEAH? NEITHER WILL YOU.
CATCH!
Crack
Crack
Crack

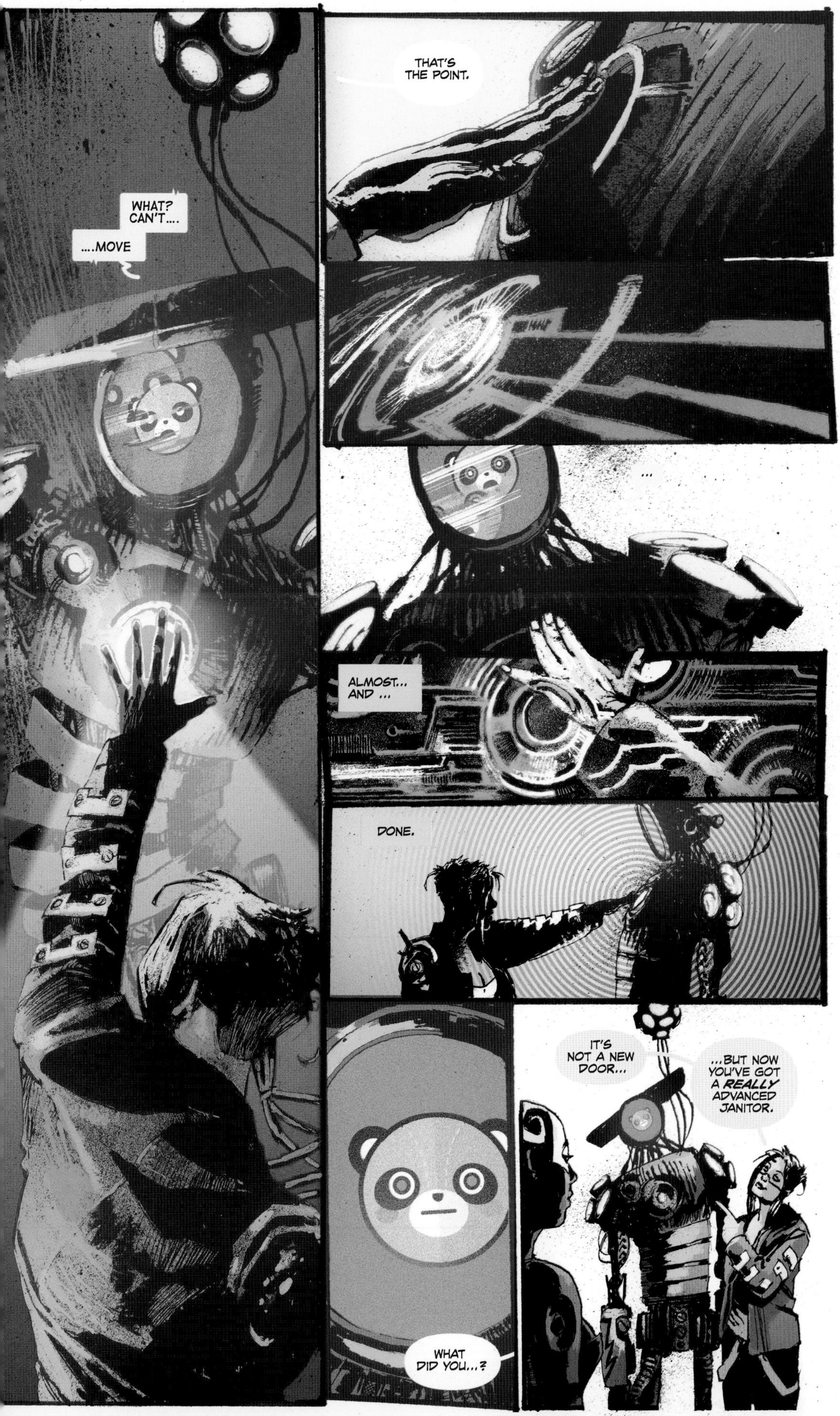
WHAT? CAN'T....
....MOVE
THAT'S THE POINT.
...
ALMOST... AND ...
DONE.
WHAT DID YOU...?
IT'S NOT A NEW DOOR...
...BUT NOW YOU'VE GOT A REALLY ADVANCED JANITOR.

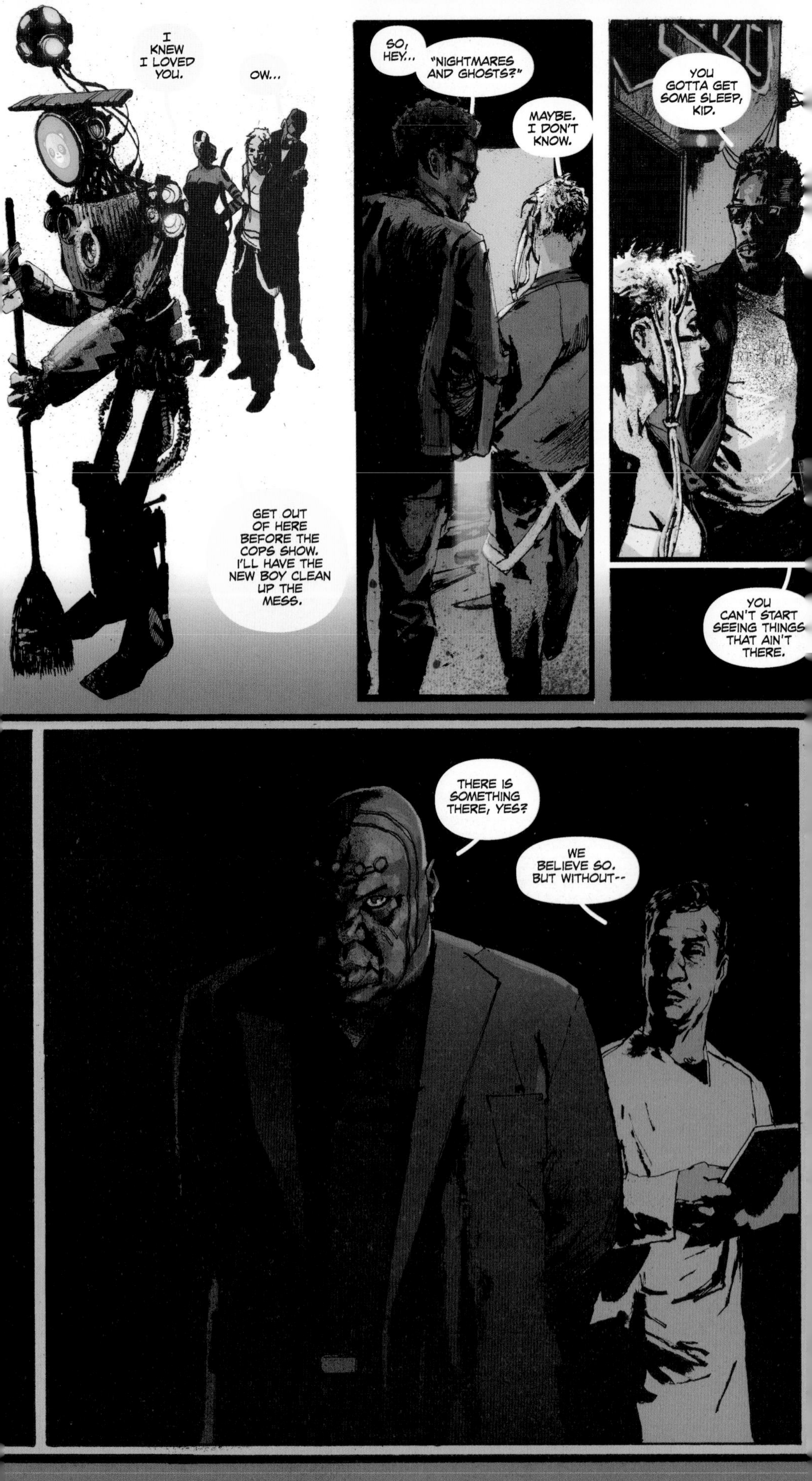
I KNEW I LOVED YOU.
OW...
GET OUT OF HERE BEFORE THE COPS SHOW. I'LL HAVE THE NEW BOY CLEAN UP THE MESS.
SO, HEY...
"NIGHTMARES AND GHOSTS?"
MAYBE. I DON'T KNOW.
YOU GOTTA GET SOME SLEEP, KID.
YOU CAN'T START SEEING THINGS THAT AIN'T THERE.
THERE IS SOMETHING THERE, YES?
WE BELIEVE SO. BUT WITHOUT--

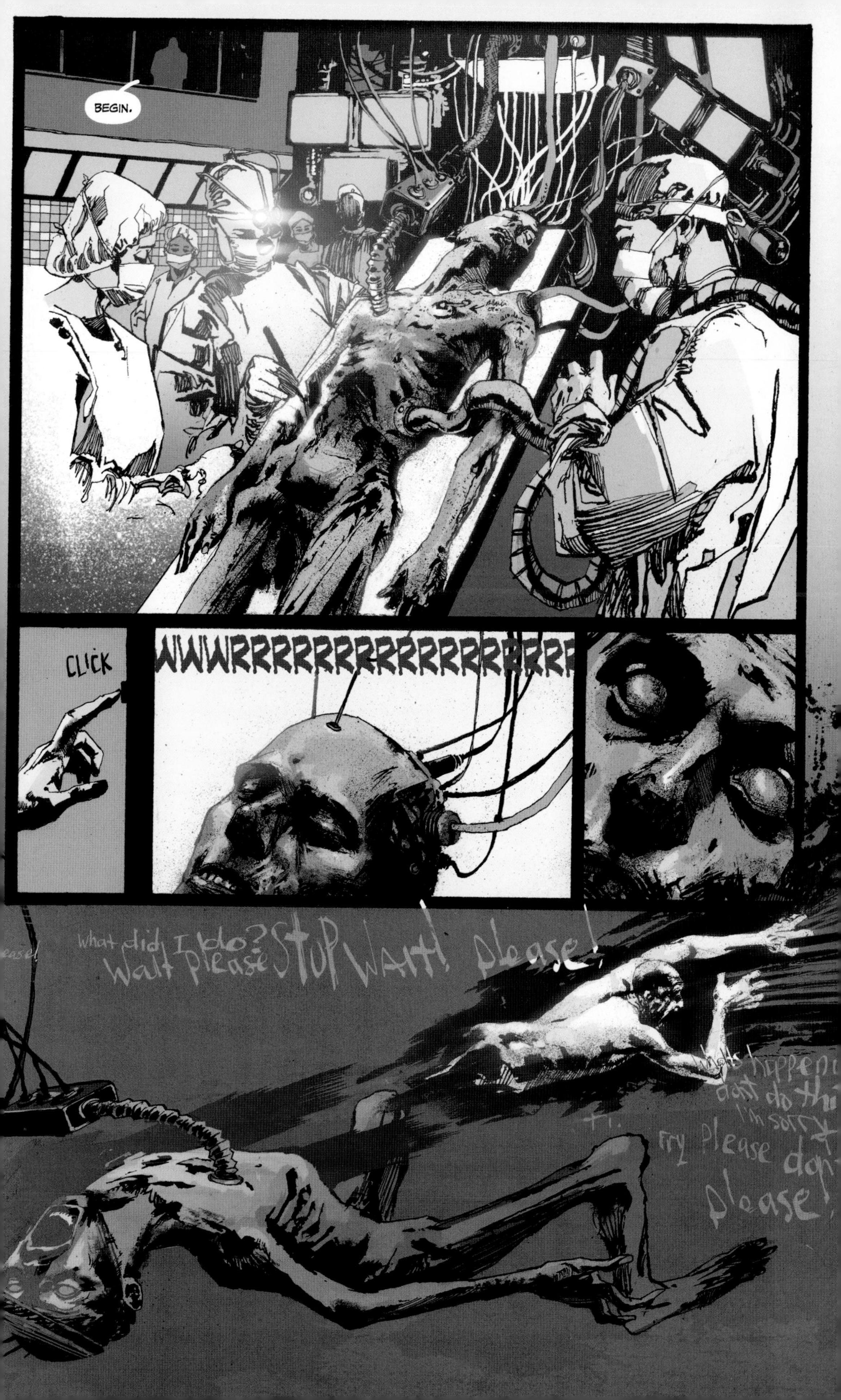
BEGIN.
CLICK
WWWRRRRRRRRRRRRRRR
what did I do?
Wait please STOP Wait! please!
i'm sorry
please
please!

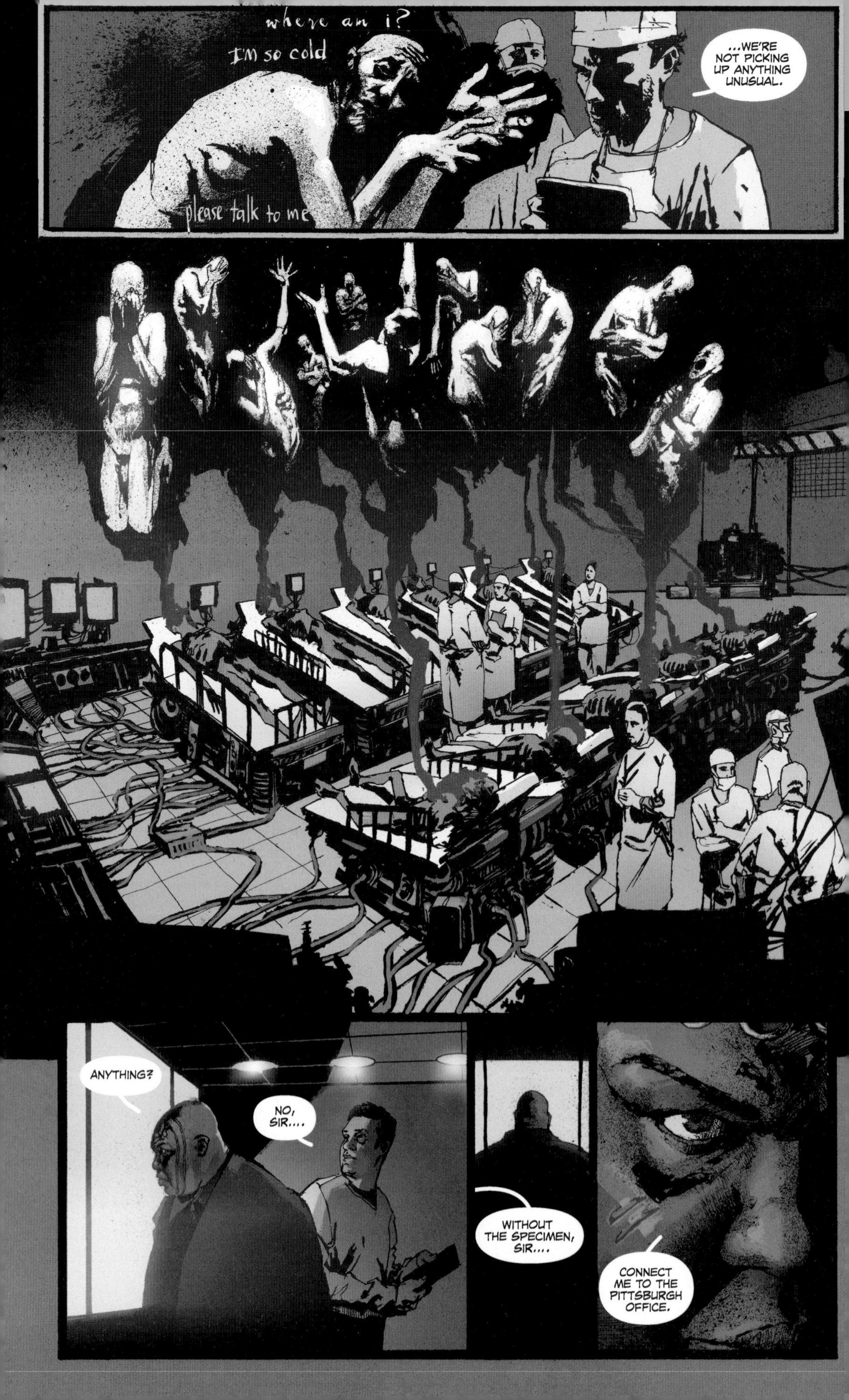
where am i?
I'M so cold
please talk to me
...WE'RE NOT PICKING UP ANYTHING UNUSUAL.
ANYTHING?
NO, SIR....
WITHOUT THE SPECIMEN, SIR....
CONNECT ME TO THE PITTSBURGH OFFICE.

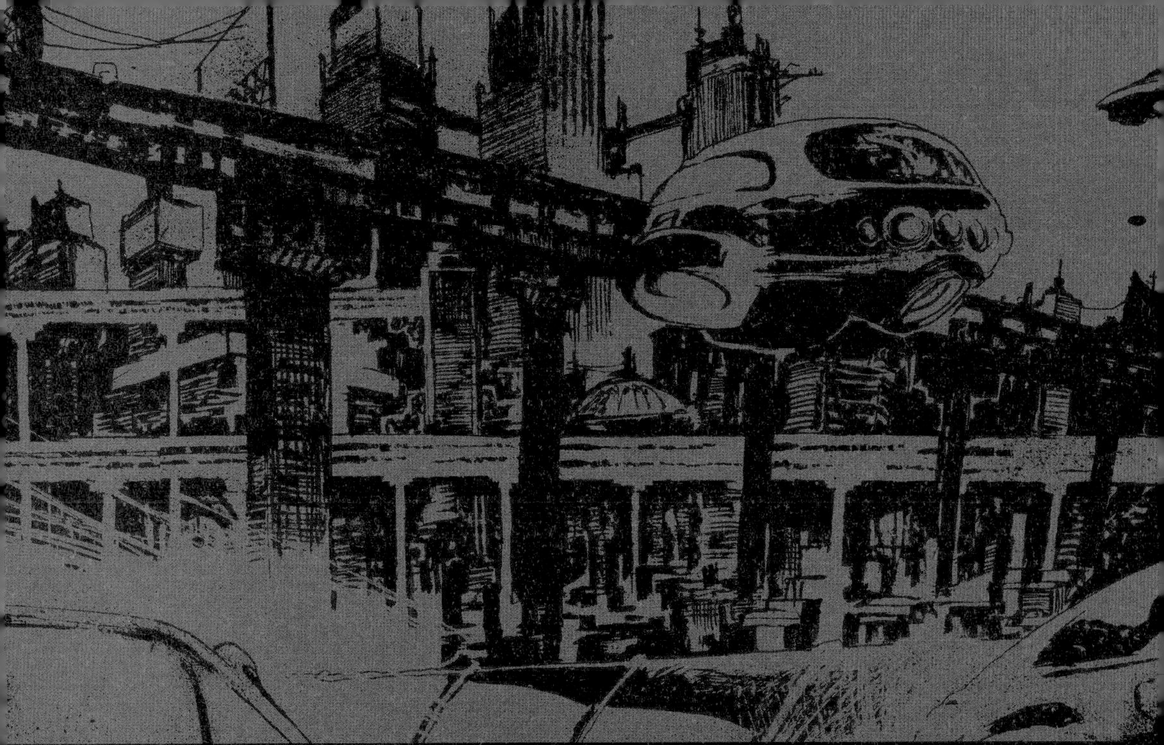

CHAPTER TWO

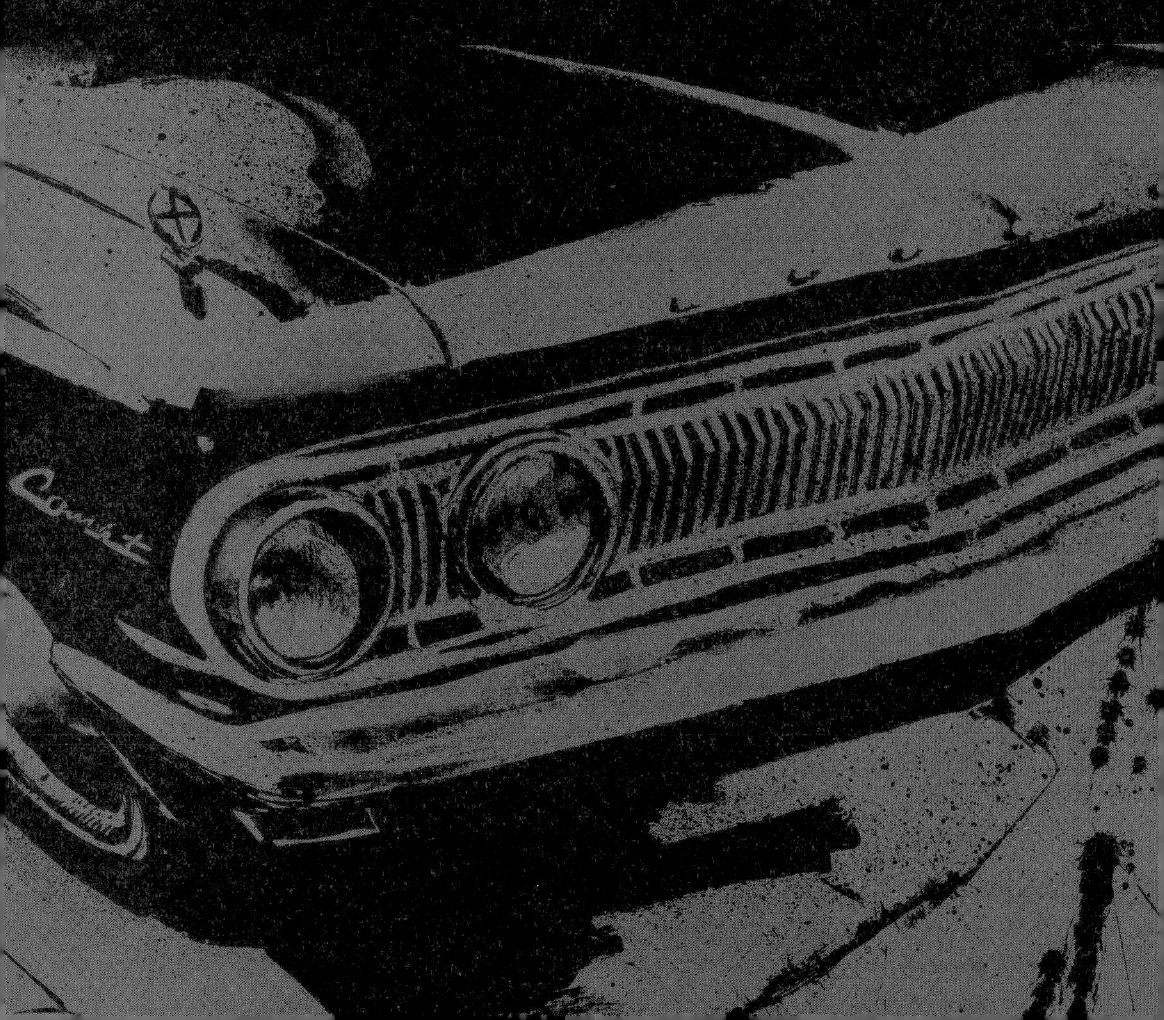
Comet

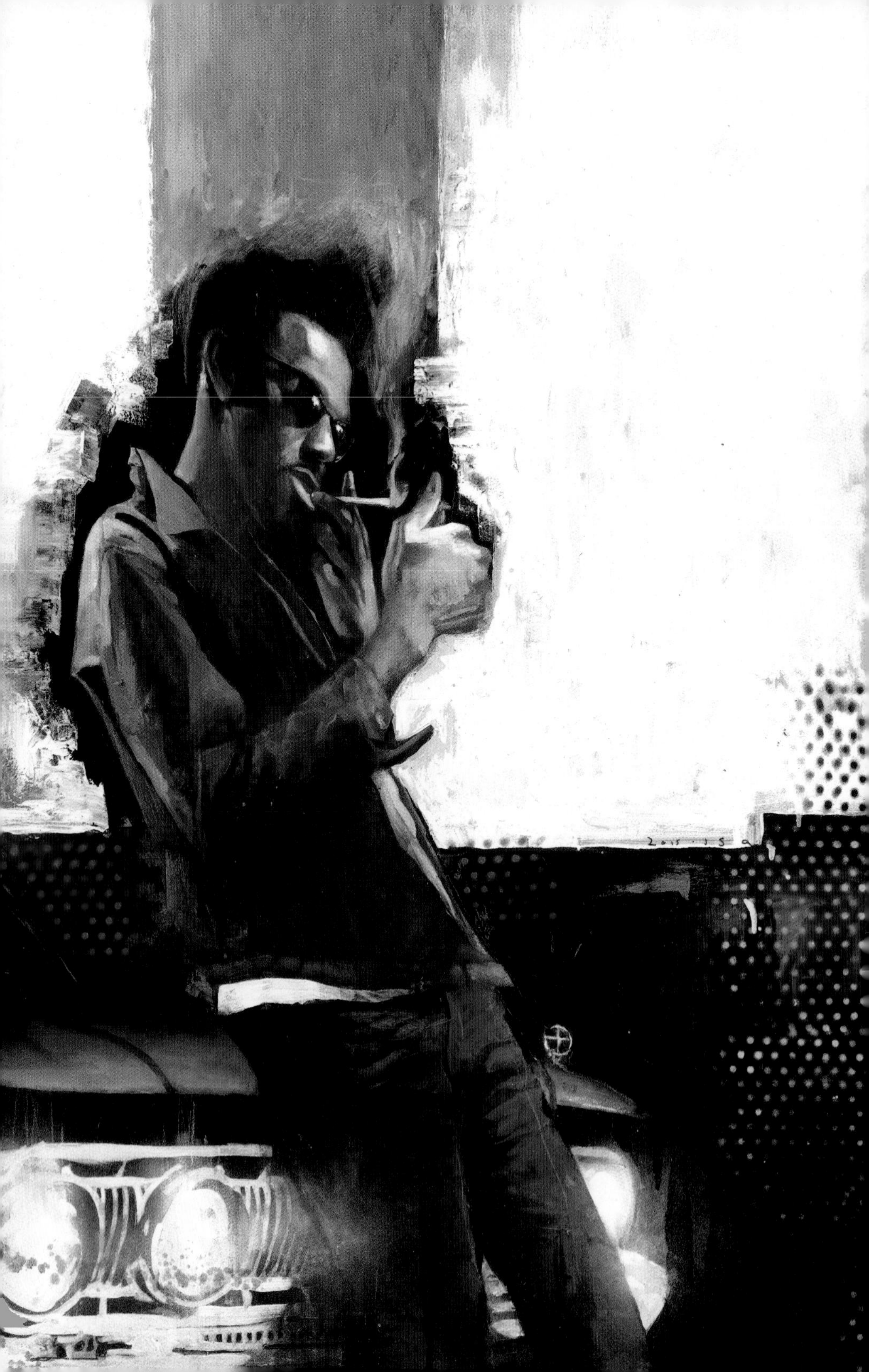

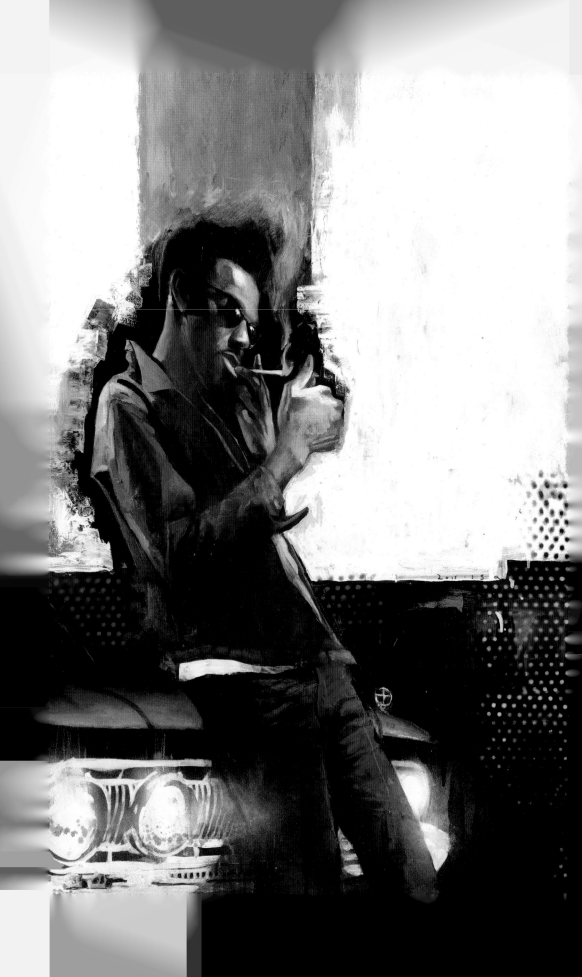

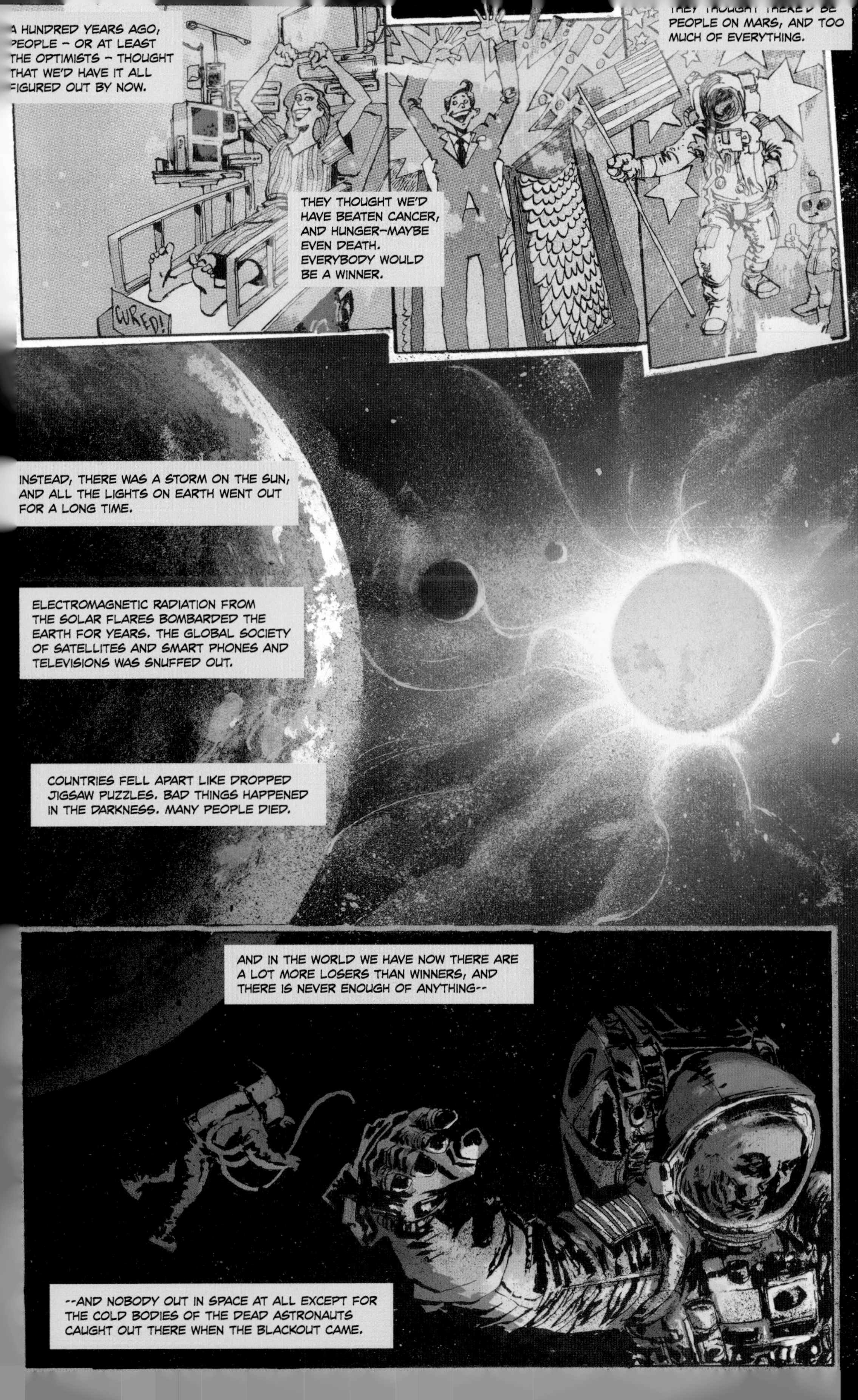
A HUNDRED YEARS AGO, PEOPLE - OR AT LEAST THE OPTIMISTS - THOUGHT THAT WE'D HAVE IT ALL FIGURED OUT BY NOW.
THEY THOUGHT WE'D HAVE BEATEN CANCER, AND HUNGER-MAYBE EVEN DEATH. EVERYBODY WOULD BE A WINNER.
CURED!
PEOPLE ON MARS, AND TOO MUCH OF EVERYTHING.
INSTEAD, THERE WAS A STORM ON THE SUN, AND ALL THE LIGHTS ON EARTH WENT OUT FOR A LONG TIME.
ELECTROMAGNETIC RADIATION FROM THE SOLAR FLARES BOMBARDED THE EARTH FOR YEARS. THE GLOBAL SOCIETY OF SATELLITES AND SMART PHONES AND TELEVISIONS WAS SNUFFED OUT.
COUNTRIES FELL APART LIKE DROPPED JIGSAW PUZZLES. BAD THINGS HAPPENED IN THE DARKNESS. MANY PEOPLE DIED.
AND IN THE WORLD WE HAVE NOW THERE ARE A LOT MORE LOSERS THAN WINNERS, AND THERE IS NEVER ENOUGH OF ANYTHING--
--AND NOBODY OUT IN SPACE AT ALL EXCEPT FOR THE COLD BODIES OF THE DEAD ASTRONAUTS CAUGHT OUT THERE WHEN THE BLACKOUT CAME.

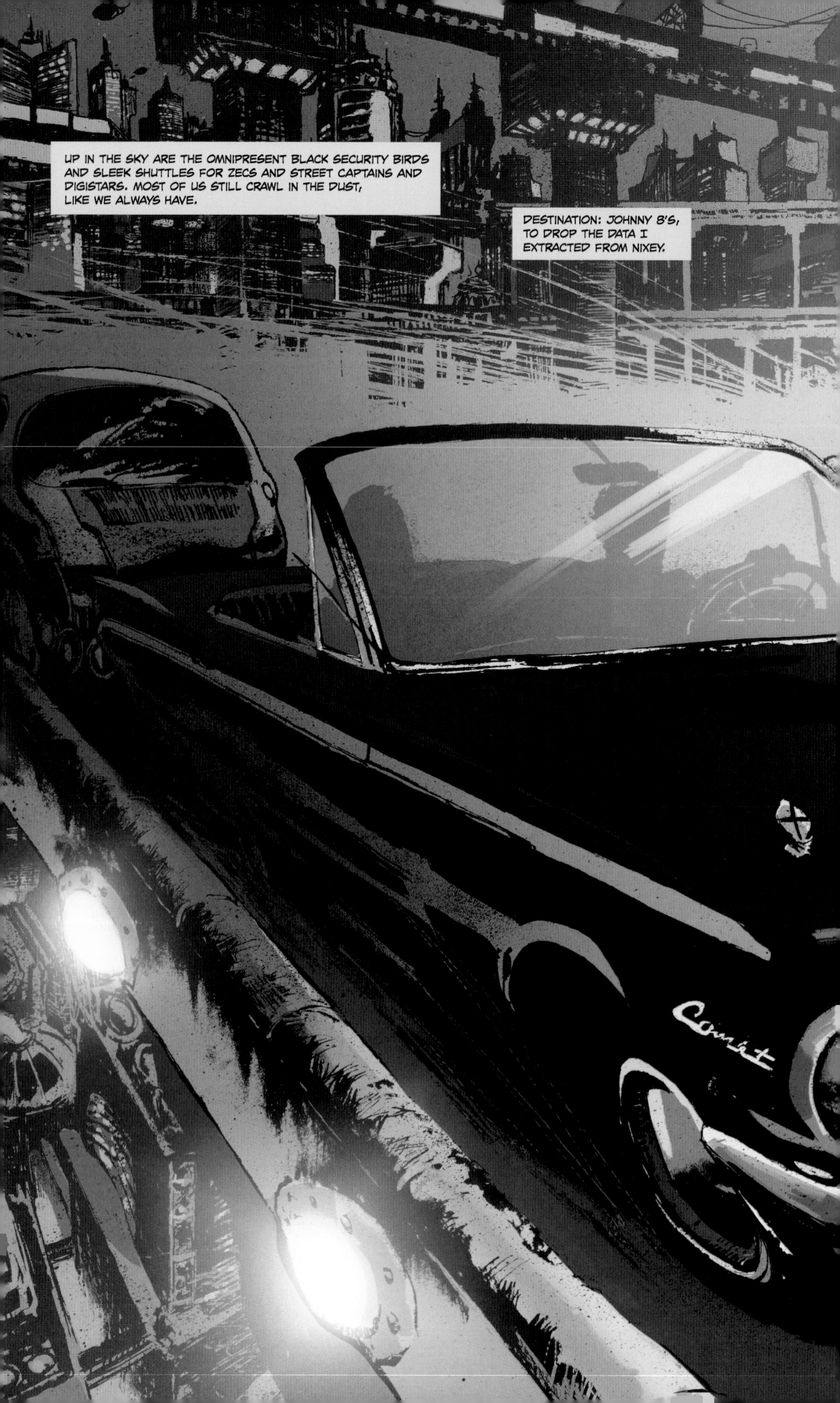
UP IN THE SKY ARE THE OMNIPRESENT BLACK SECURITY BIRDS AND SLEEK SHUTTLES FOR ZECS AND STREET CAPTAINS AND DIGISTARS. MOST OF US STILL CRAWL IN THE DUST, LIKE WE ALWAYS HAVE.
DESTINATION: JOHNNY 8'S, TO DROP THE DATA I EXTRACTED FROM NIXEY.

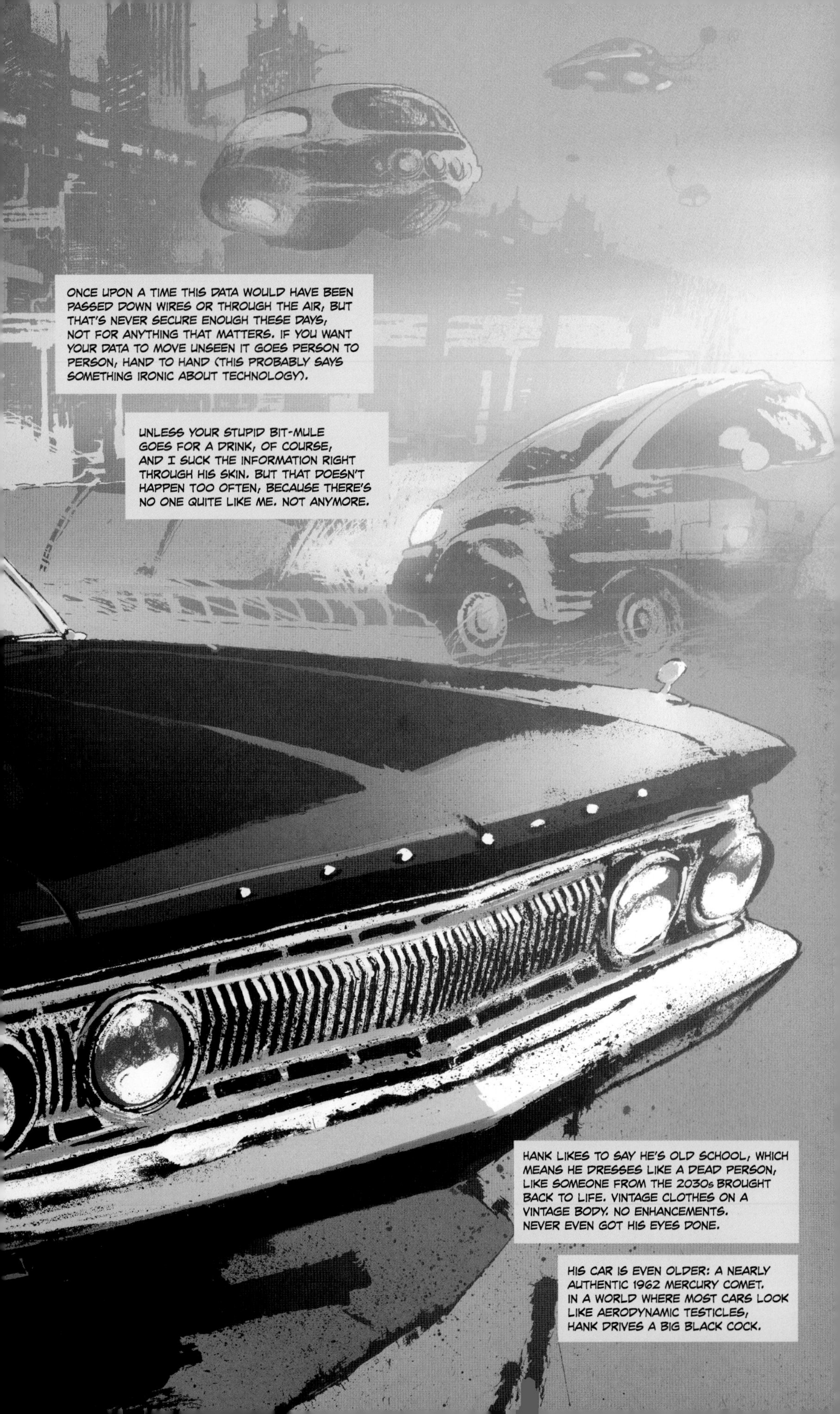
ONCE UPON A TIME THIS DATA WOULD HAVE BEEN PASSED DOWN WIRES OR THROUGH THE AIR, BUT THAT'S NEVER SECURE ENOUGH THESE DAYS, NOT FOR ANYTHING THAT MATTERS. IF YOU WANT YOUR DATA TO MOVE UNSEEN IT GOES PERSON TO PERSON, HAND TO HAND (THIS PROBABLY SAYS SOMETHING IRONIC ABOUT TECHNOLOGY).
UNLESS YOUR STUPID BIT-MULE GOES FOR A DRINK, OF COURSE, AND I SUCK THE INFORMATION RIGHT THROUGH HIS SKIN. BUT THAT DOESN'T HAPPEN TOO OFTEN, BECAUSE THERE'S NO ONE QUITE LIKE ME. NOT ANYMORE.
HANK LIKES TO SAY HE'S OLD SCHOOL, WHICH MEANS HE DRESSES LIKE A DEAD PERSON, LIKE SOMEONE FROM THE 2030s BROUGHT BACK TO LIFE. VINTAGE CLOTHES ON A VINTAGE BODY. NO ENHANCEMENTS. NEVER EVEN GOT HIS EYES DONE.
HIS CAR IS EVEN OLDER: A NEARLY AUTHENTIC 1962 MERCURY COMET. IN A WORLD WHERE MOST CARS LOOK LIKE AERODYNAMIC TESTICLES, HANK DRIVES A BIG BLACK COCK.

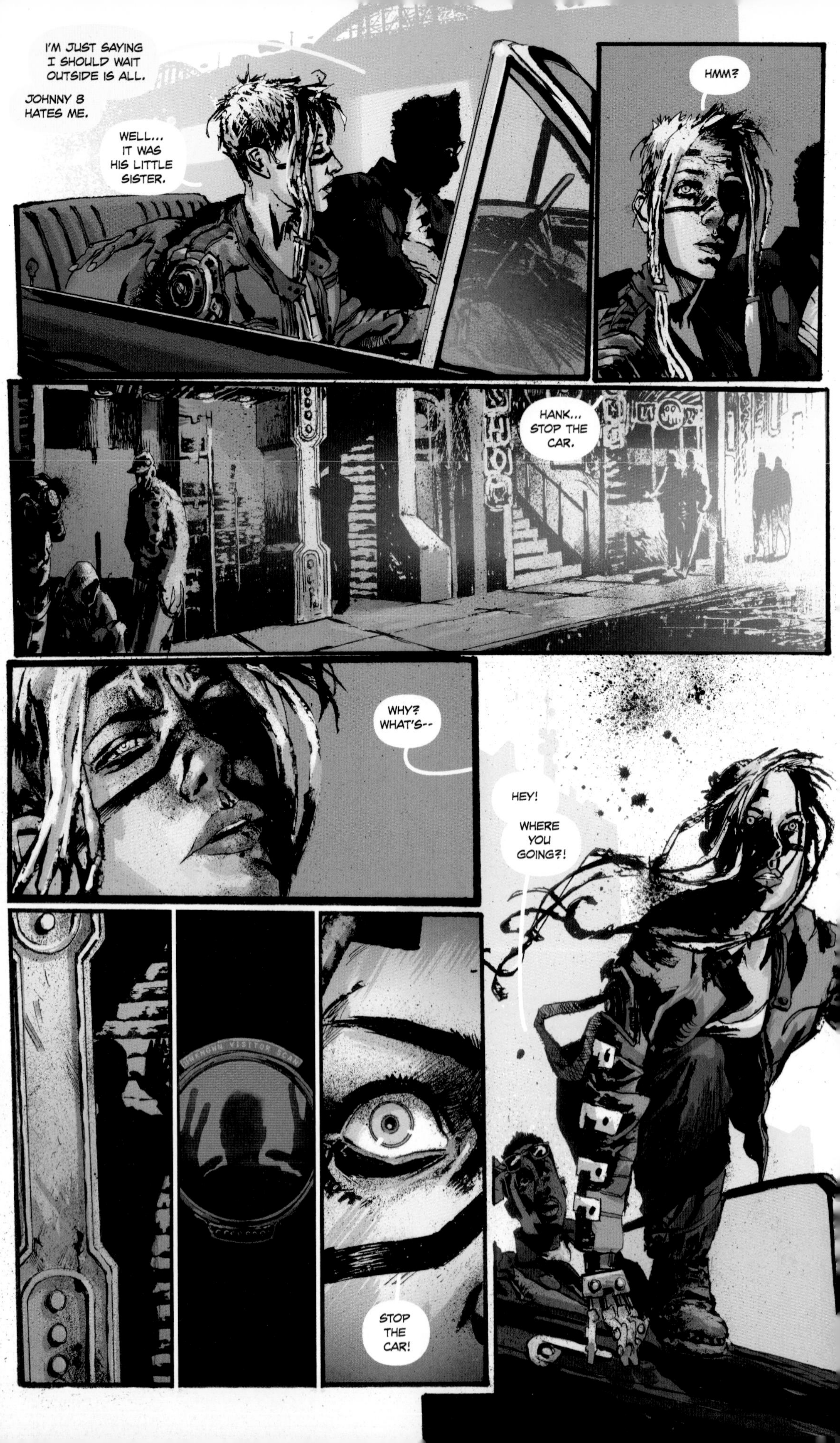
I'M JUST SAYING I SHOULD WAIT OUTSIDE IS ALL.
JOHNNY 8 HATES ME.
WELL... IT WAS HIS LITTLE SISTER.
HMM?
HANK... STOP THE CAR.
WHY? WHAT'S--
UNKNOWN VISITOR SCAN
STOP THE CAR!
HEY!
WHERE YOU GOING?!

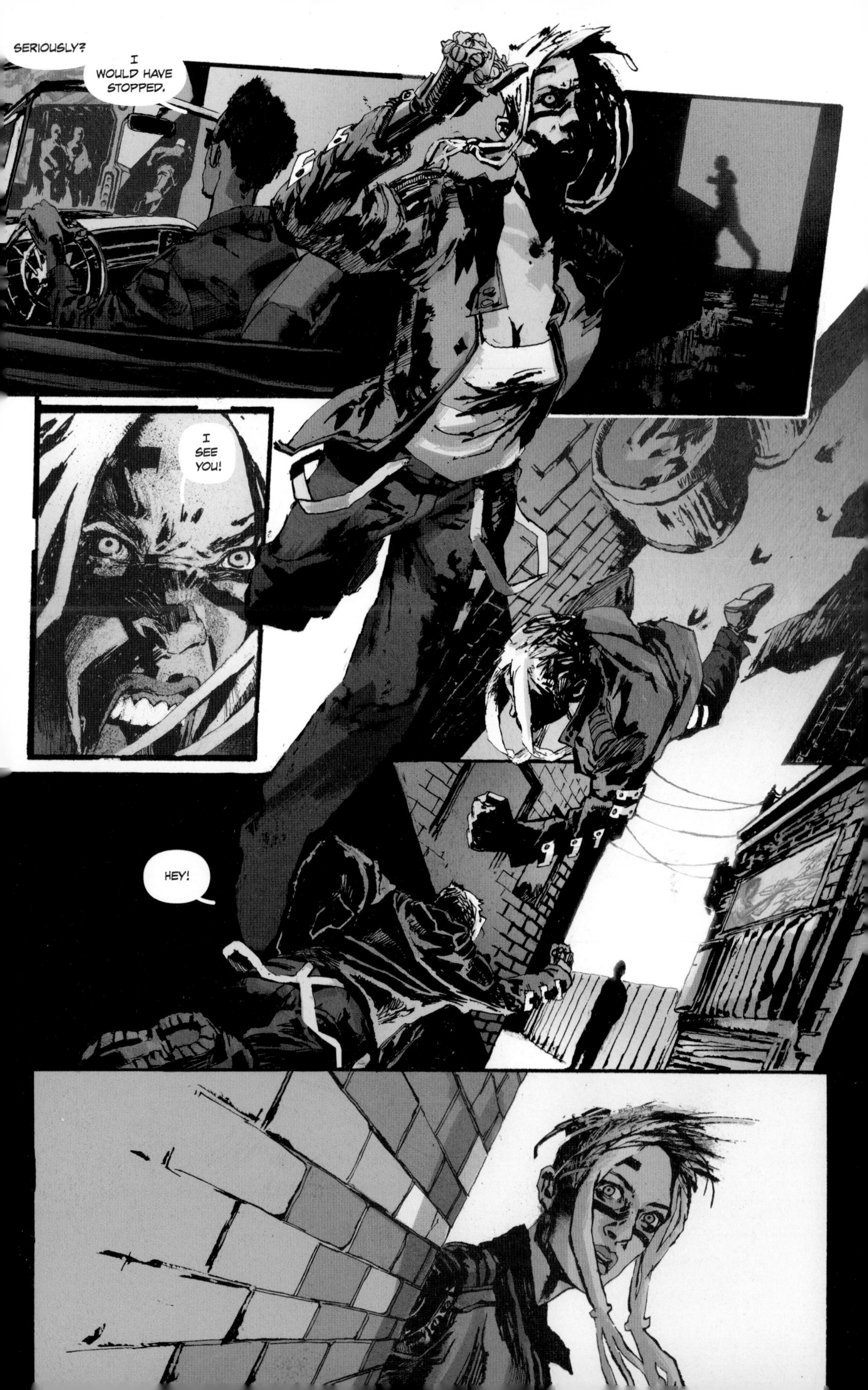
SERIOUSLY?
I WOULD HAVE STOPPED.
I SEE YOU!
HEY!

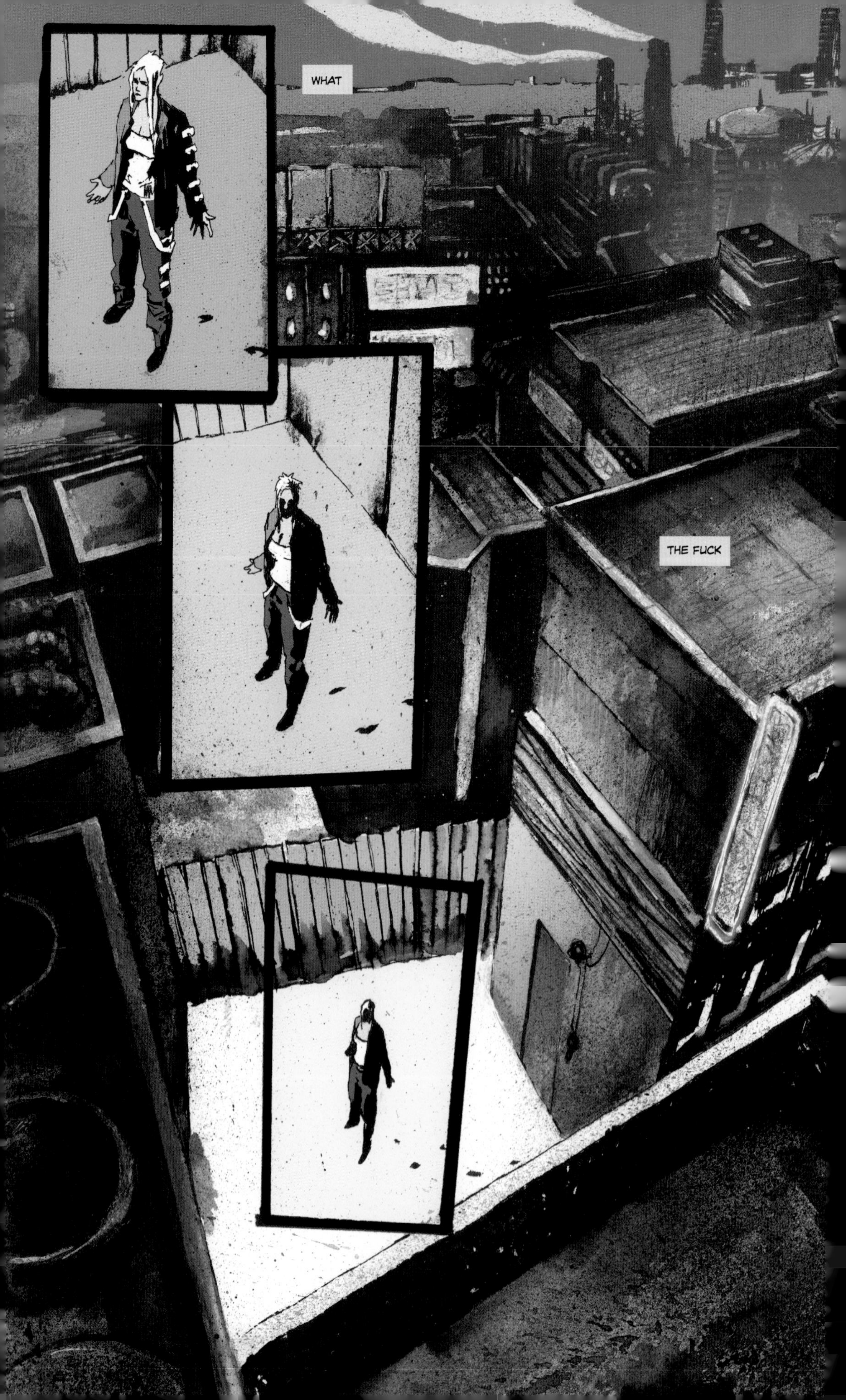
WHAT
THE FUCK

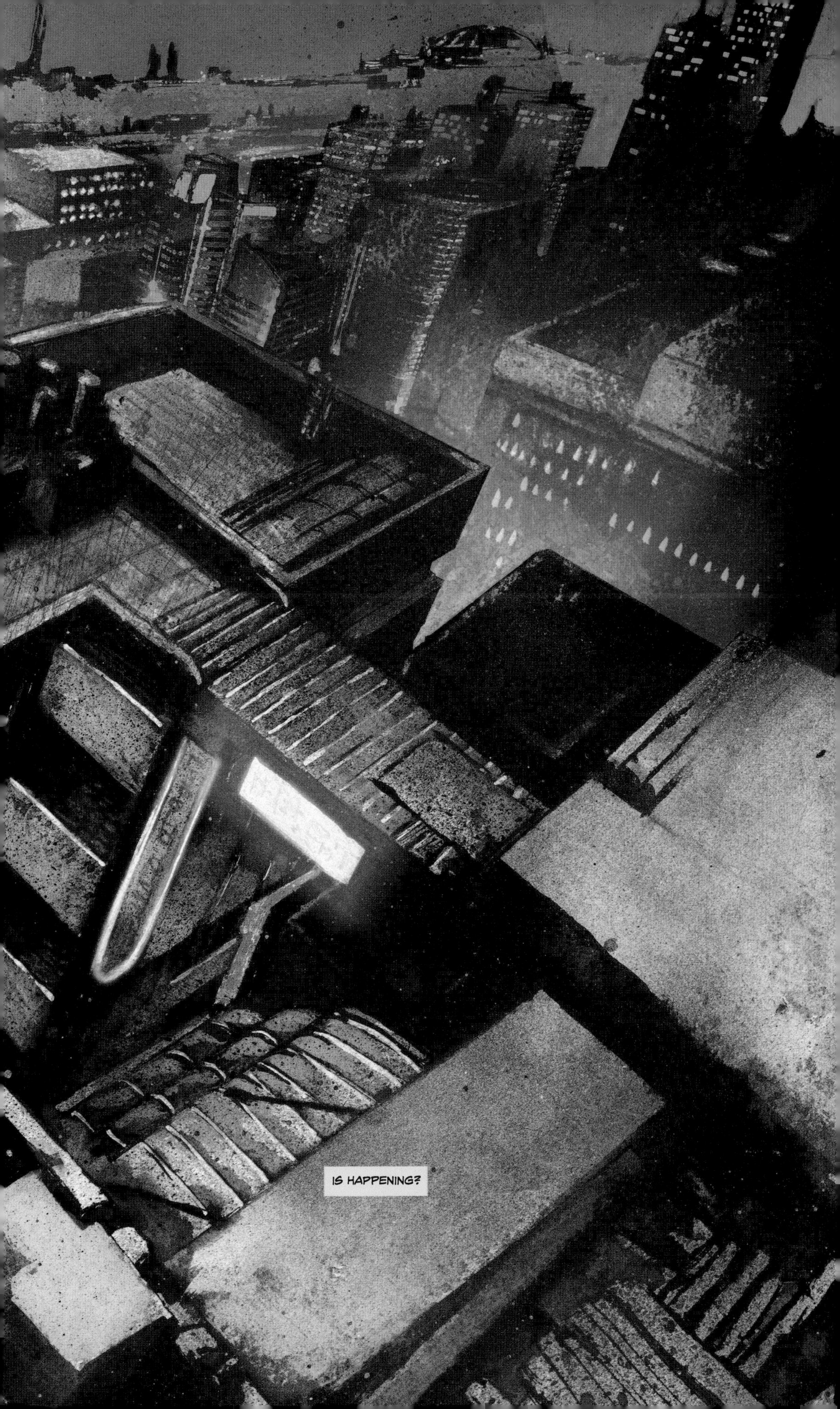
IS HAPPENING?

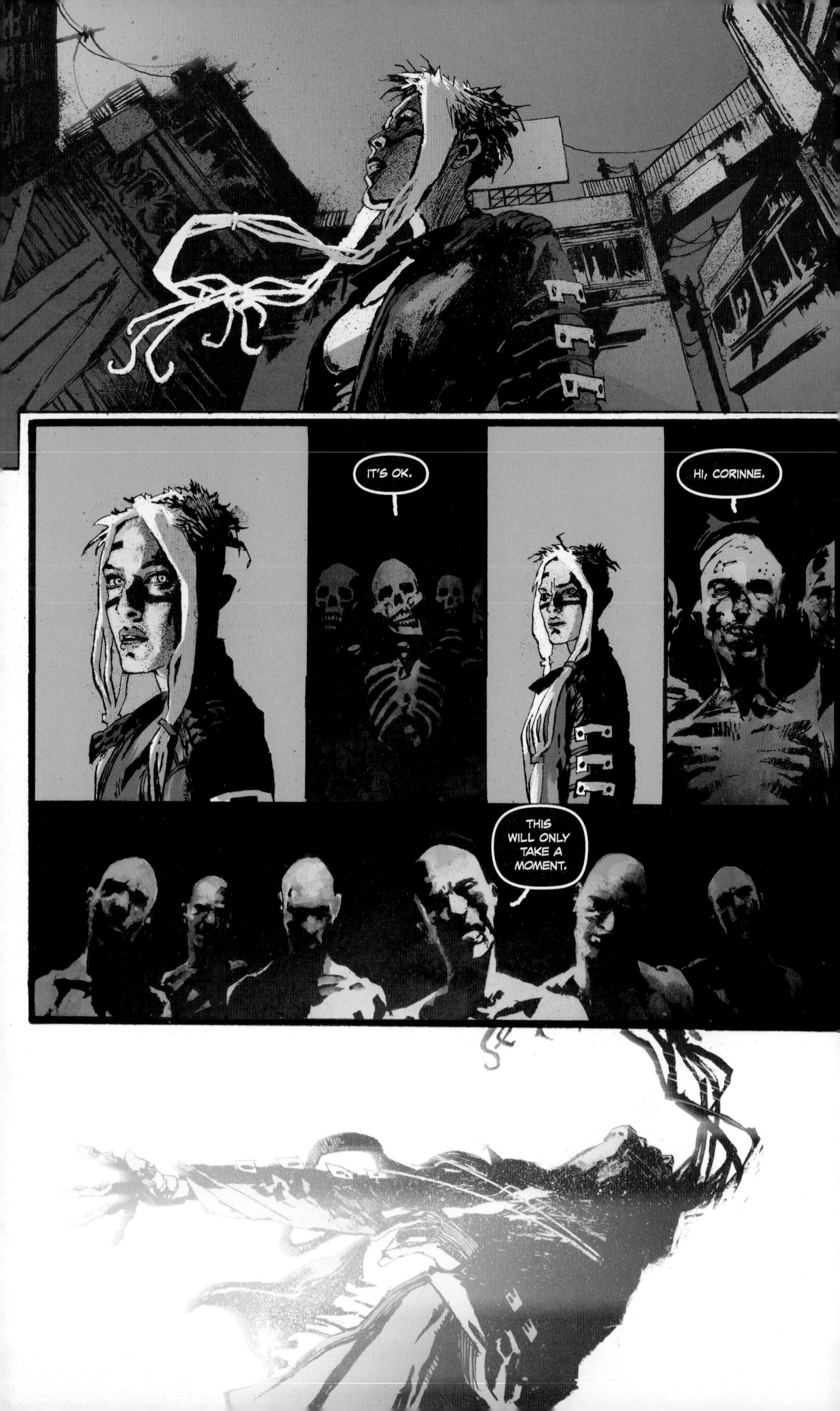

IT'S OK.
HI, CORINNE.
THIS WILL ONLY TAKE A MOMENT.

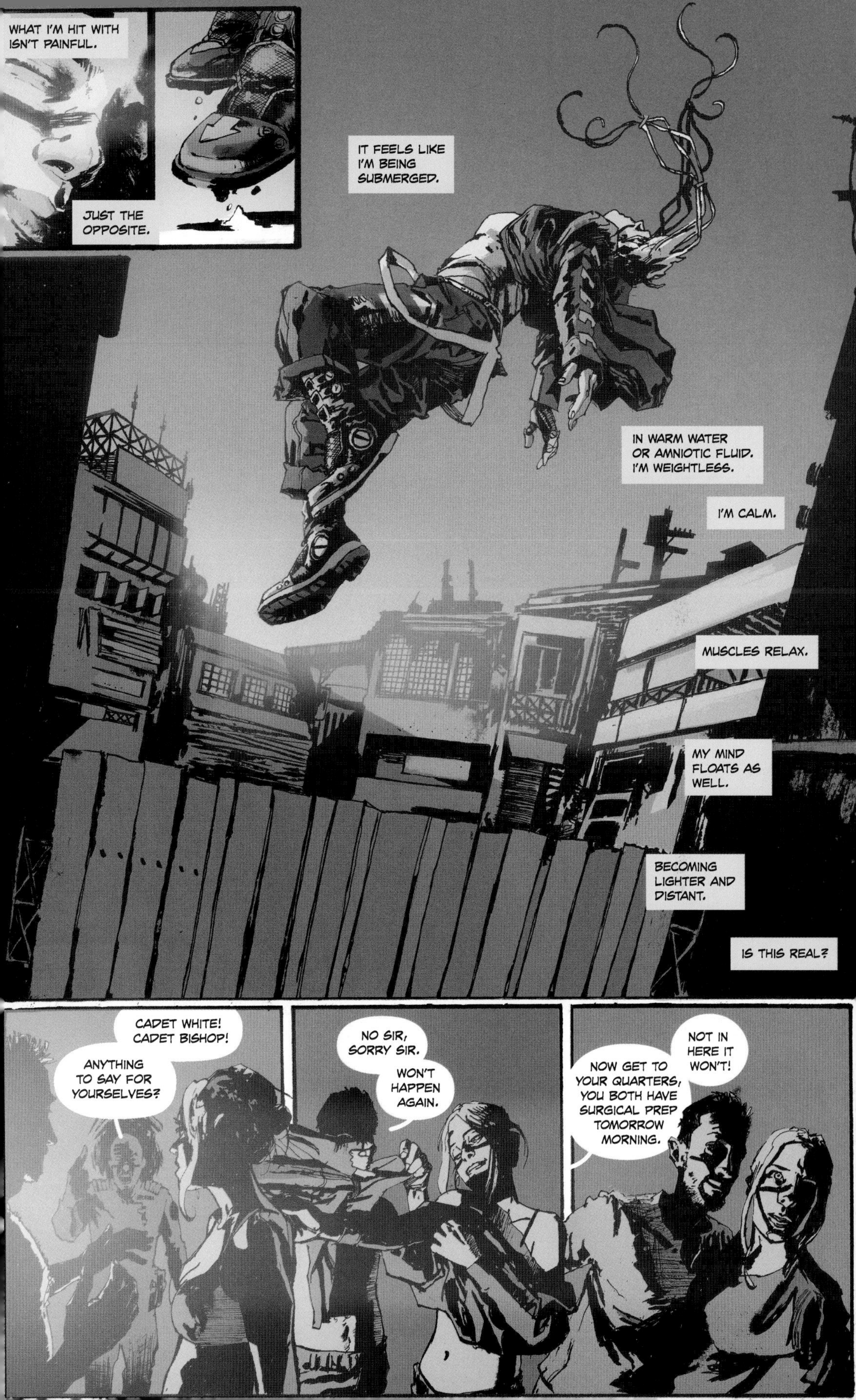
WHAT I'M HIT WITH ISN'T PAINFUL.
JUST THE OPPOSITE.
IT FEELS LIKE I'M BEING SUBMERGED.
IN WARM WATER OR AMNIOTIC FLUID. I'M WEIGHTLESS.
I'M CALM.
MUSCLES RELAX.
MY MIND FLOATS AS WELL.
BECOMING LIGHTER AND DISTANT.
IS THIS REAL?
CADET WHITE! CADET BISHOP!
ANYTHING TO SAY FOR YOURSELVES?
NO SIR, SORRY SIR.
WON'T HAPPEN AGAIN.
NOT IN HERE IT WON'T!
NOW GET TO YOUR QUARTERS, YOU BOTH HAVE SURGICAL PREP TOMORROW MORNING.

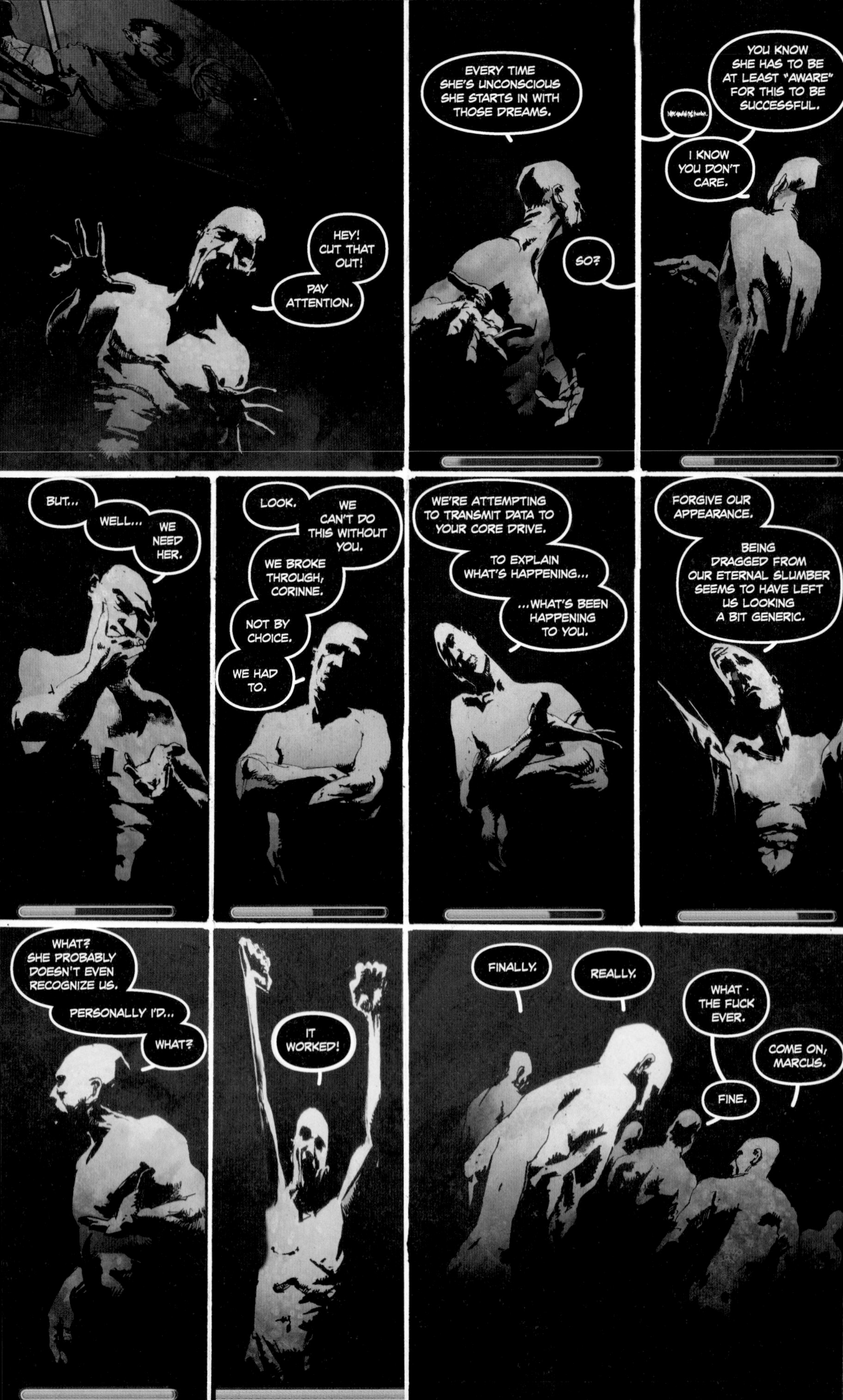
HEY! CUT THAT OUT!
PAY ATTENTION.
EVERY TIME SHE'S UNCONSCIOUS SHE STARTS IN WITH THOSE DREAMS.
SO?
YOU KNOW SHE HAS TO BE AT LEAST "AWARE" FOR THIS TO BE SUCCESSFUL.
I KNOW YOU DON'T CARE.
BUT...
WELL...
WE NEED HER.
LOOK.
WE CAN'T DO THIS WITHOUT YOU.
WE BROKE THROUGH, CORINNE.
NOT BY CHOICE.
WE HAD TO.
WE'RE ATTEMPTING TO TRANSMIT DATA TO YOUR CORE DRIVE.
TO EXPLAIN WHAT'S HAPPENING...
...WHAT'S BEEN HAPPENING TO YOU.
FORGIVE OUR APPEARANCE.
BEING DRAGGED FROM OUR ETERNAL SLUMBER SEEMS TO HAVE LEFT US LOOKING A BIT GENERIC.
WHAT? SHE PROBABLY DOESN'T EVEN RECOGNIZE US.
PERSONALLY I'D...
WHAT?
IT WORKED!
FINALLY.
REALLY.
WHAT THE FUCK EVER.
COME ON, MARCUS.
FINE.

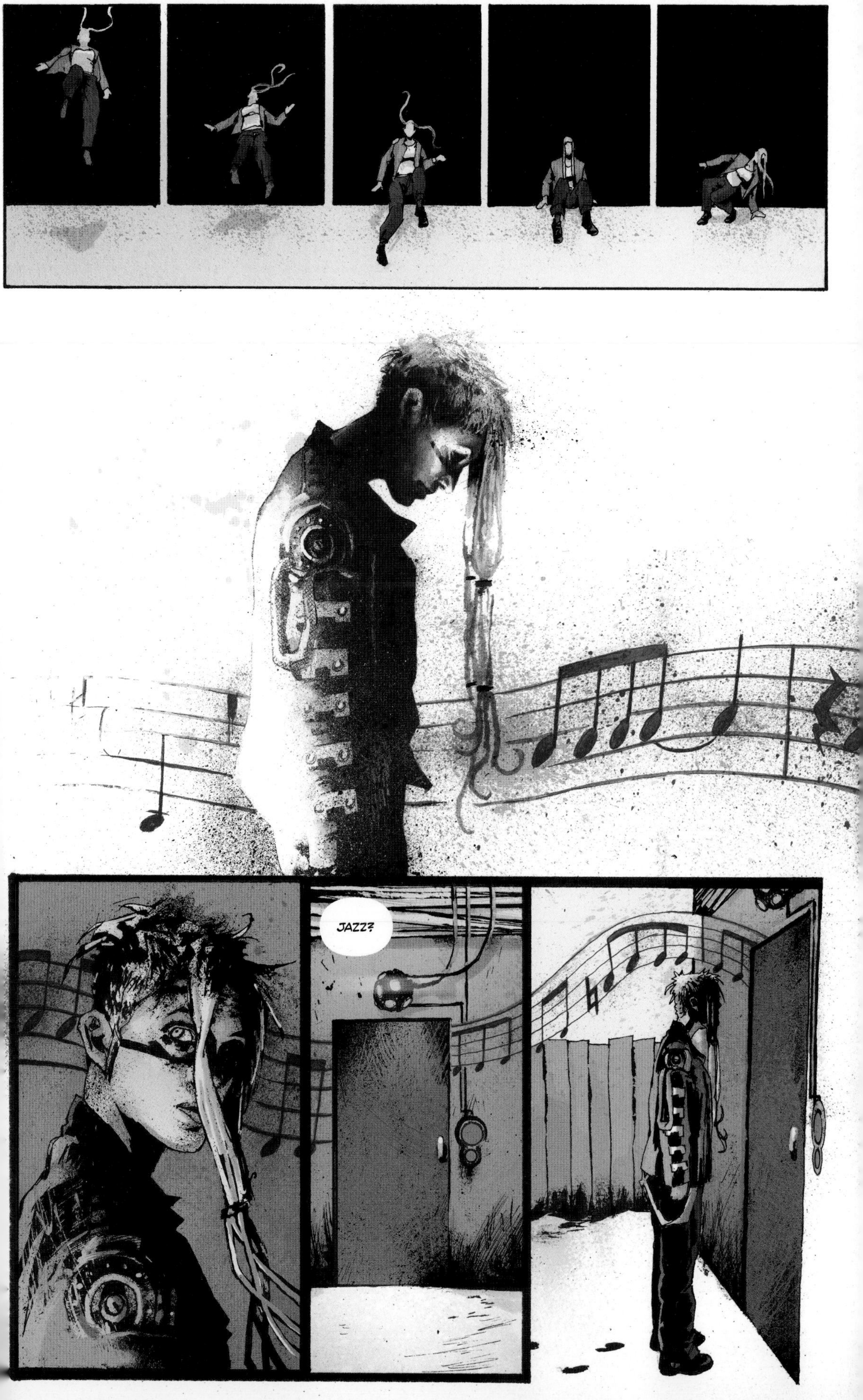
JAZZ?

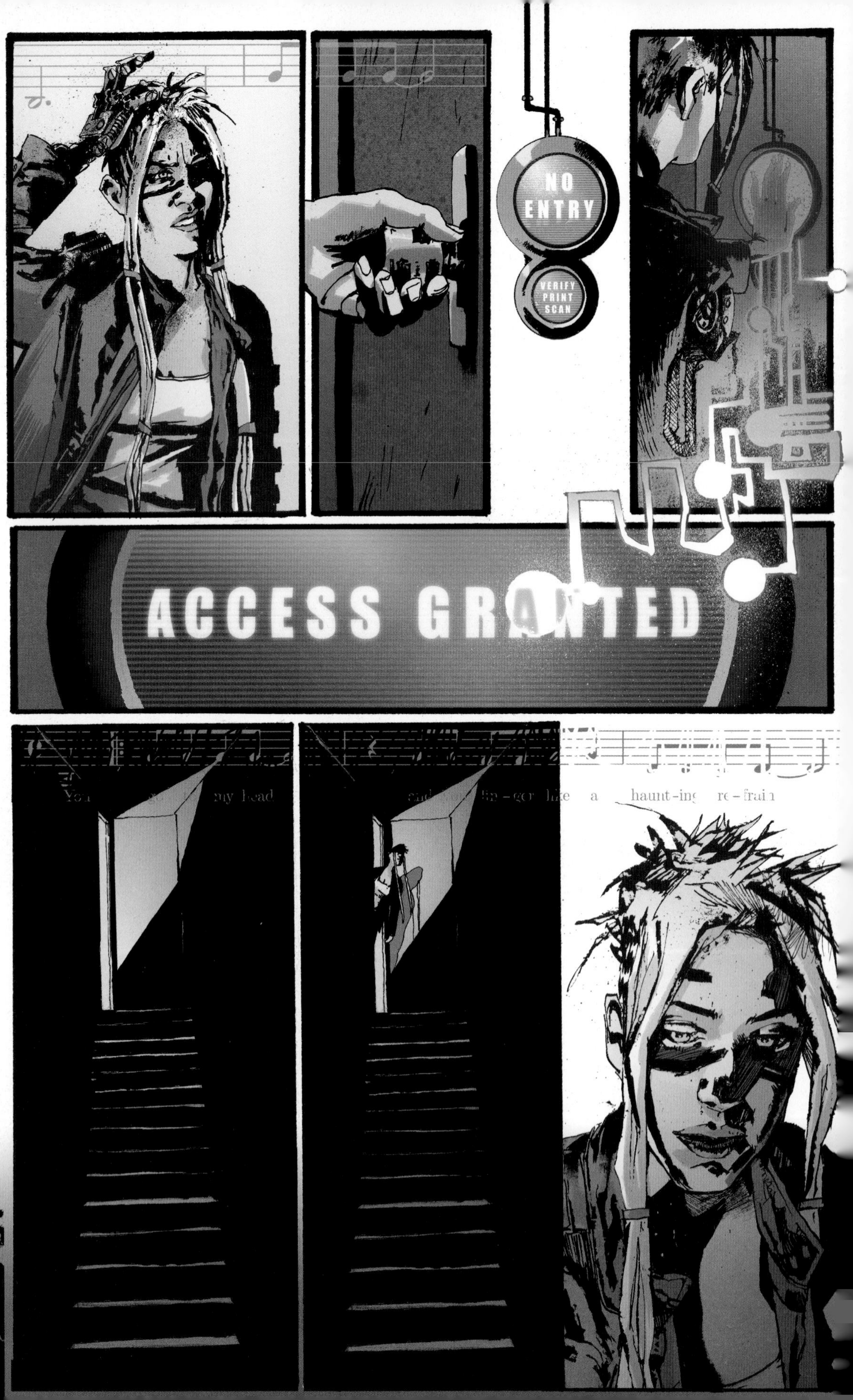
NO ENTRY
VERIFY PRINT SCAN
ACCESS GRANTED
my head
like a haunt-ing re-frain

ghost of a chance ... to my head.

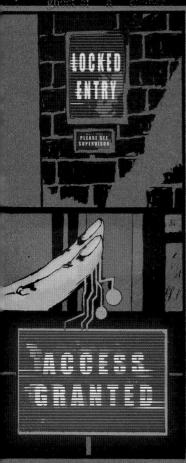

LOCKED ENTRY

PLEASE SEE SUPERVISOR

ACCESS GRANTED

HELLO?

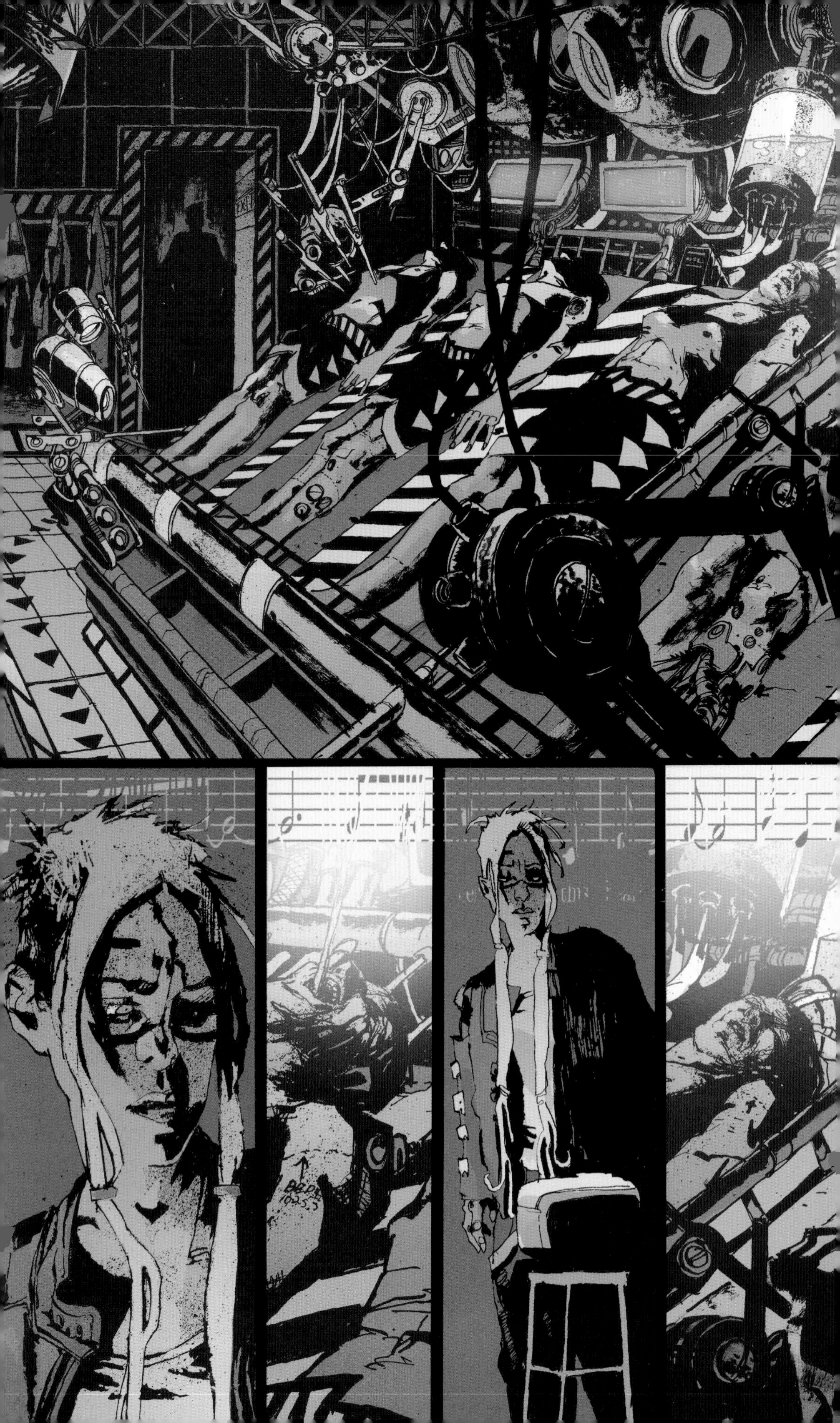

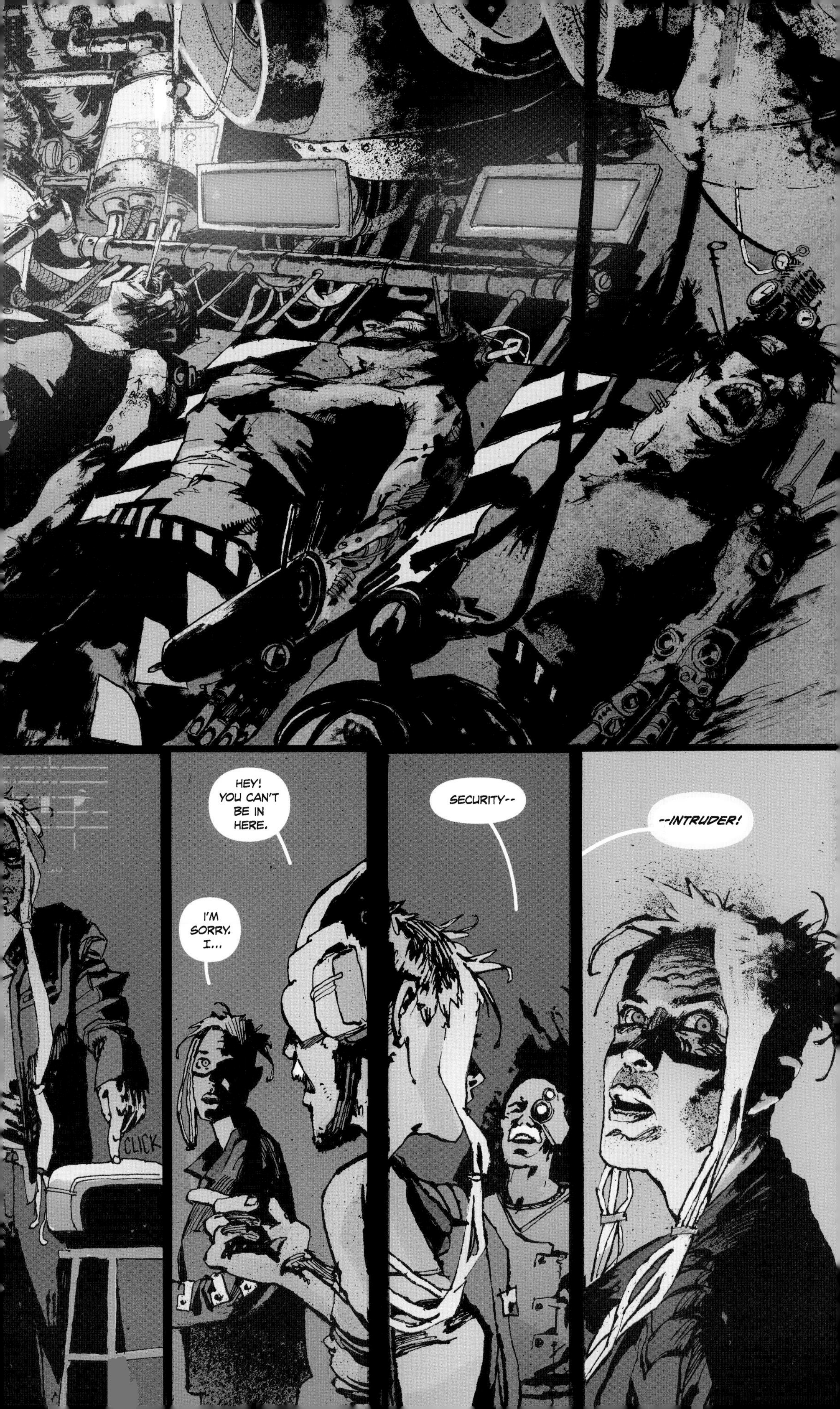
CLICK
HEY! YOU CAN'T BE IN HERE.
I'M SORRY. I...
SECURITY--
--INTRUDER!

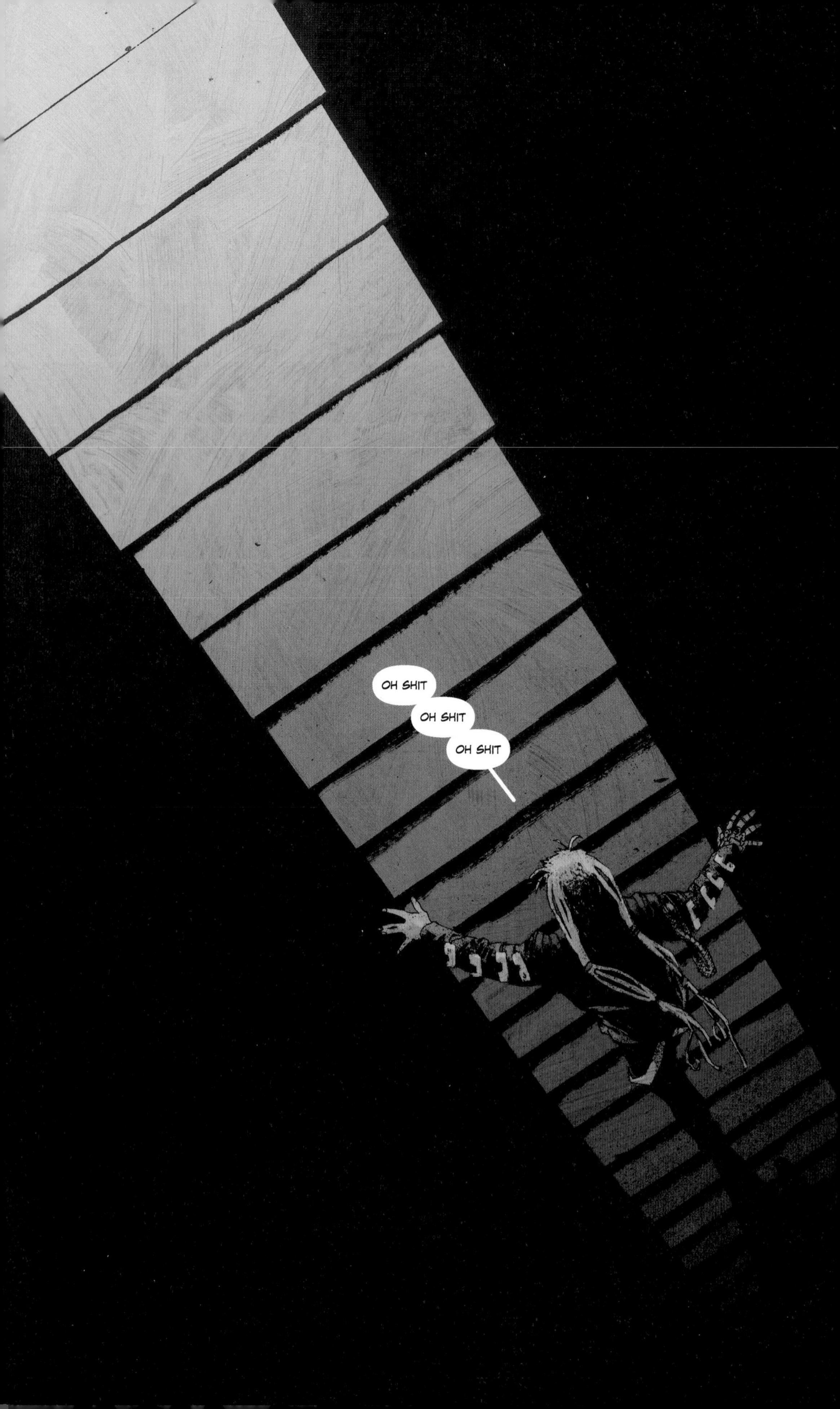
OH SHIT
OH SHIT
OH SHIT

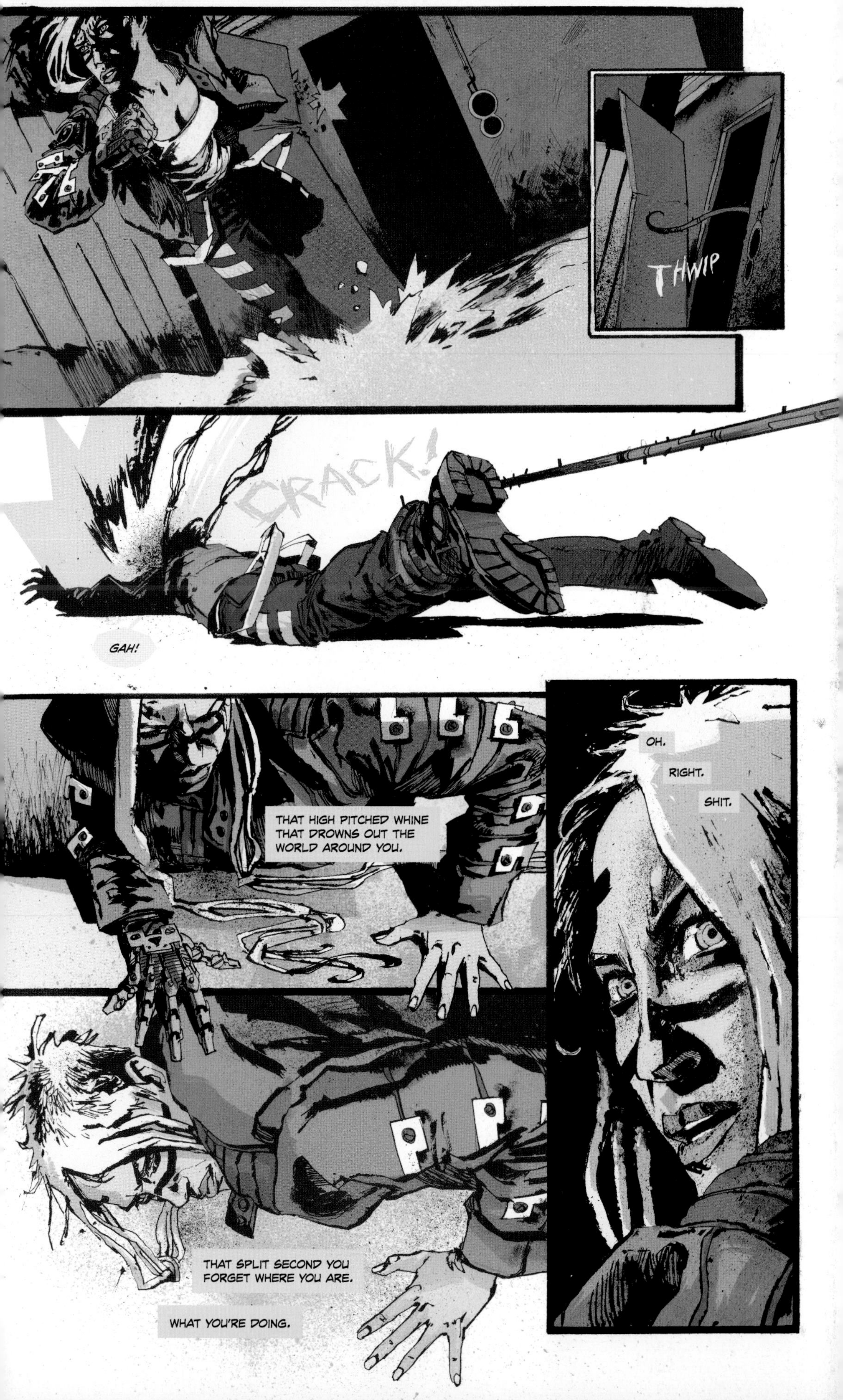
THWIP
CRACK!
GAH!
THAT HIGH PITCHED WHINE THAT DROWNS OUT THE WORLD AROUND YOU.
THAT SPLIT SECOND YOU FORGET WHERE YOU ARE.
WHAT YOU'RE DOING.
OH.
RIGHT.
SHIT.

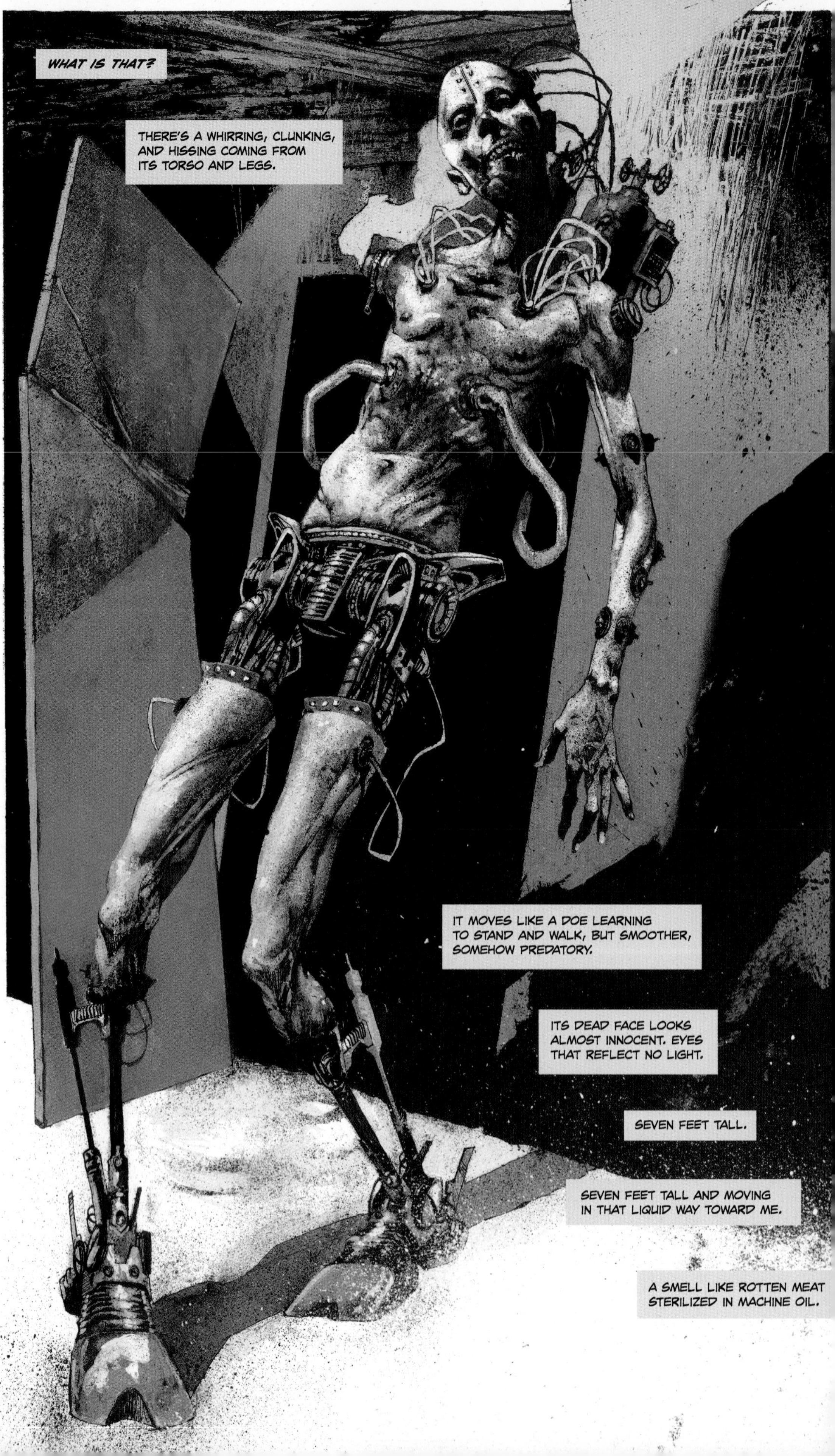
WHAT IS THAT?
THERE'S A WHIRRING, CLUNKING, AND HISSING COMING FROM ITS TORSO AND LEGS.
IT MOVES LIKE A DOE LEARNING TO STAND AND WALK, BUT SMOOTHER, SOMEHOW PREDATORY.
ITS DEAD FACE LOOKS ALMOST INNOCENT. EYES THAT REFLECT NO LIGHT.
SEVEN FEET TALL.
SEVEN FEET TALL AND MOVING IN THAT LIQUID WAY TOWARD ME.
A SMELL LIKE ROTTEN MEAT STERILIZED IN MACHINE OIL.

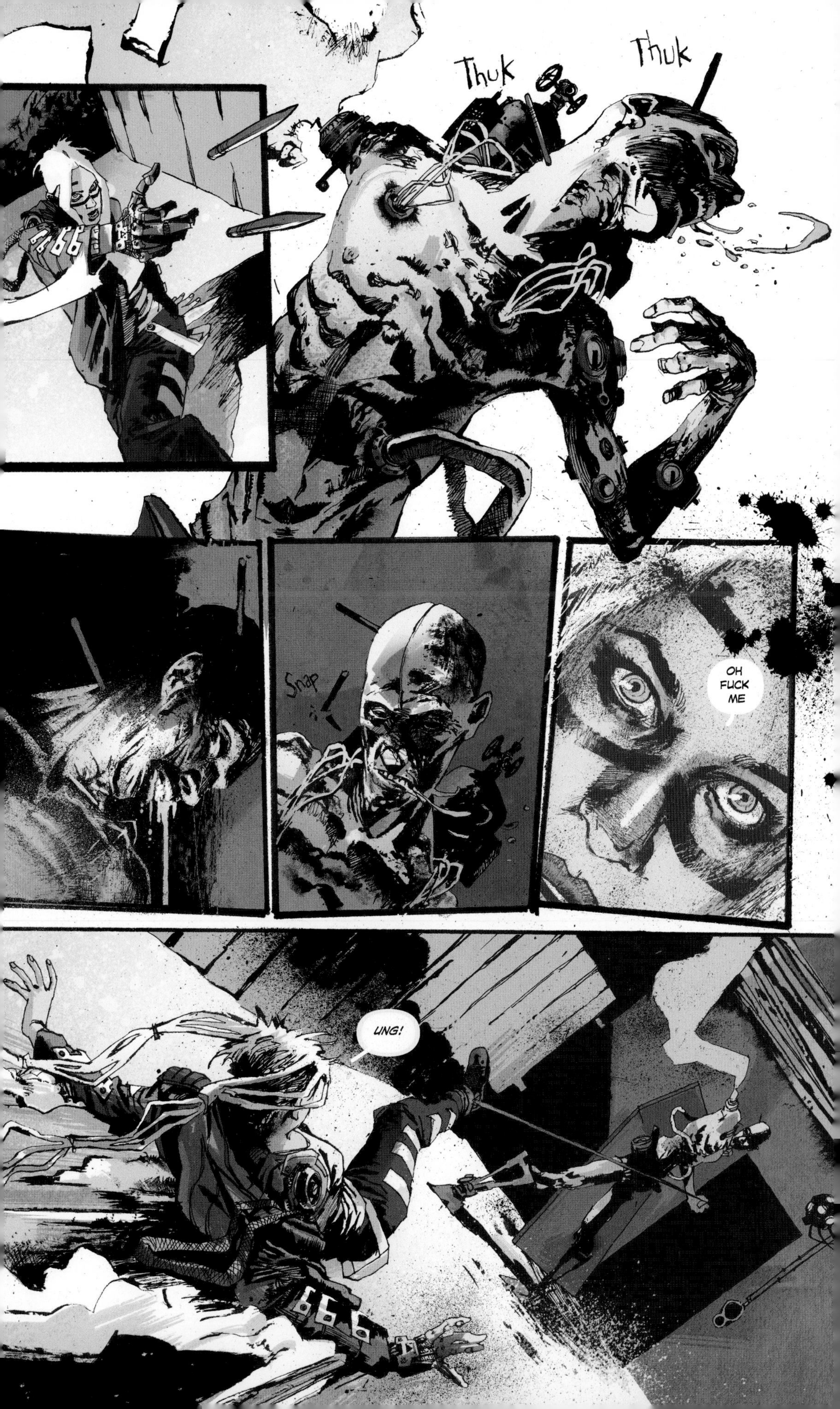

Thuk
Thuk
Snap
OH FUCK ME
UNG!

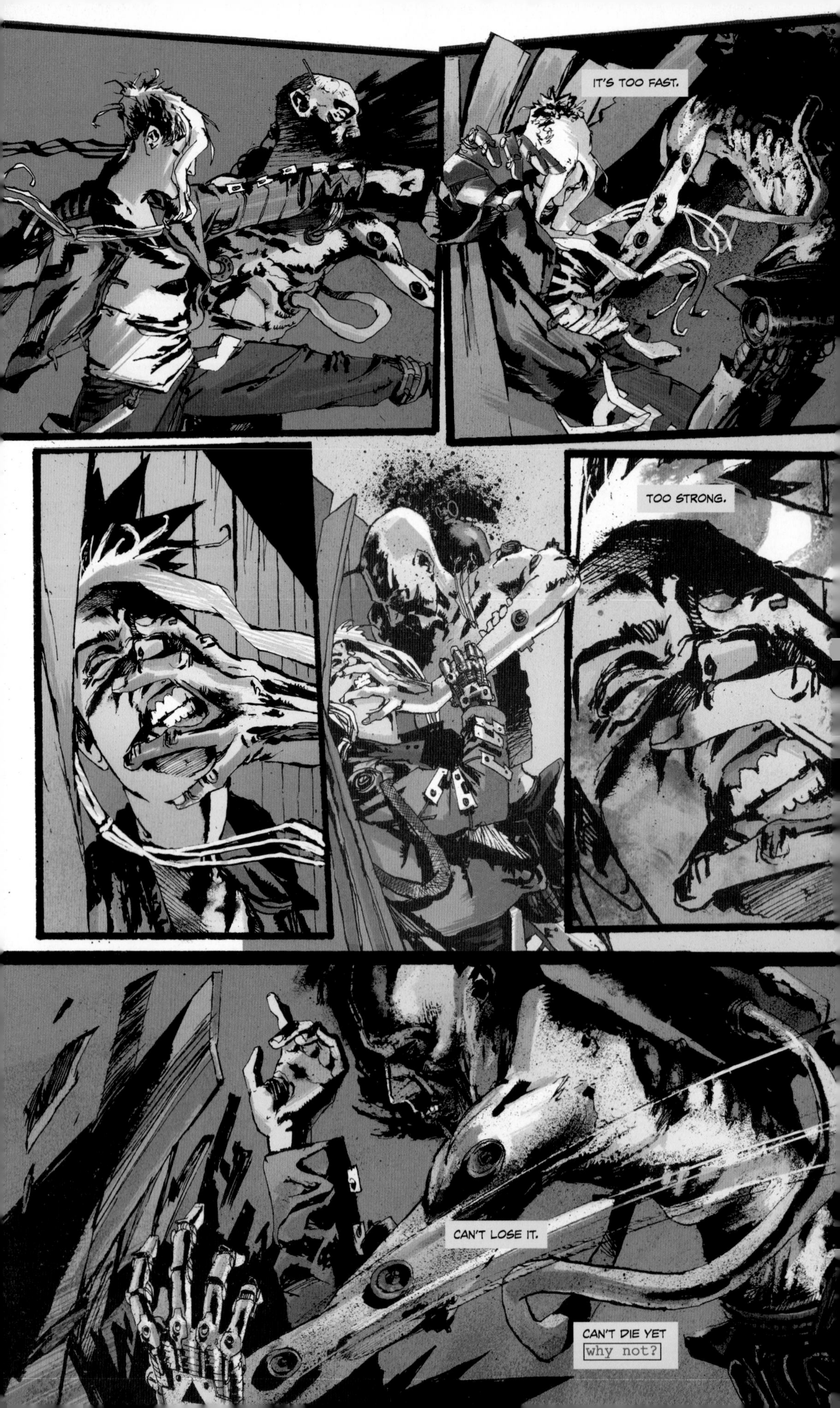
IT'S TOO FAST.
TOO STRONG.
CAN'T LOSE IT.
CAN'T DIE YET
why not?

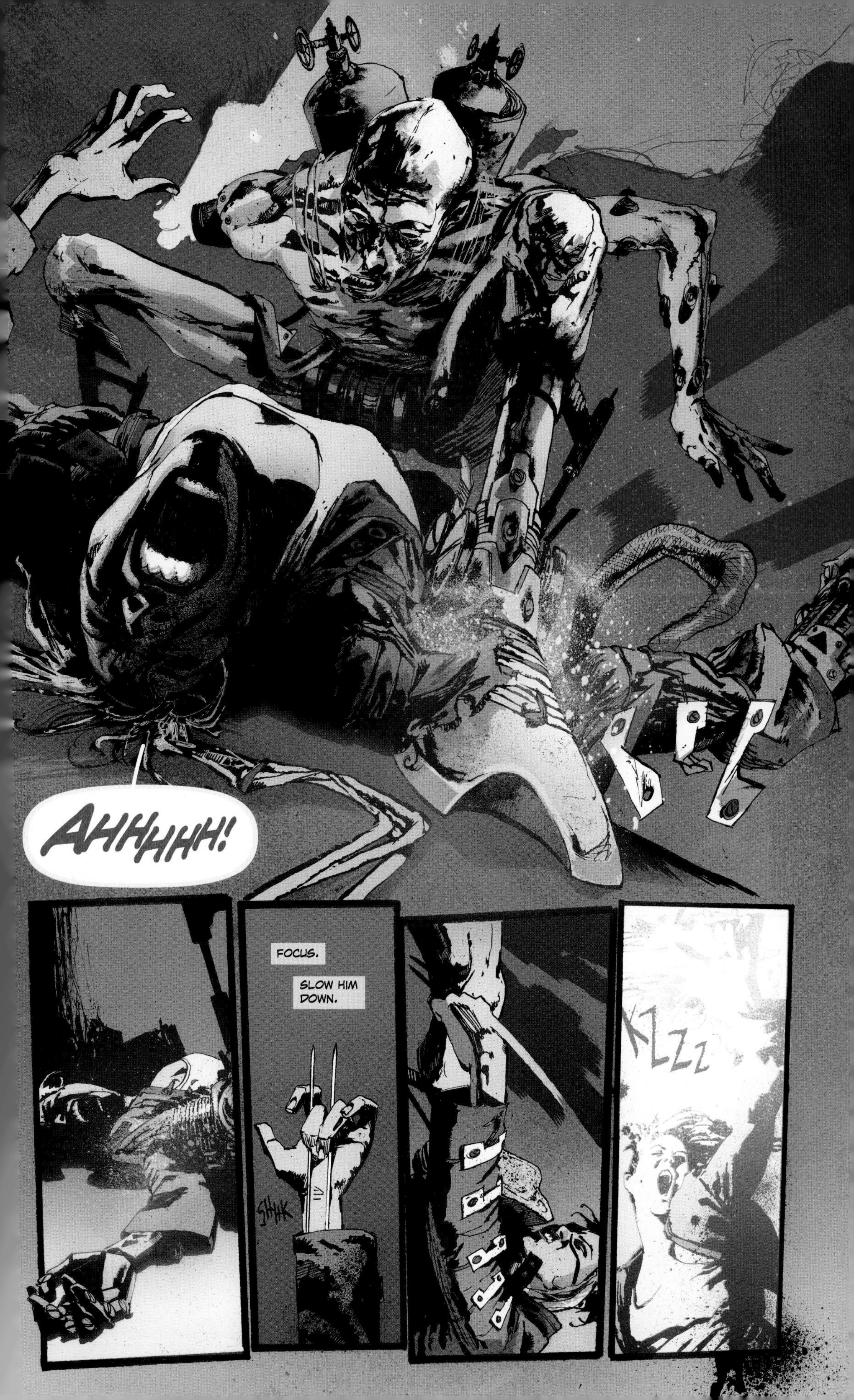
AHHHHH!
FOCUS.
SLOW HIM DOWN.
SHIK
KZZZ

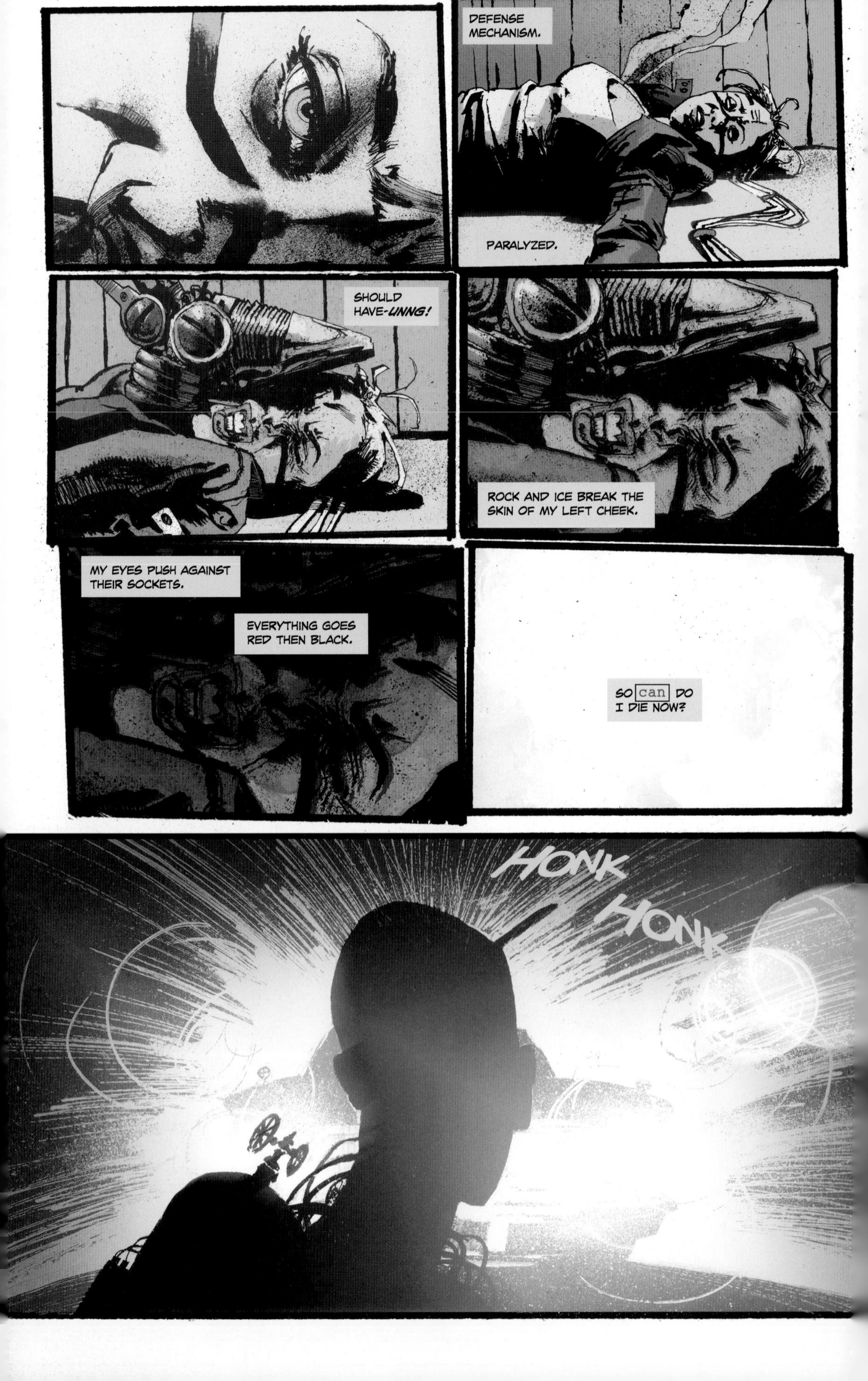
DEFENSE MECHANISM.
PARALYZED.
SHOULD HAVE-UNNG!
ROCK AND ICE BREAK THE SKIN OF MY LEFT CHEEK.
MY EYES PUSH AGAINST THEIR SOCKETS.
EVERYTHING GOES RED THEN BLACK.
SO can DO I DIE NOW?
HONK
HONK

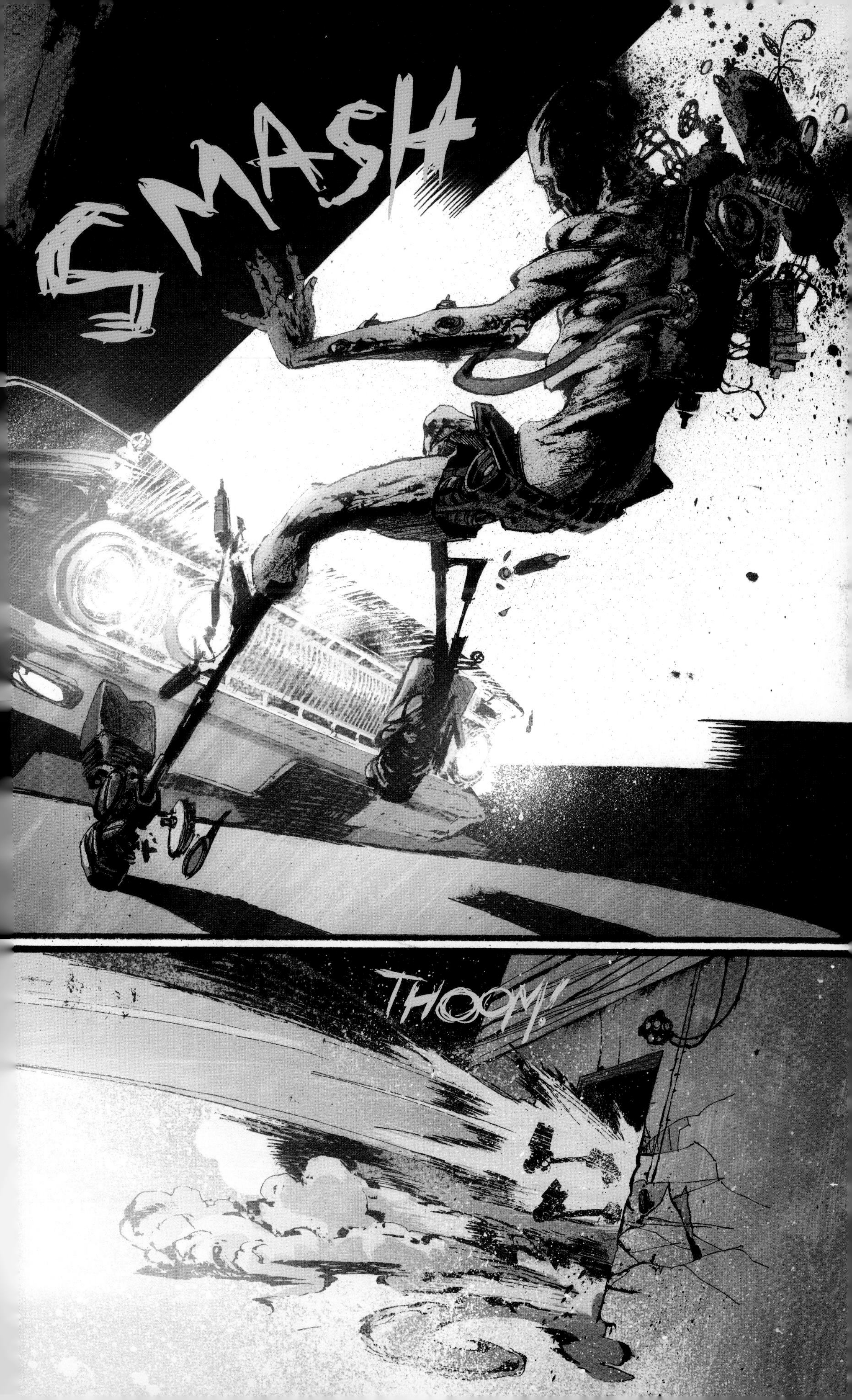
SMASH
THOOM!

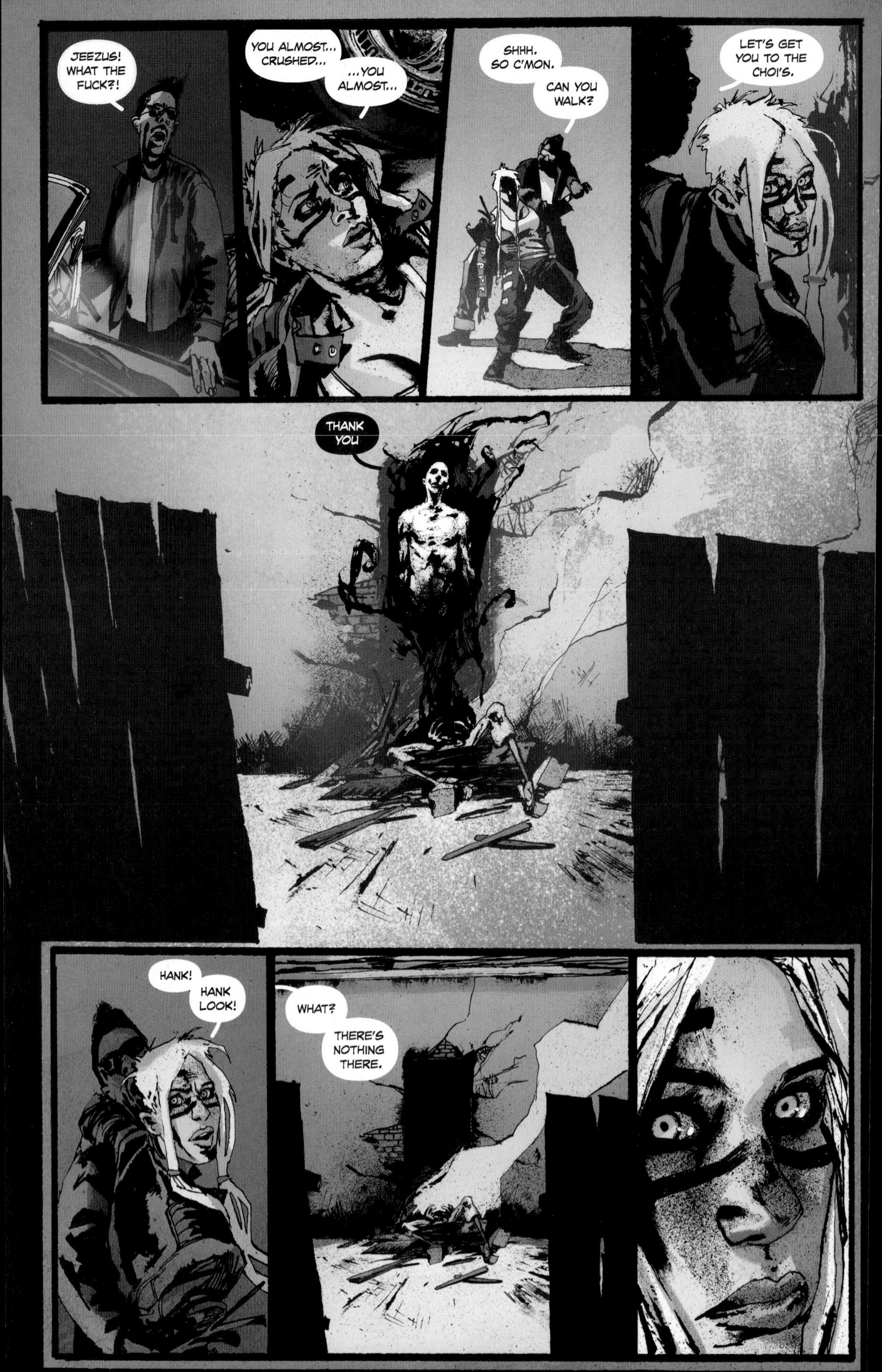
JEEZUS! WHAT THE FUCK?!
YOU ALMOST... CRUSHED...
...YOU ALMOST...
SHHH. SO C'MON.
CAN YOU WALK?
LET'S GET YOU TO THE CHOI'S.
THANK YOU
HANK!
HANK LOOK!
WHAT?
THERE'S NOTHING THERE.

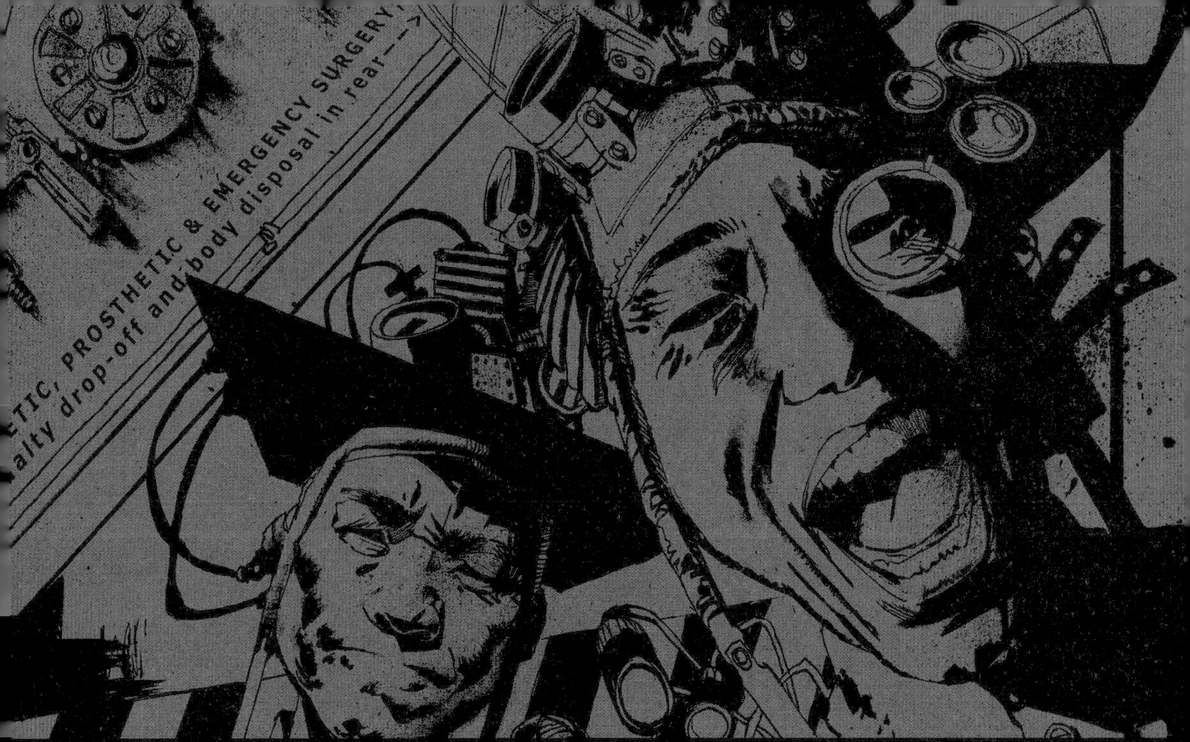
ETIC, PROSTHETIC & EMERGENCY SURGERY
alty drop-off and body disposal in rear-->

CHAPTER THREE

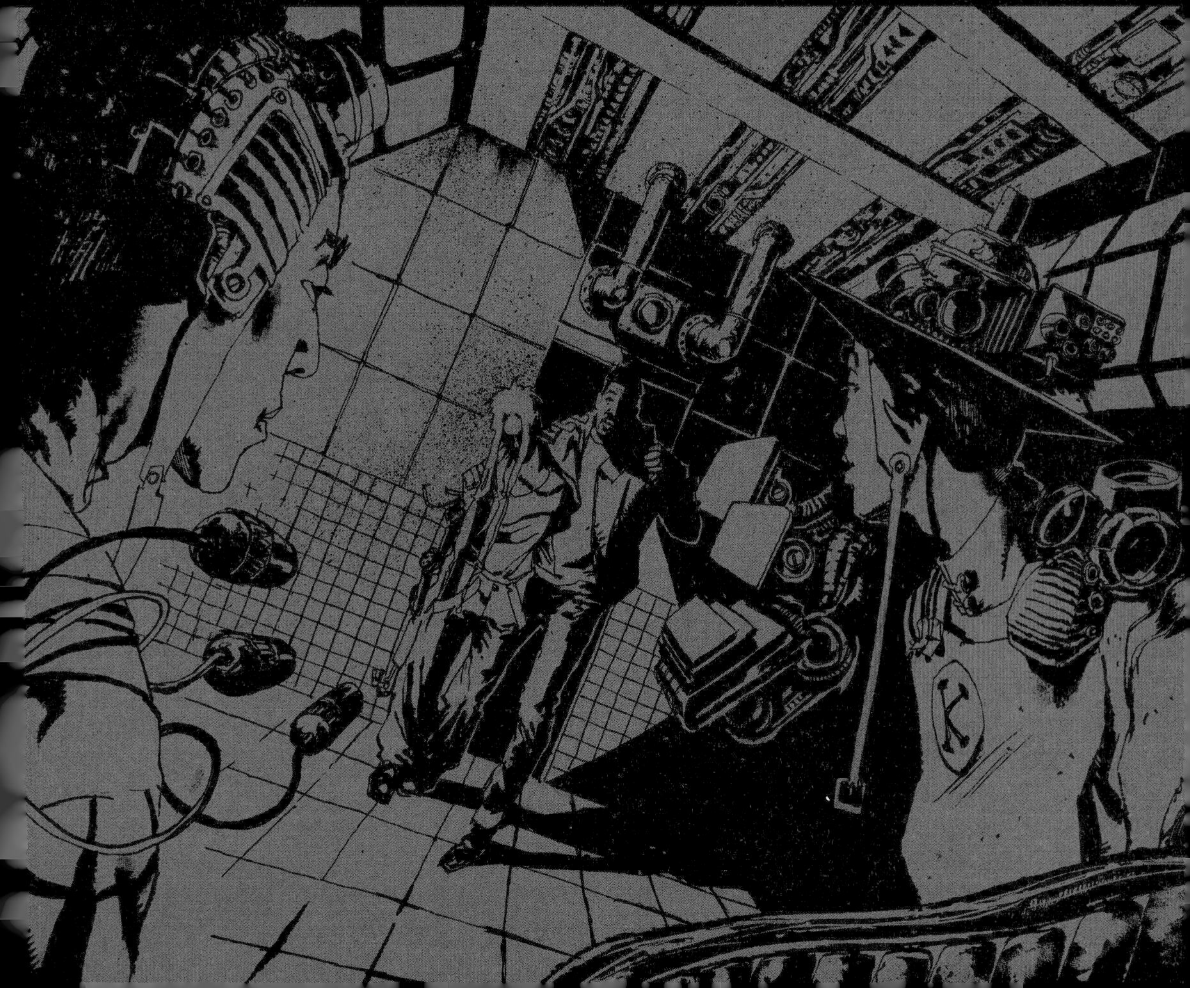

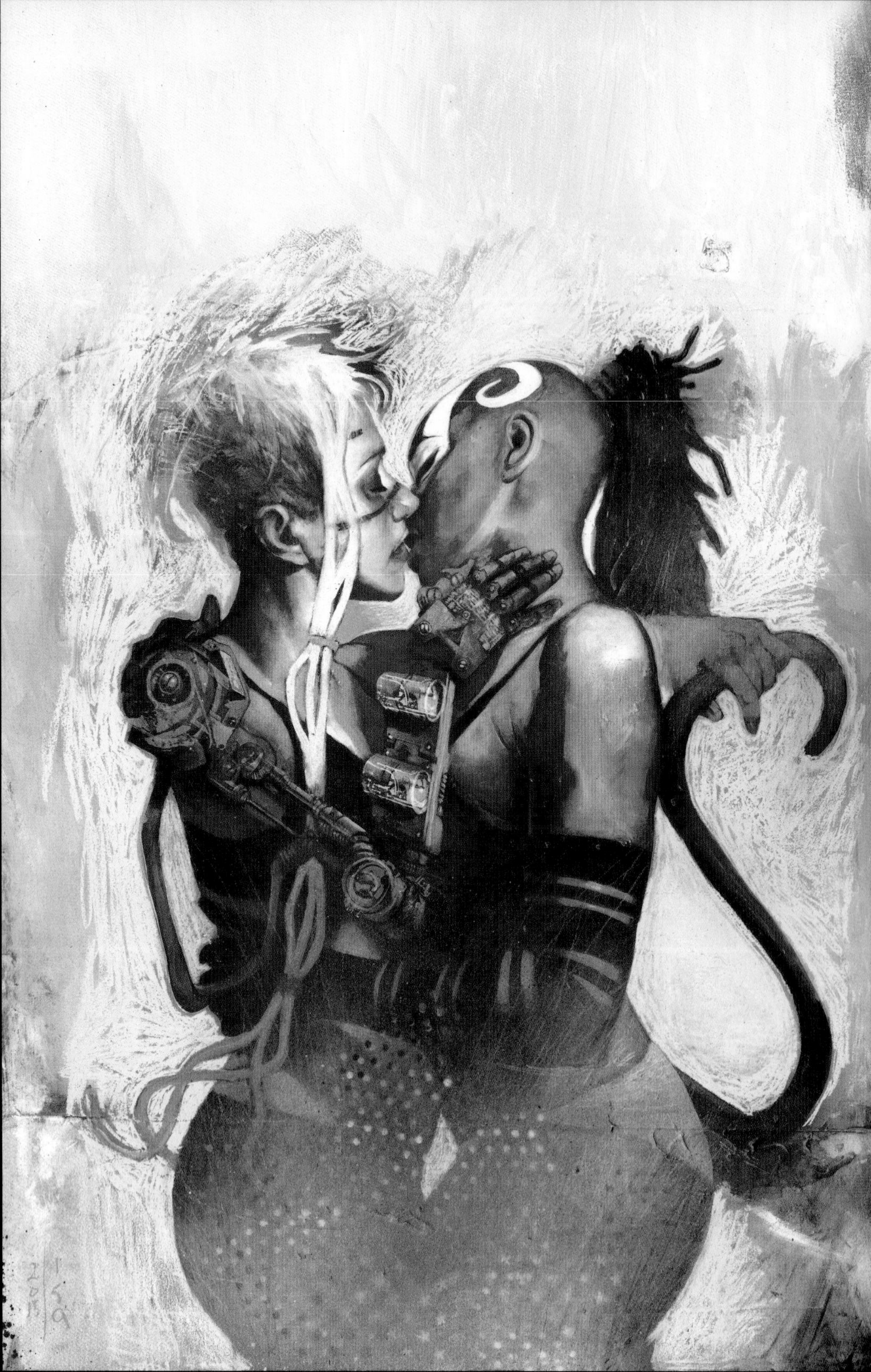

30 x 40 in. ink, acrylic, oil, pastel, spray paint, paper, & digital collage on canvas

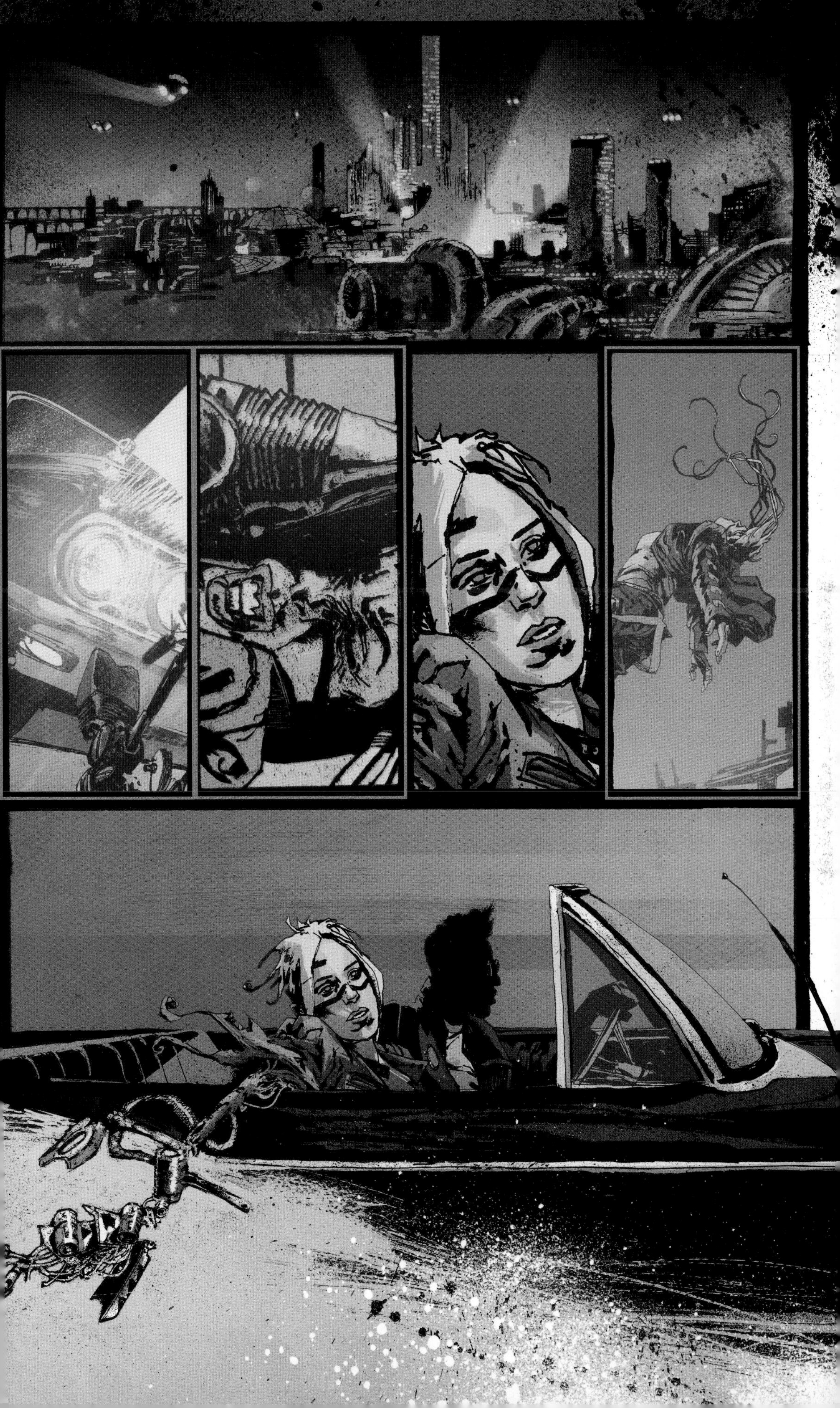

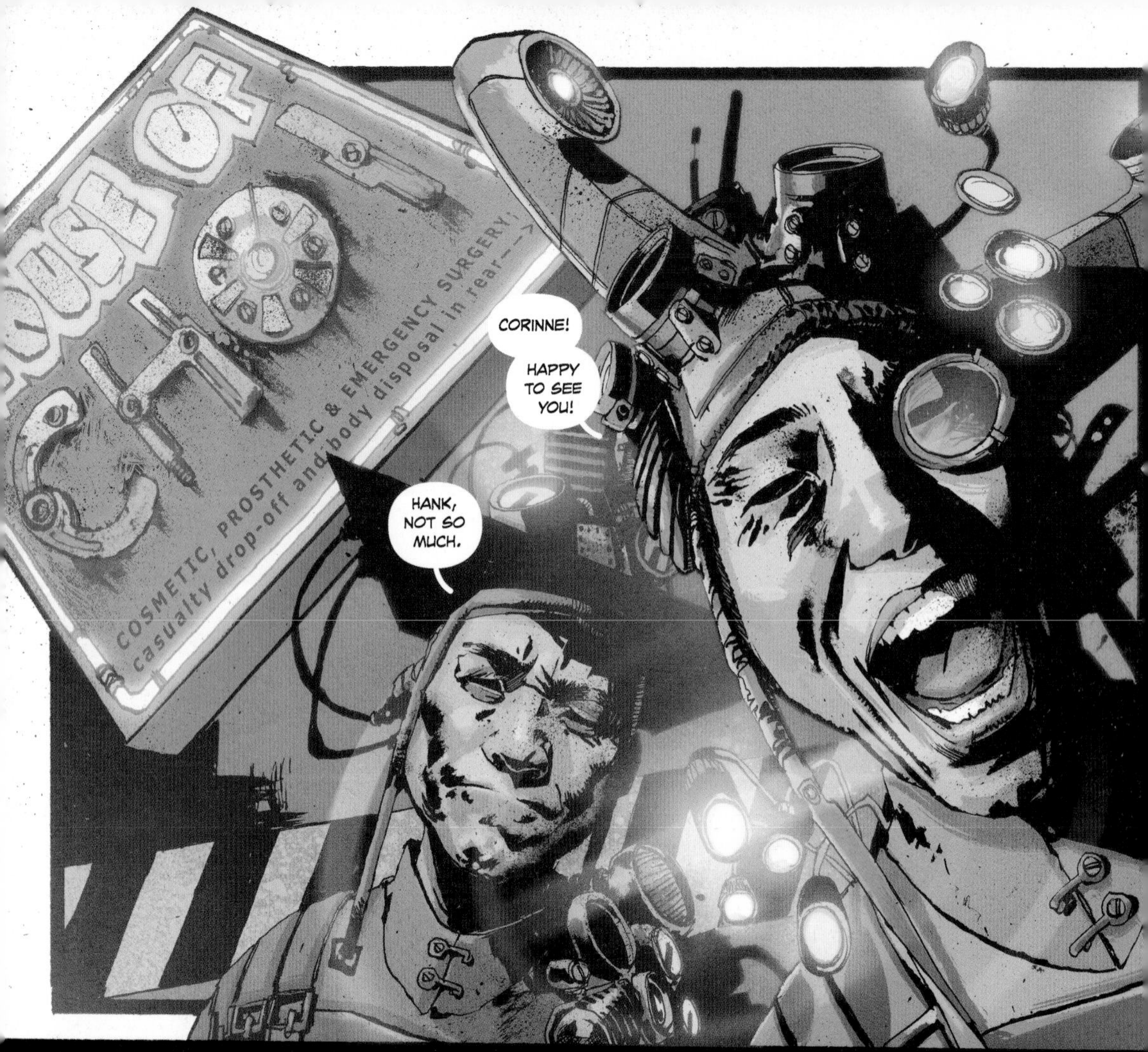
HOUSE OF
COSMETIC, PROSTHETIC & EMERGENCY SURGERY!
casualty drop-off and body disposal in rear--->
CORINNE!
HAPPY TO SEE YOU!
HANK, NOT SO MUCH.

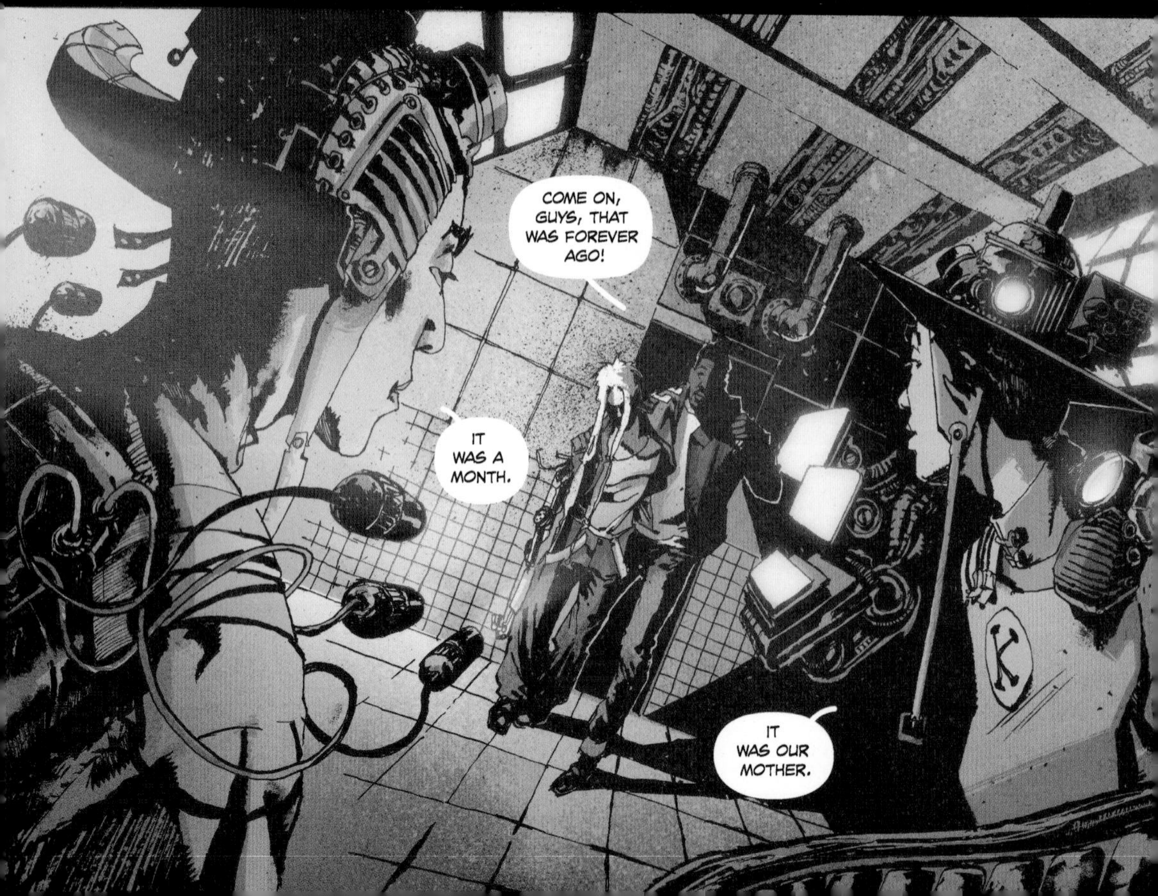
COME ON, GUYS, THAT WAS FOREVER AGO!
IT WAS A MONTH.
IT WAS OUR MOTHER.

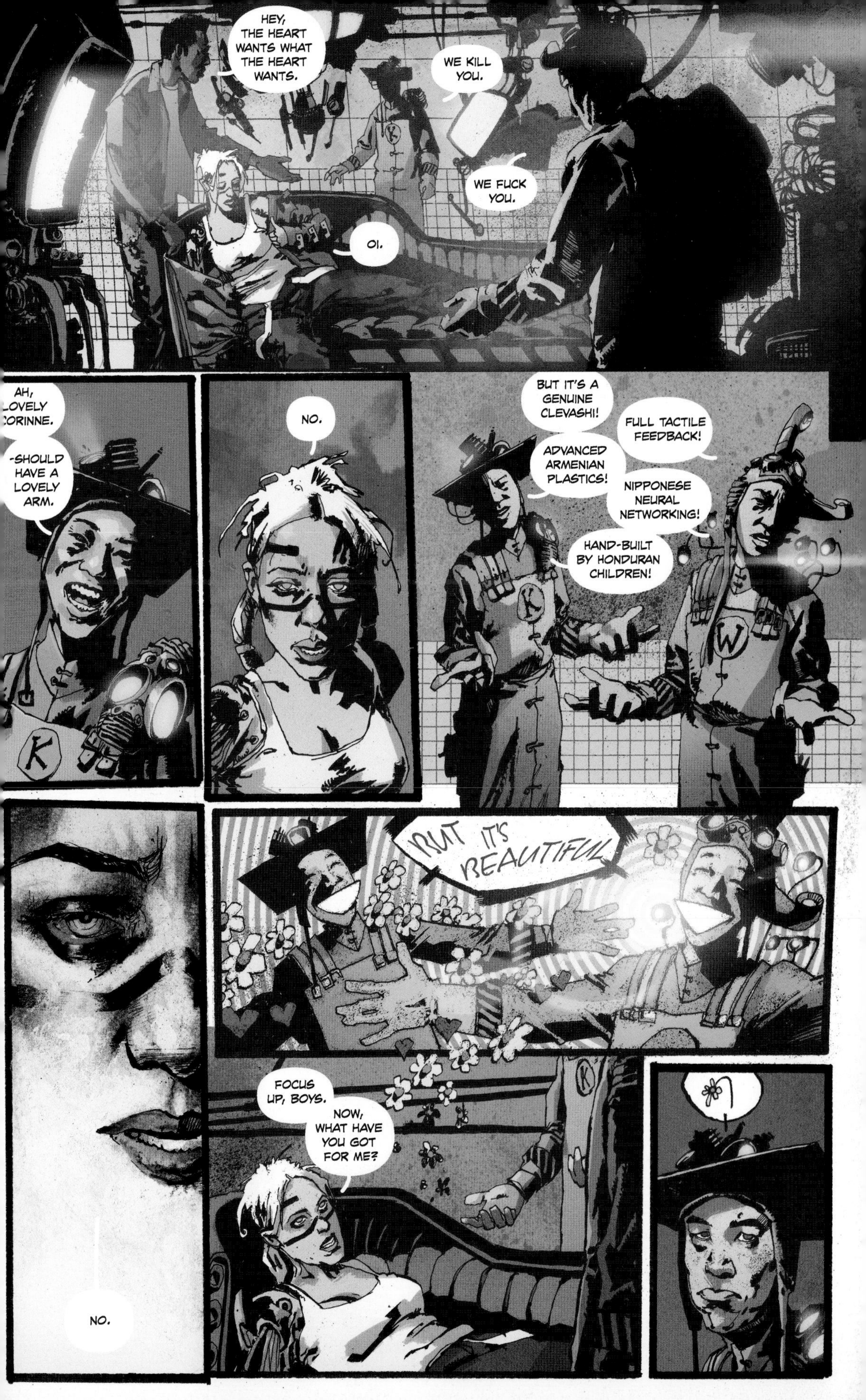
HEY, THE HEART WANTS WHAT THE HEART WANTS.
WE KILL YOU.
WE FUCK YOU.
OI.
AH, LOVELY CORINNE.
-SHOULD HAVE A LOVELY ARM.
NO.
BUT IT'S A GENUINE CLEVASHI!
FULL TACTILE FEEDBACK!
ADVANCED ARMENIAN PLASTICS!
NIPPONESE NEURAL NETWORKING!
HAND-BUILT BY HONDURAN CHILDREN!
NO.
BUT IT'S BEAUTIFUL
FOCUS UP, BOYS.
NOW, WHAT HAVE YOU GOT FOR ME?

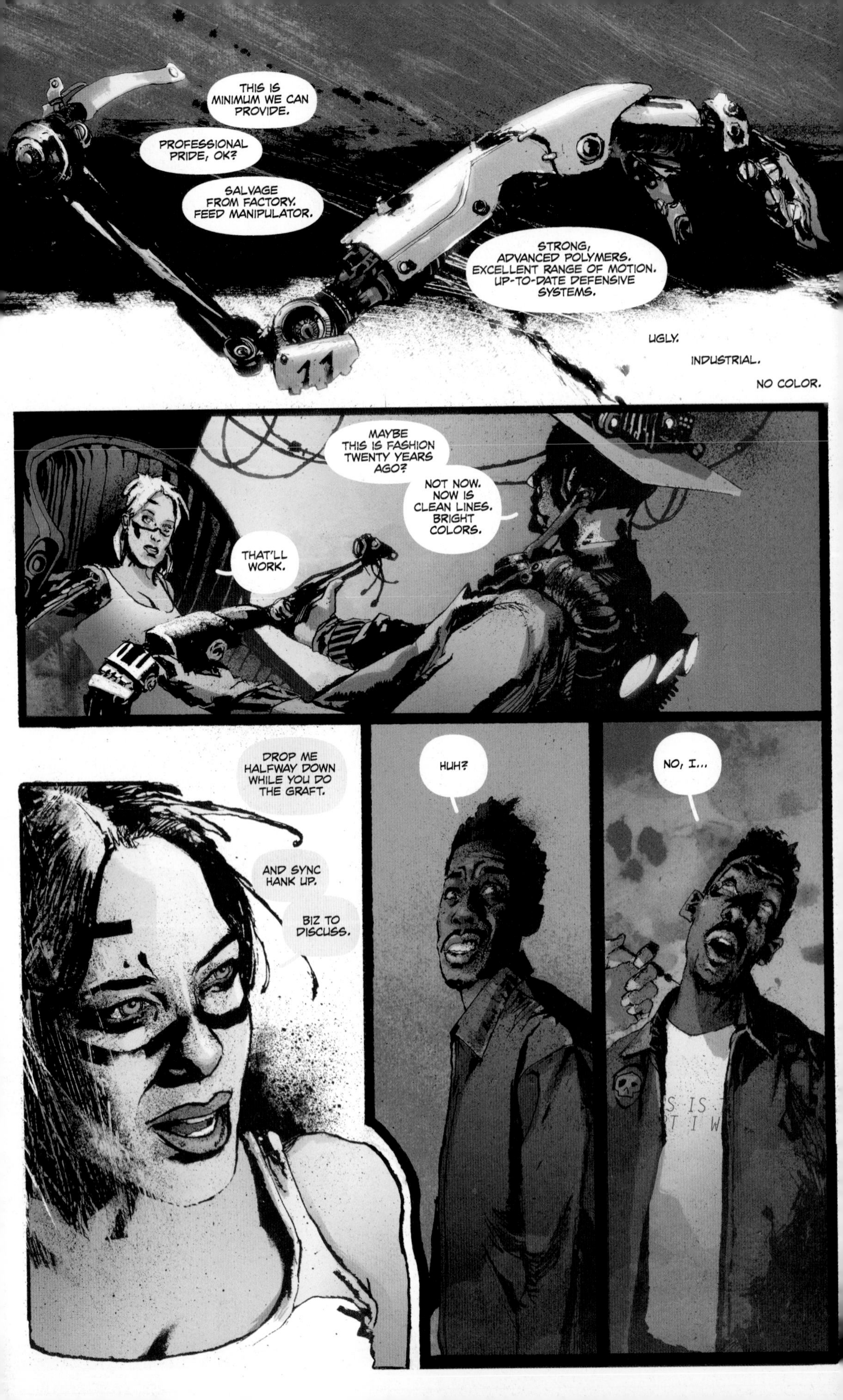
THIS IS MINIMUM WE CAN PROVIDE.
PROFESSIONAL PRIDE, OK?
SALVAGE FROM FACTORY. FEED MANIPULATOR.
STRONG, ADVANCED POLYMERS. EXCELLENT RANGE OF MOTION. UP-TO-DATE DEFENSIVE SYSTEMS.
UGLY.
INDUSTRIAL.
NO COLOR.
MAYBE THIS IS FASHION TWENTY YEARS AGO?
NOT NOW. NOW IS CLEAN LINES. BRIGHT COLORS.
THAT'LL WORK.
DROP ME HALFWAY DOWN WHILE YOU DO THE GRAFT.
AND SYNC HANK UP.
BIZ TO DISCUSS.
HUH?
NO, I...

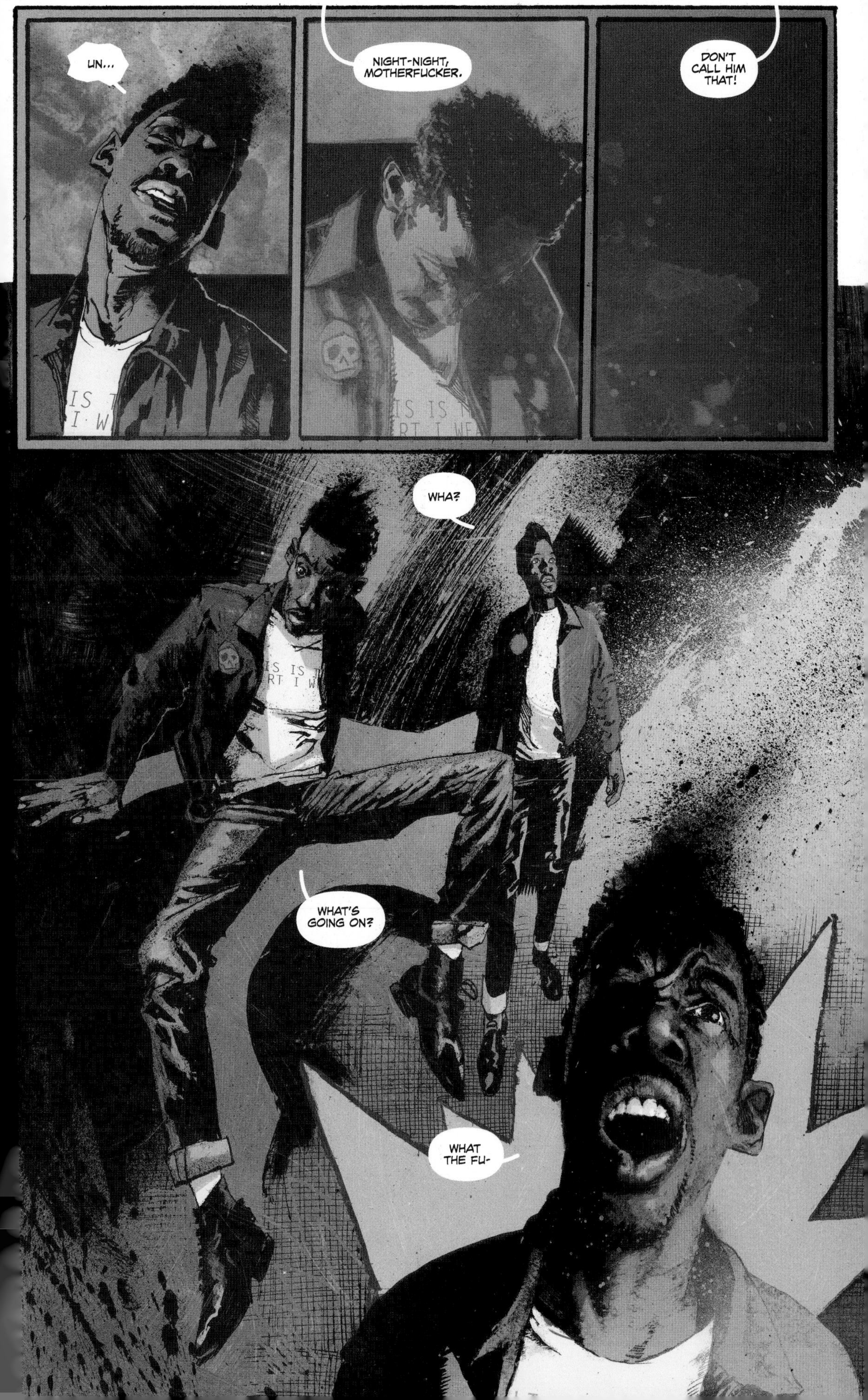
UN...
NIGHT-NIGHT, MOTHERFUCKER.
DON'T CALL HIM THAT!
WHA?
WHAT'S GOING ON?
WHAT THE FU-

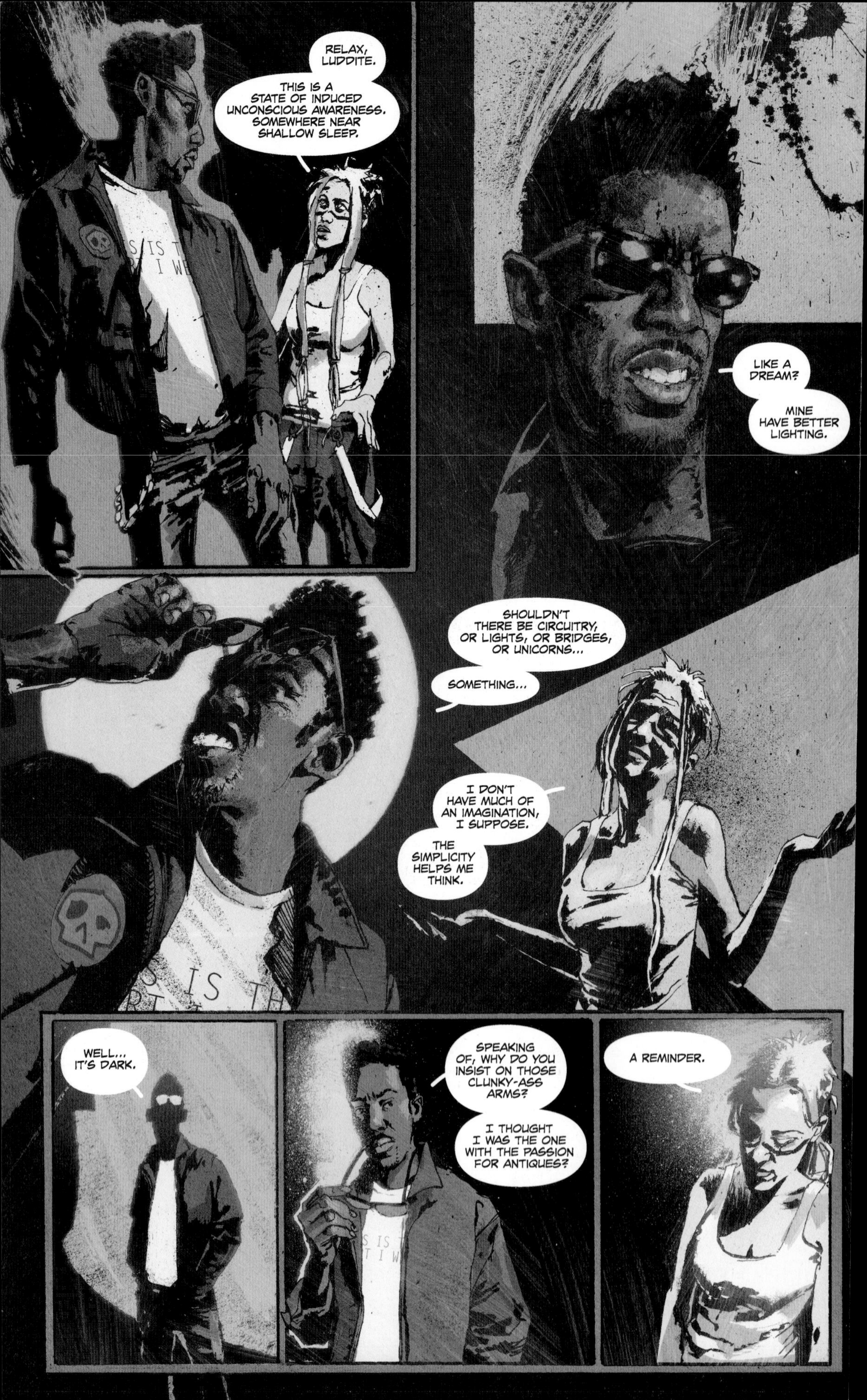
RELAX, LUDDITE.
THIS IS A STATE OF INDUCED UNCONSCIOUS AWARENESS. SOMEWHERE NEAR SHALLOW SLEEP.
LIKE A DREAM?
MINE HAVE BETTER LIGHTING.
SHOULDN'T THERE BE CIRCUITRY, OR LIGHTS, OR BRIDGES, OR UNICORNS...
SOMETHING...
I DON'T HAVE MUCH OF AN IMAGINATION, I SUPPOSE.
THE SIMPLICITY HELPS ME THINK.
WELL... IT'S DARK.
SPEAKING OF, WHY DO YOU INSIST ON THOSE CLUNKY-ASS ARMS?
I THOUGHT I WAS THE ONE WITH THE PASSION FOR ANTIQUES?
A REMINDER.

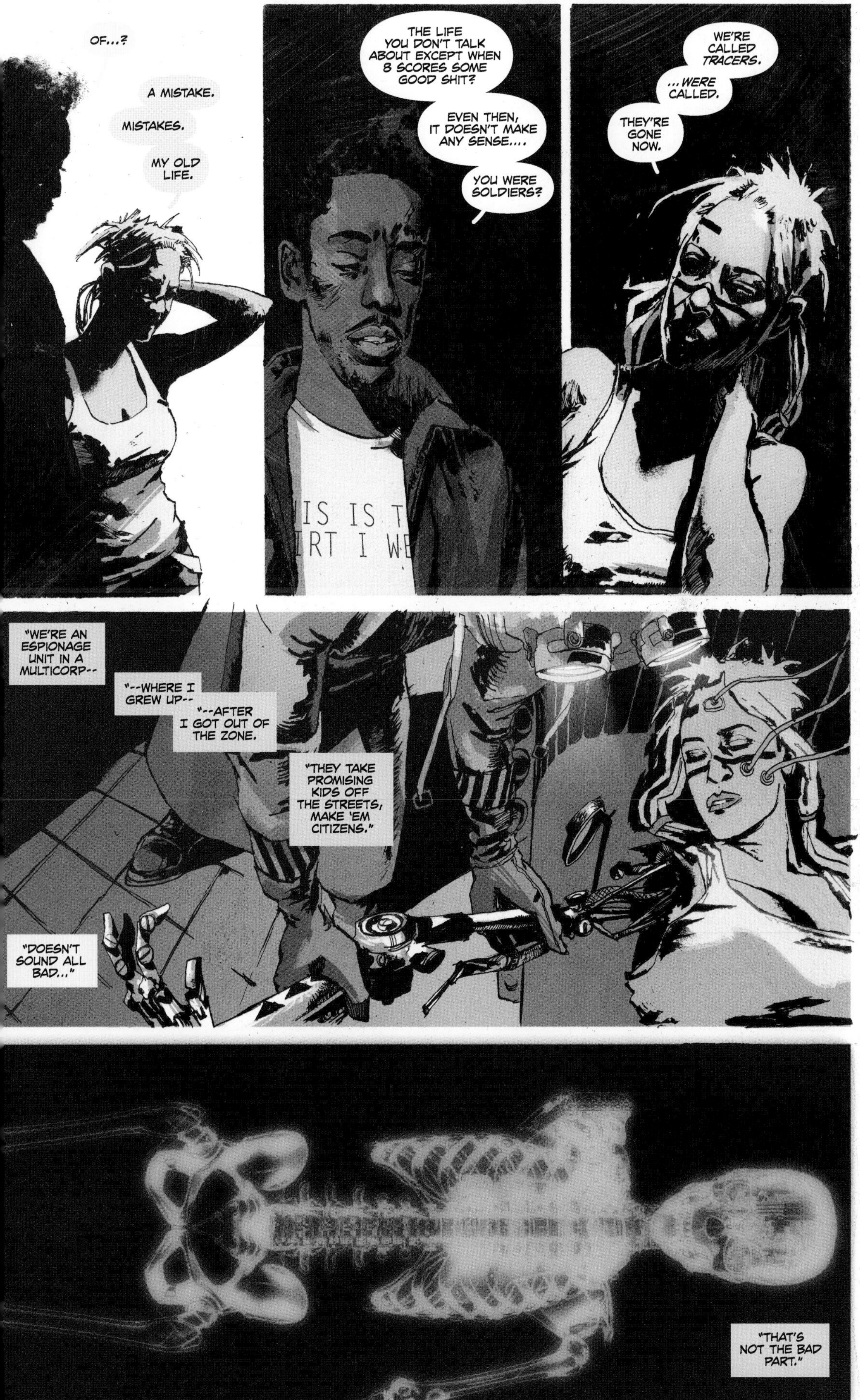
OF...?
A MISTAKE.
MISTAKES.
MY OLD LIFE.
THE LIFE YOU DON'T TALK ABOUT EXCEPT WHEN 8 SCORES SOME GOOD SHIT?
EVEN THEN, IT DOESN'T MAKE ANY SENSE....
YOU WERE SOLDIERS?
IS IS T
IRT I WE
WE'RE CALLED *TRACERS*.
...*WERE* CALLED.
THEY'RE GONE NOW.
"WE'RE AN ESPIONAGE UNIT IN A MULTICORP--
"--WHERE I GREW UP--
"--AFTER I GOT OUT OF THE ZONE.
"THEY TAKE PROMISING KIDS OFF THE STREETS, MAKE 'EM CITIZENS."
"DOESN'T SOUND ALL BAD..."
"THAT'S NOT THE BAD PART."

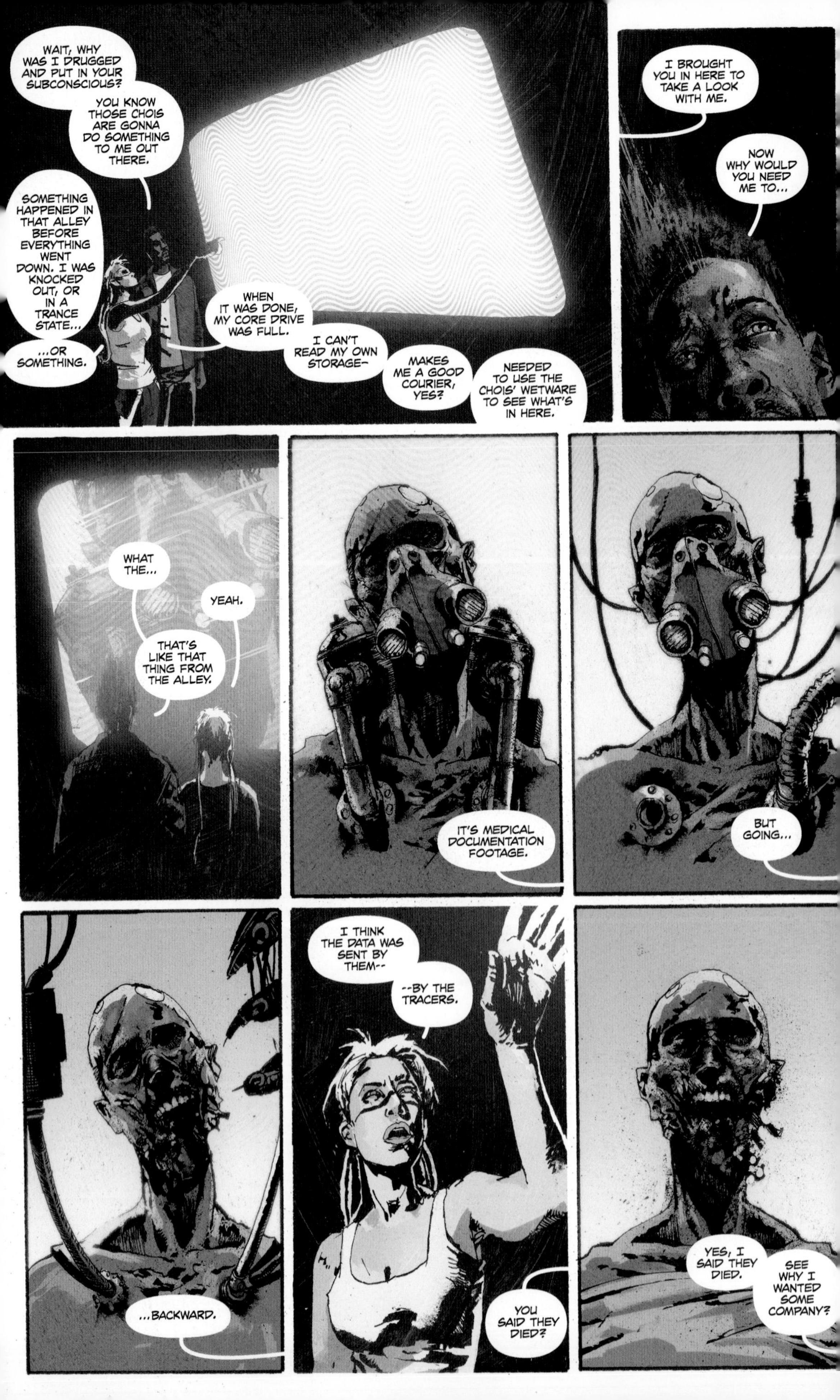
WAIT, WHY WAS I DRUGGED AND PUT IN YOUR SUBCONSCIOUS?
YOU KNOW THOSE CHOIS ARE GONNA DO SOMETHING TO ME OUT THERE.
SOMETHING HAPPENED IN THAT ALLEY BEFORE EVERYTHING WENT DOWN. I WAS KNOCKED OUT, OR IN A TRANCE STATE...
...OR SOMETHING.
WHEN IT WAS DONE, MY CORE DRIVE WAS FULL.
I CAN'T READ MY OWN STORAGE--
MAKES ME A GOOD COURIER, YES?
NEEDED TO USE THE CHOIS' WETWARE TO SEE WHAT'S IN HERE.
I BROUGHT YOU IN HERE TO TAKE A LOOK WITH ME.
NOW WHY WOULD YOU NEED ME TO...
WHAT THE...
YEAH.
THAT'S LIKE THAT THING FROM THE ALLEY.
IT'S MEDICAL DOCUMENTATION FOOTAGE.
BUT GOING...
...BACKWARD.
I THINK THE DATA WAS SENT BY THEM--
--BY THE TRACERS.
YOU SAID THEY DIED?
YES, I SAID THEY DIED.
SEE WHY I WANTED SOME COMPANY?

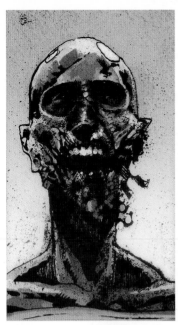

HOW COULD ANYONE POSSIBLY SNEAK ANYTHING ONTO YOUR CORE DRIVE?

I MEAN, THAT'S PRETTY MUCH IMPO—

WHAT THE FUCK?

WAIT, YOU KNOW THAT CAT?

SIMMONS?

HOW IS ANY OF THIS...

THE FOOTAGE IS STILL GOING. WAIT, IS THAT...

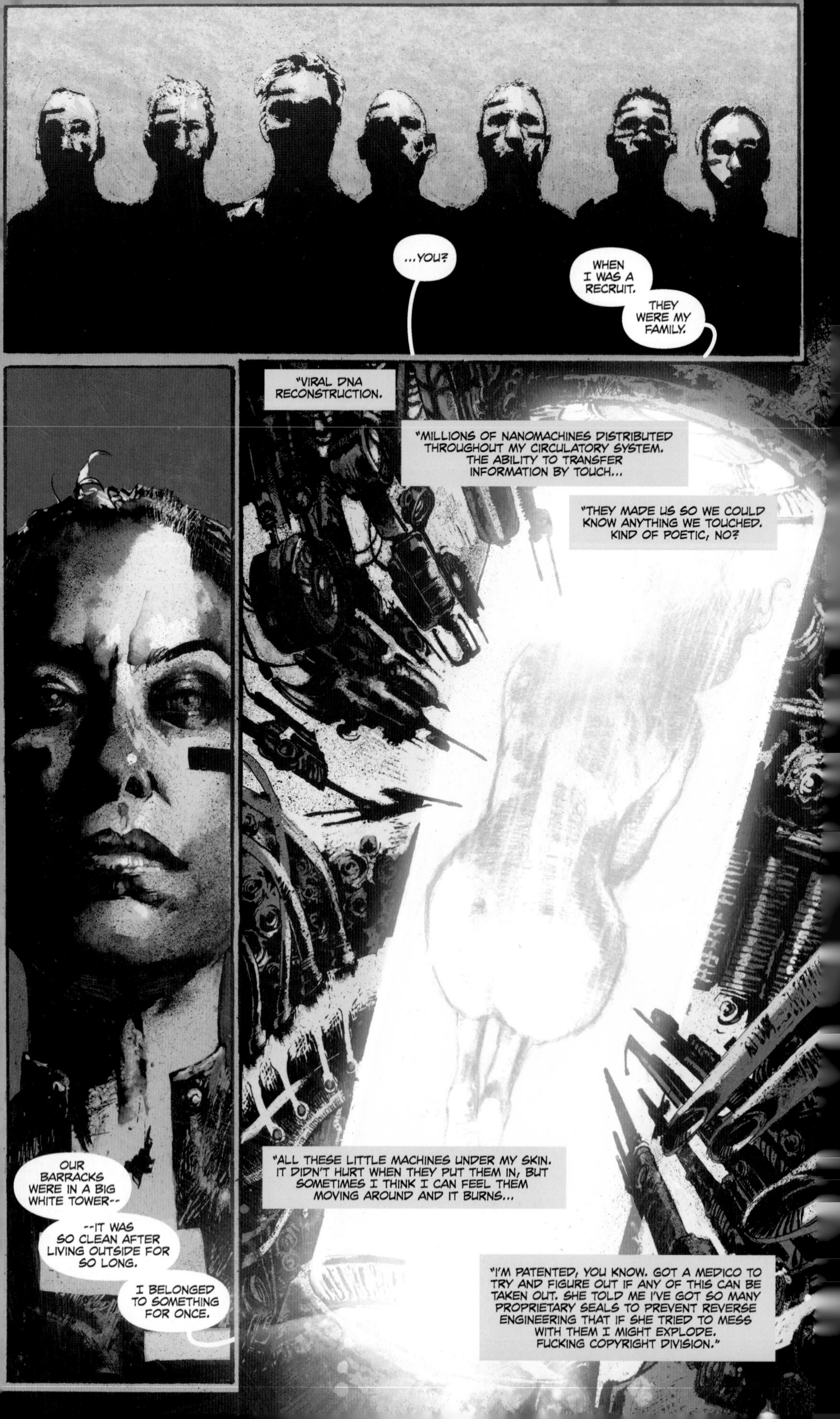
...YOU?
WHEN I WAS A RECRUIT.
THEY WERE MY FAMILY.
"VIRAL DNA RECONSTRUCTION.
"MILLIONS OF NANOMACHINES DISTRIBUTED THROUGHOUT MY CIRCULATORY SYSTEM. THE ABILITY TO TRANSFER INFORMATION BY TOUCH...
"THEY MADE US SO WE COULD KNOW ANYTHING WE TOUCHED. KIND OF POETIC, NO?
"ALL THESE LITTLE MACHINES UNDER MY SKIN. IT DIDN'T HURT WHEN THEY PUT THEM IN, BUT SOMETIMES I THINK I CAN FEEL THEM MOVING AROUND AND IT BURNS...
OUR BARRACKS WERE IN A BIG WHITE TOWER--
--IT WAS SO CLEAN AFTER LIVING OUTSIDE FOR SO LONG.
I BELONGED TO SOMETHING FOR ONCE.
"I'M PATENTED, YOU KNOW. GOT A MEDICO TO TRY AND FIGURE OUT IF ANY OF THIS CAN BE TAKEN OUT. SHE TOLD ME I'VE GOT SO MANY PROPRIETARY SEALS TO PREVENT REVERSE ENGINEERING THAT IF SHE TRIED TO MESS WITH THEM I MIGHT EXPLODE. FUCKING COPYRIGHT DIVISION."

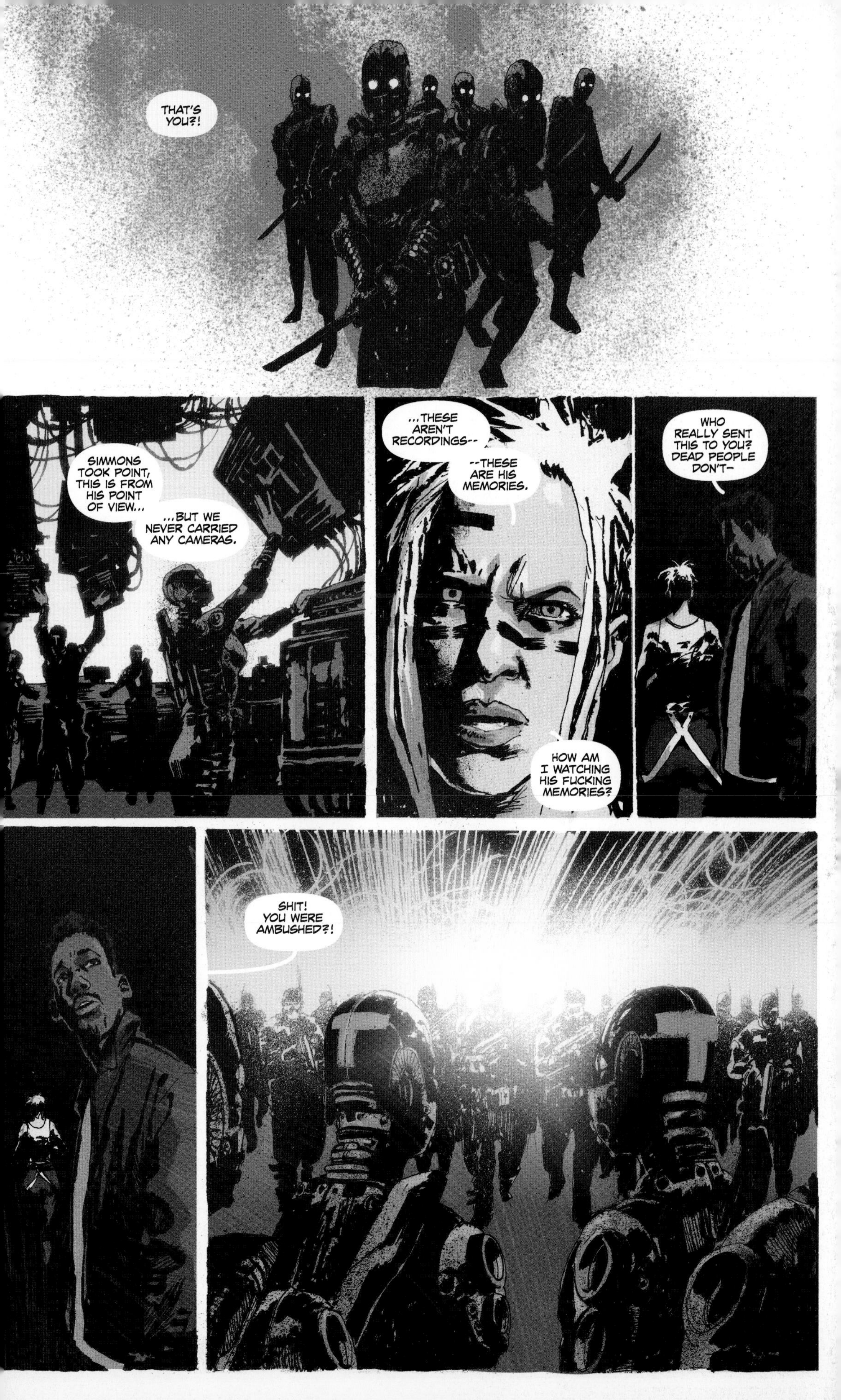

THAT'S YOU?!
SIMMONS TOOK POINT, THIS IS FROM HIS POINT OF VIEW...
...BUT WE NEVER CARRIED ANY CAMERAS.
...THESE AREN'T RECORDINGS--
--THESE ARE HIS MEMORIES.
HOW AM I WATCHING HIS FUCKING MEMORIES?
WHO REALLY SENT THIS TO YOU? DEAD PEOPLE DON'T-
SHIT! YOU WERE AMBUSHED?!

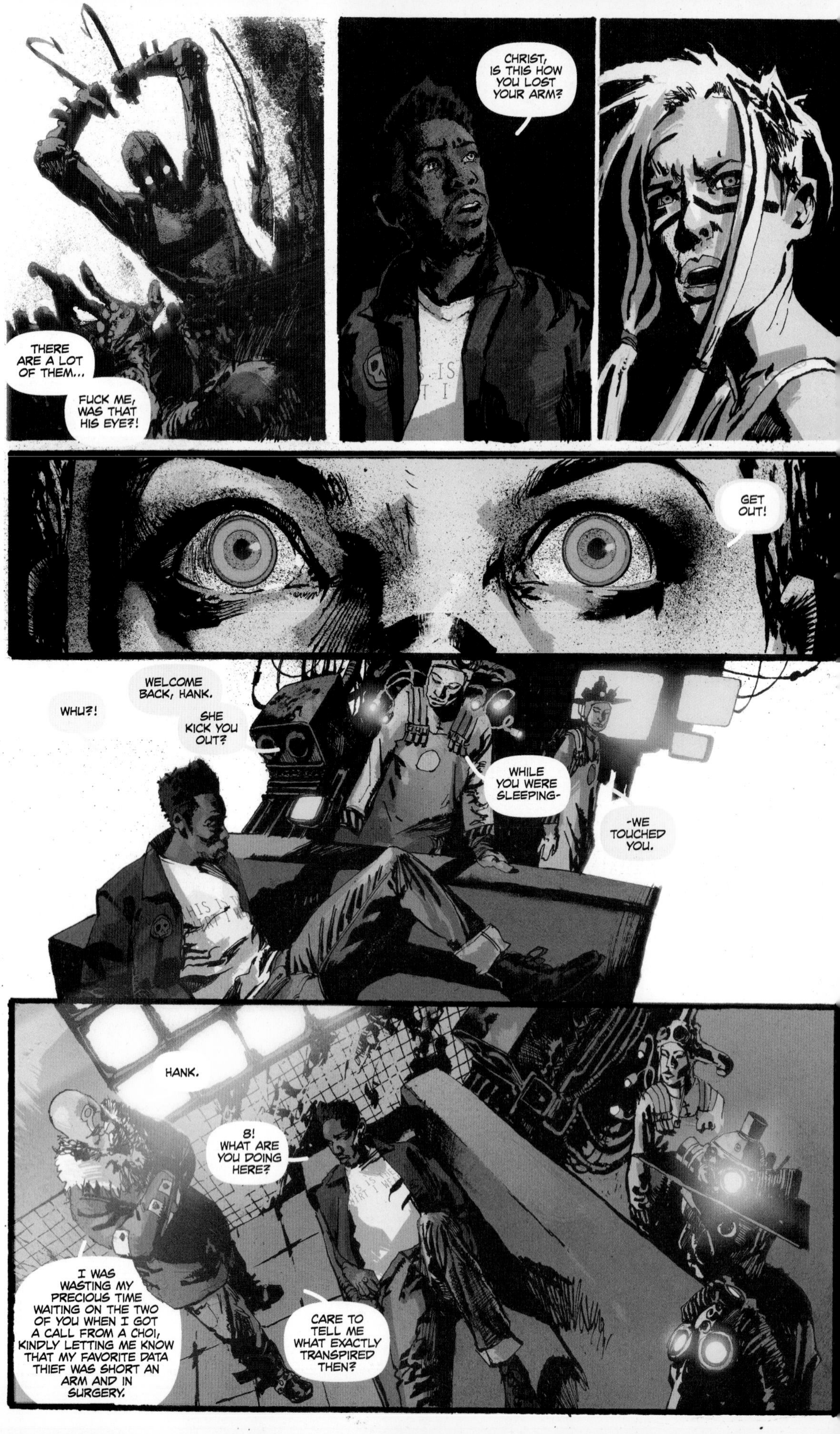

THERE ARE A LOT OF THEM...
FUCK ME, WAS THAT HIS EYE?!
CHRIST, IS THIS HOW YOU LOST YOUR ARM?
GET OUT!
WHU?!
WELCOME BACK, HANK.
SHE KICK YOU OUT?
WHILE YOU WERE SLEEPING-
-WE TOUCHED YOU.
HANK.
8! WHAT ARE YOU DOING HERE?
I WAS WASTING MY PRECIOUS TIME WAITING ON THE TWO OF YOU WHEN I GOT A CALL FROM A CHOI, KINDLY LETTING ME KNOW THAT MY FAVORITE DATA THIEF WAS SHORT AN ARM AND IN SURGERY.
CARE TO TELL ME WHAT EXACTLY TRANSPIRED THEN?

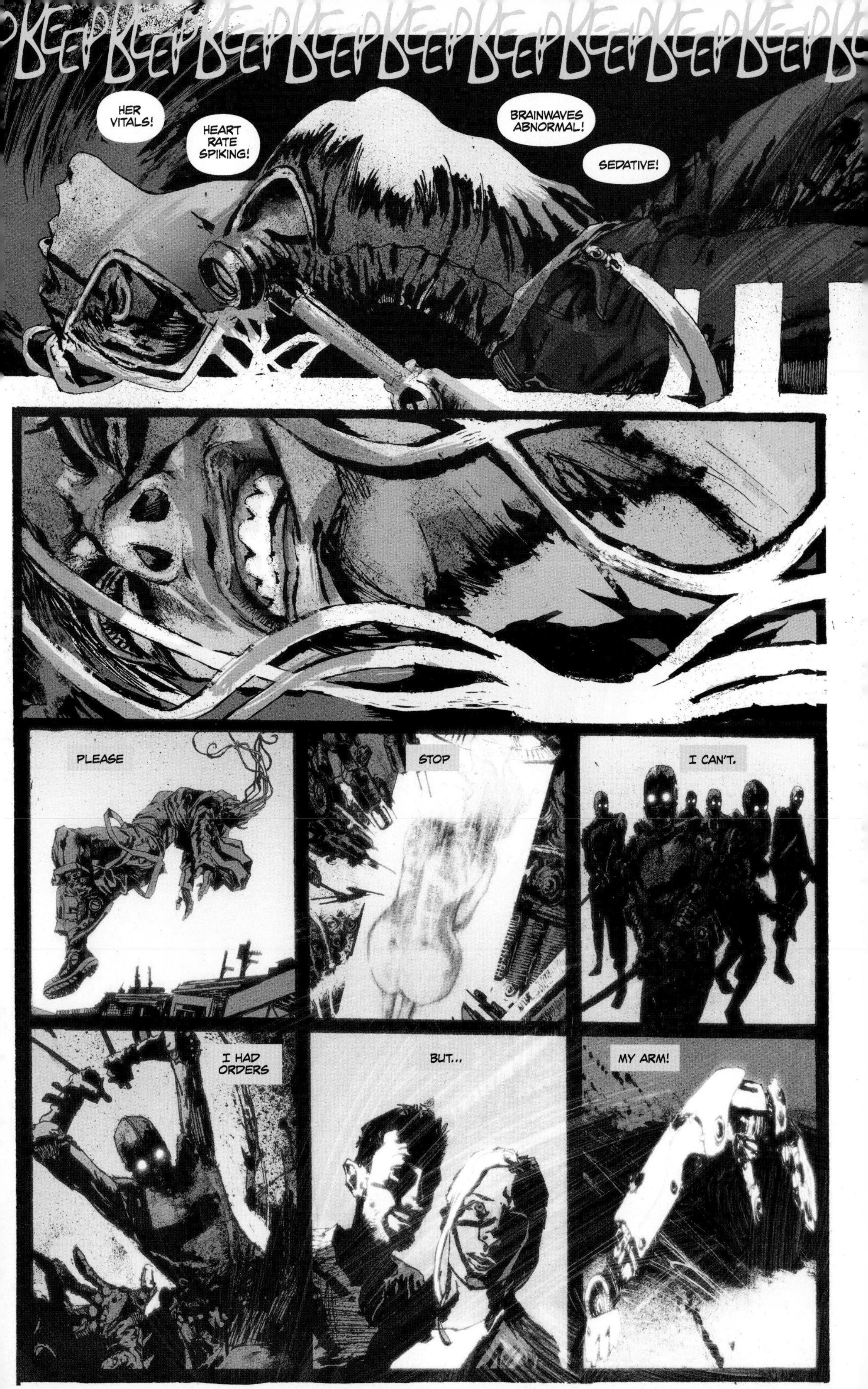
BEEP BEEP BEEP BEEP BEEP BEEP BEEP BEEP BEEP
HER VITALS!
HEART RATE SPIKING!
BRAINWAVES ABNORMAL!
SEDATIVE!
PLEASE
STOP
I CAN'T.
I HAD ORDERS
BUT...
MY ARM!

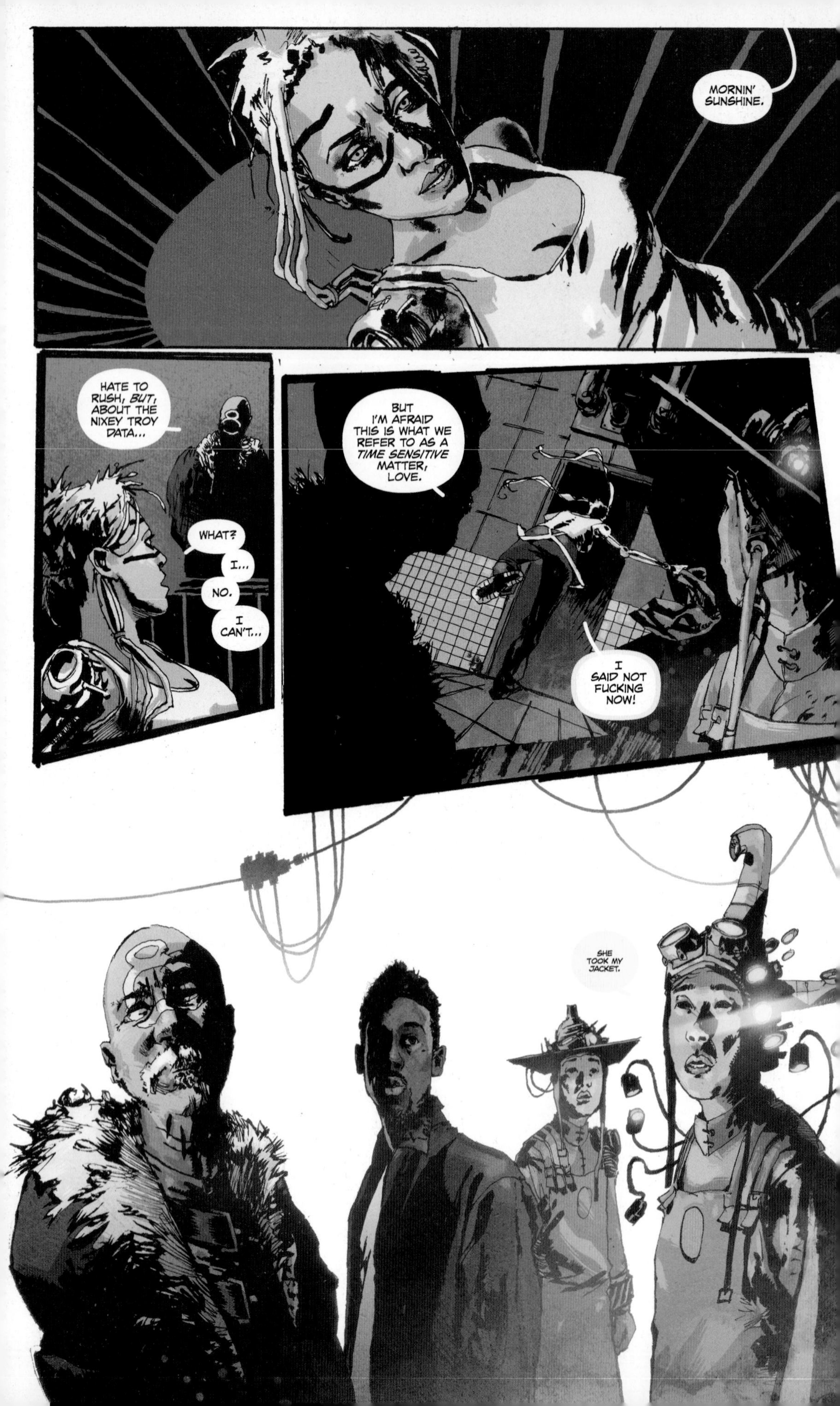
MORNIN' SUNSHINE.
HATE TO RUSH, *BUT,* ABOUT THE NIXEY TROY DATA...
WHAT?
I...
NO.
I CAN'T...
BUT I'M AFRAID THIS IS WHAT WE REFER TO AS A *TIME SENSITIVE* MATTER, LOVE.
I SAID NOT FUCKING NOW!
SHE TOOK MY JACKET.

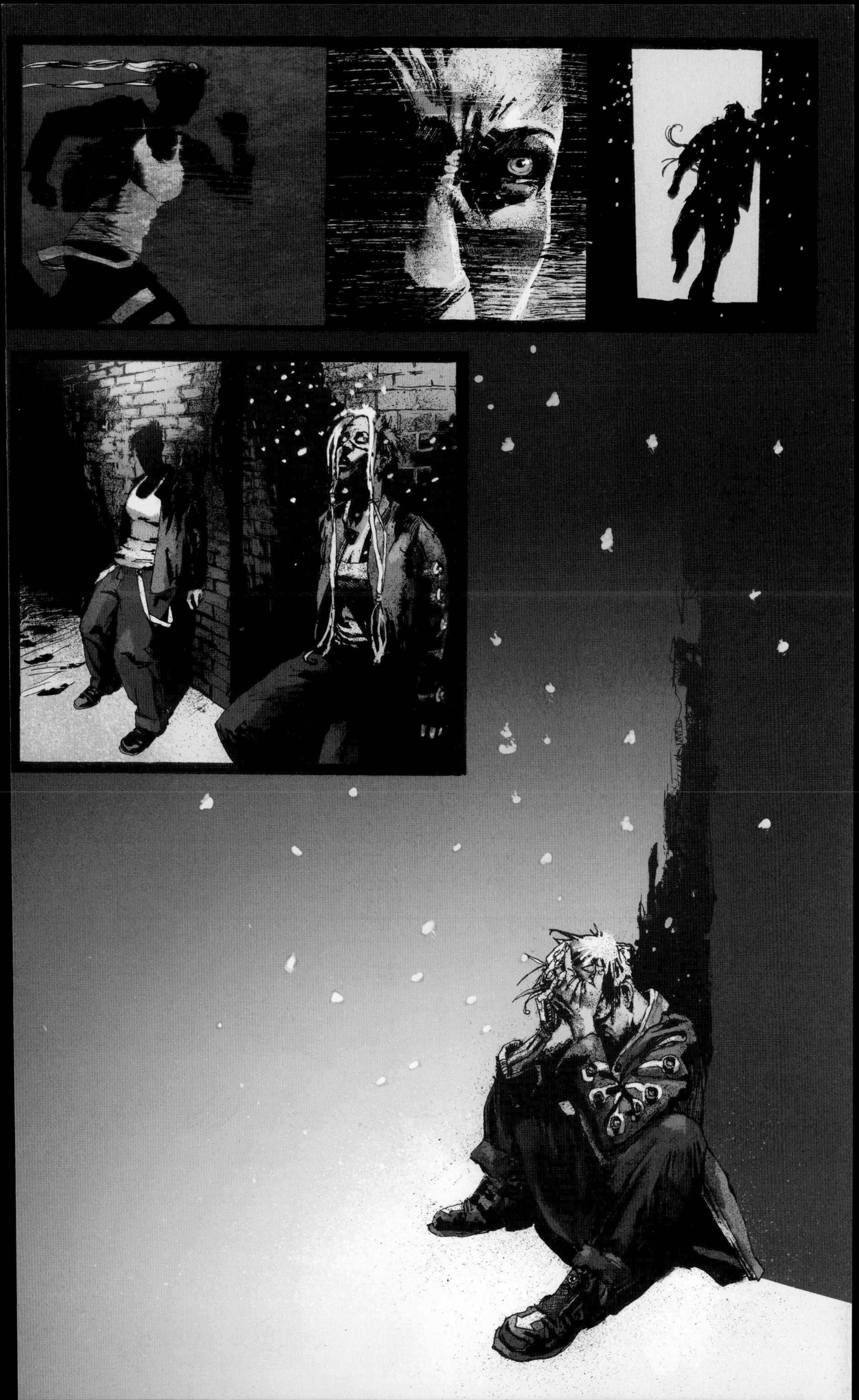

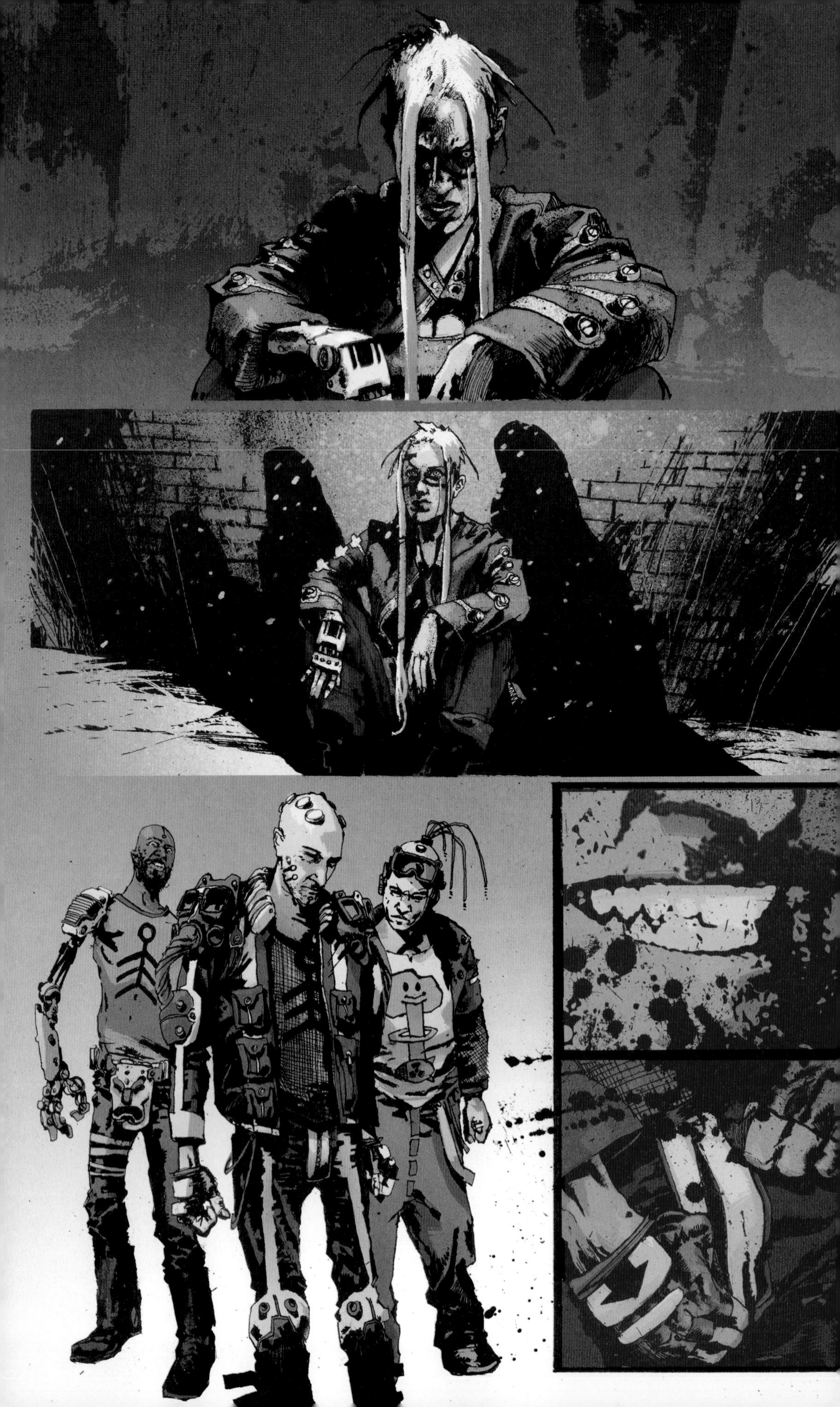

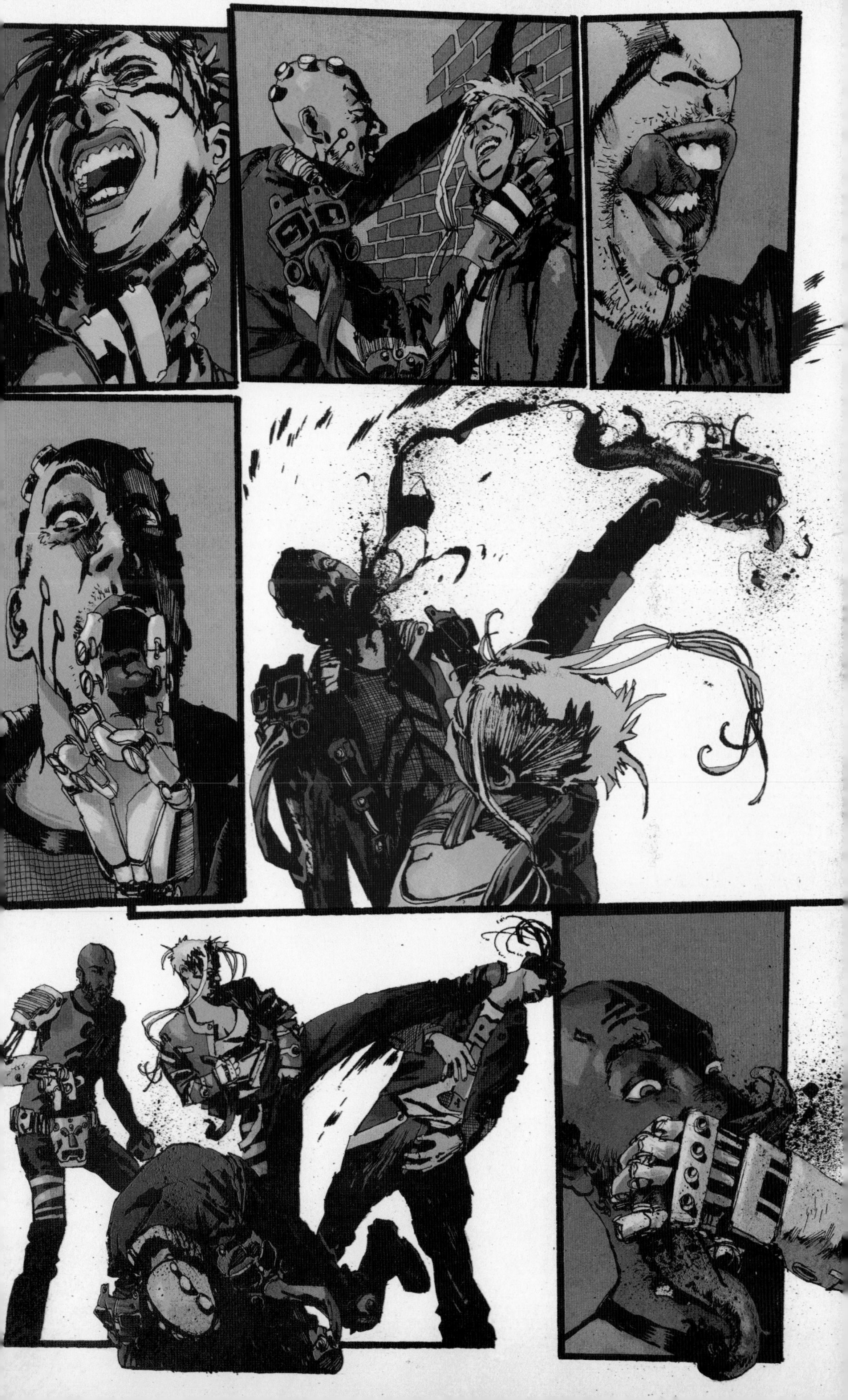

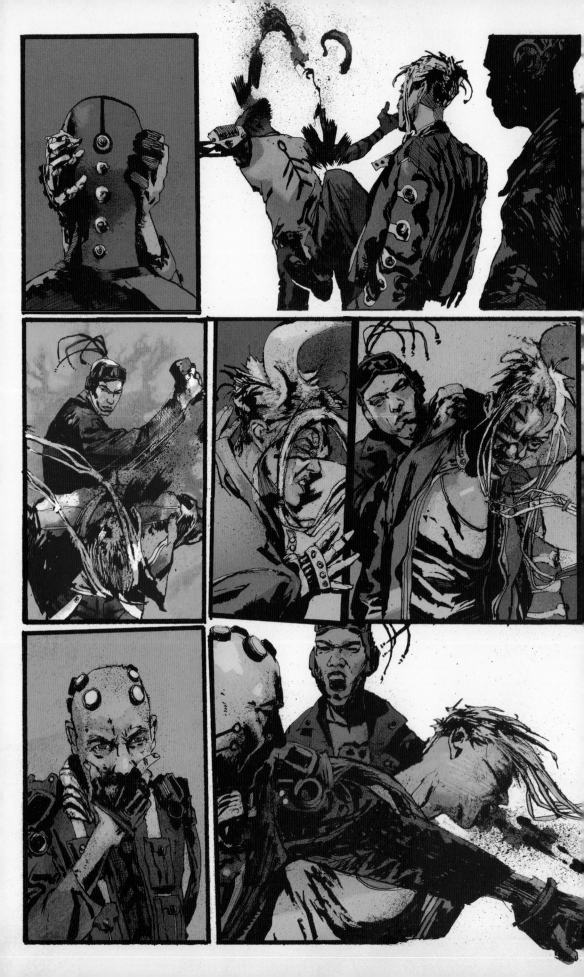

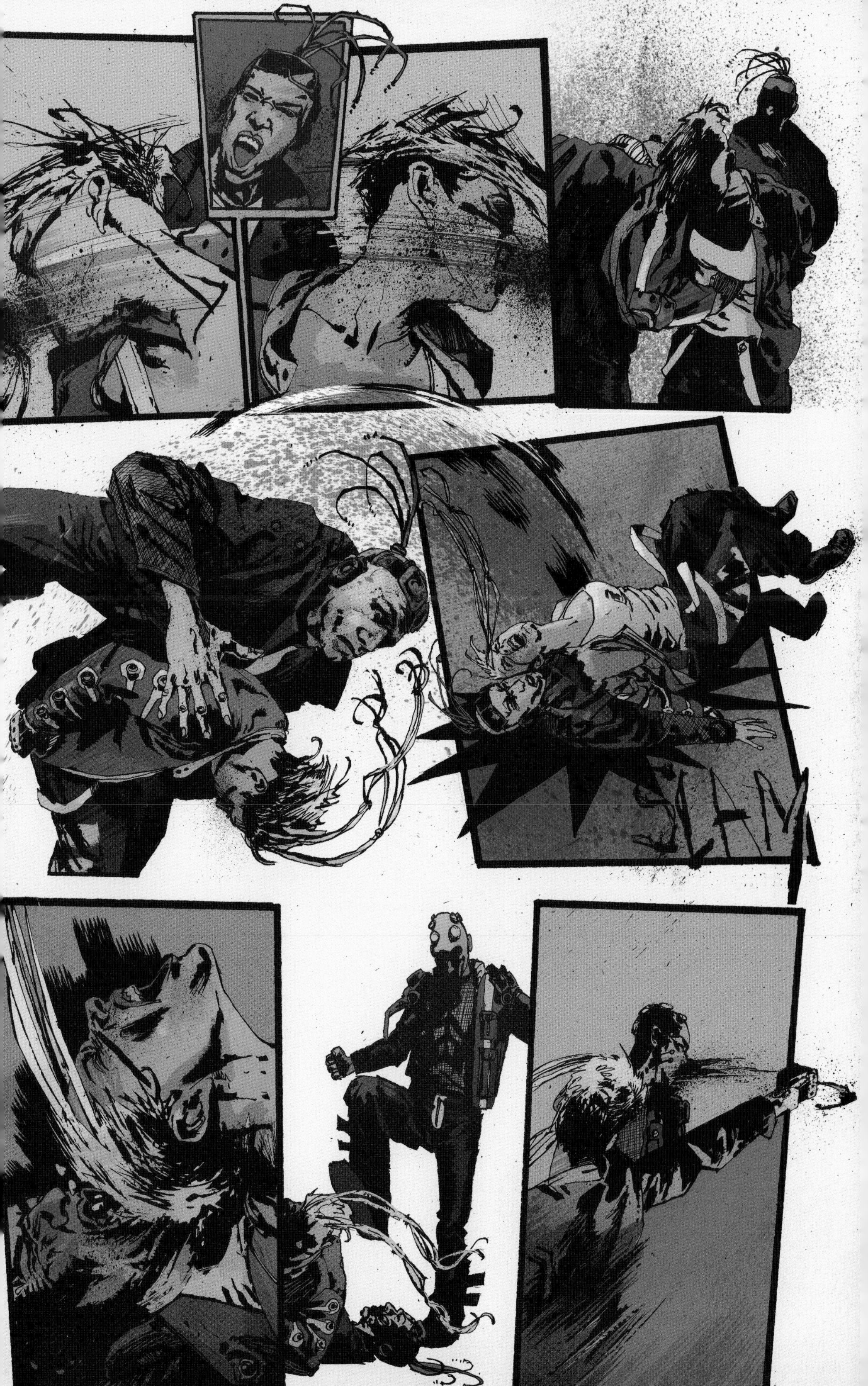

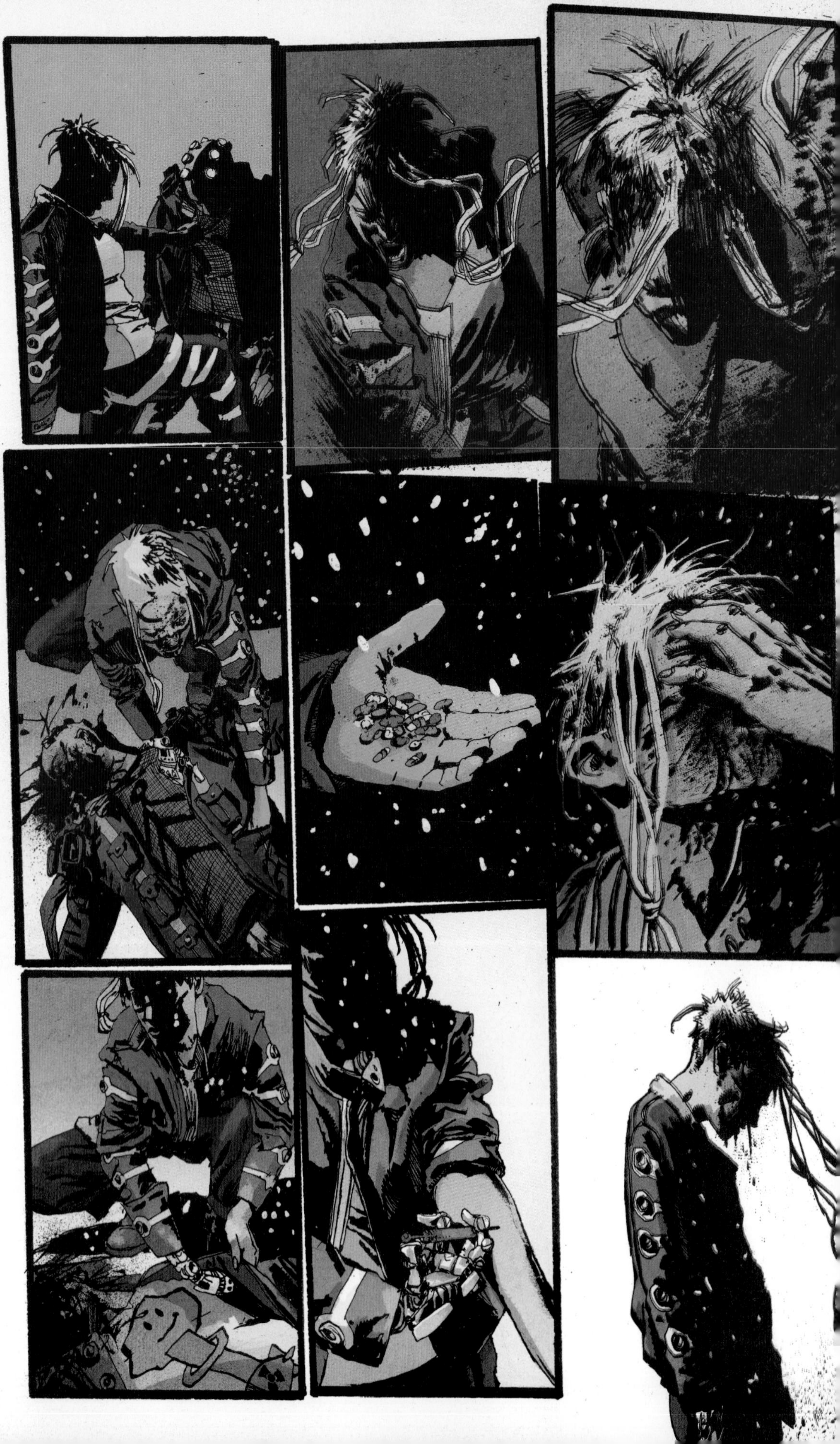

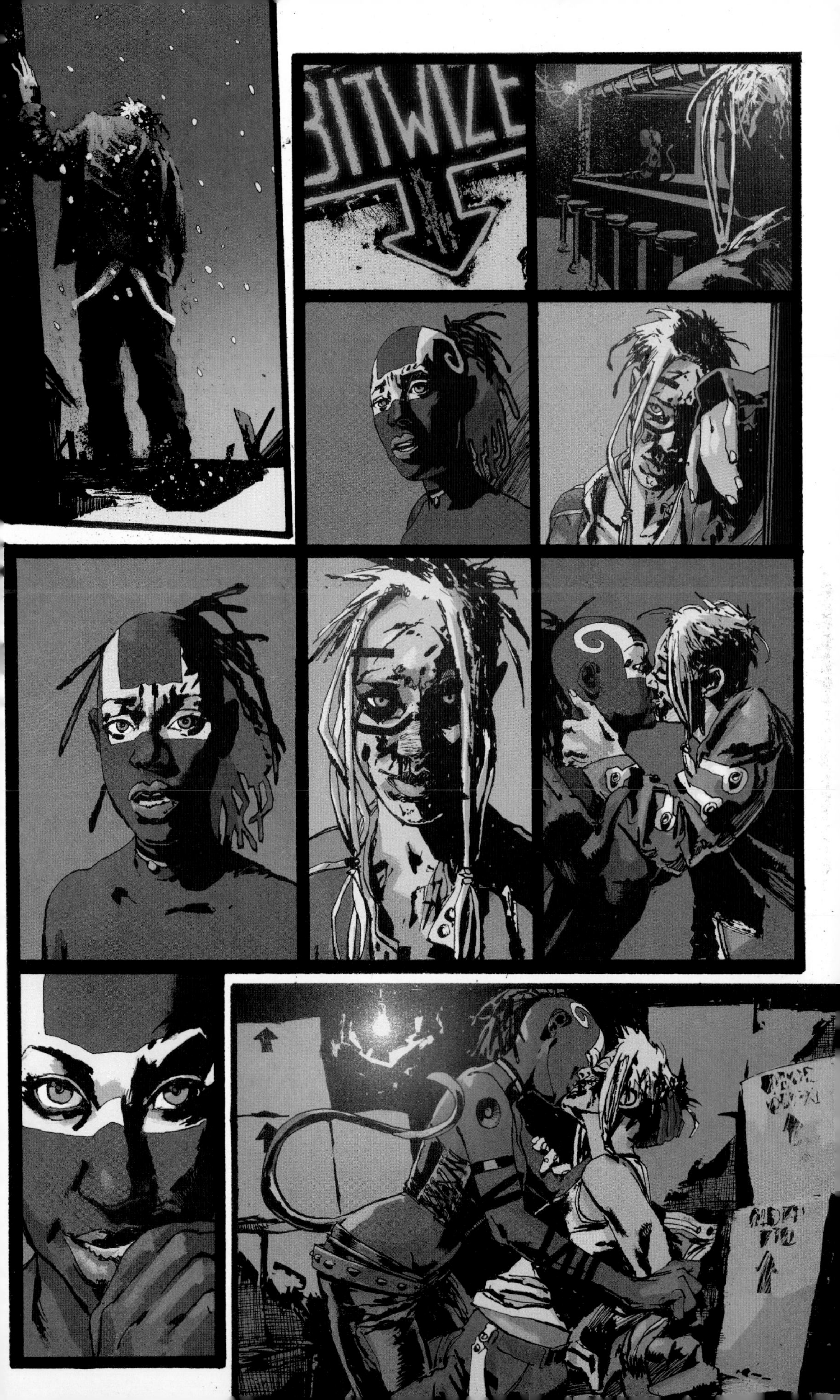
BITWIZE

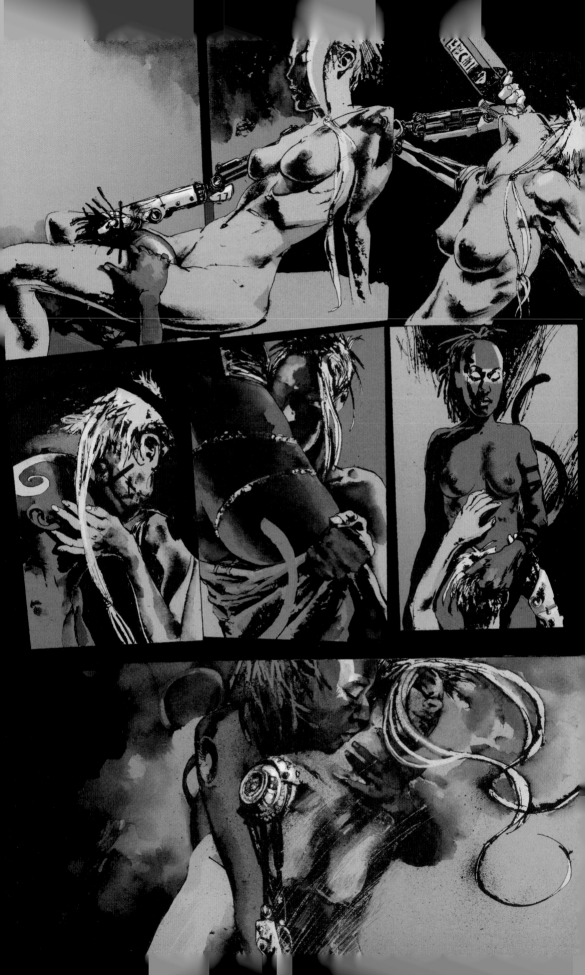

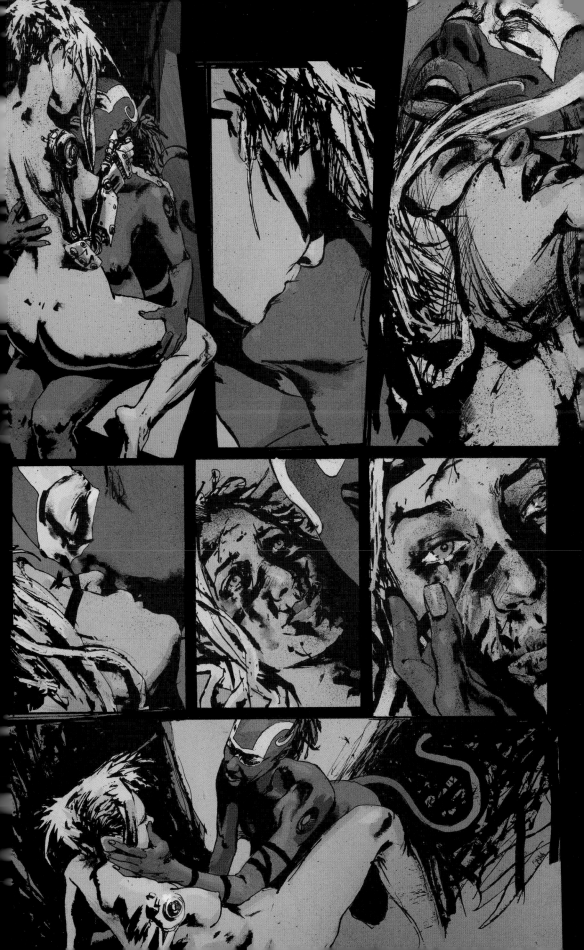

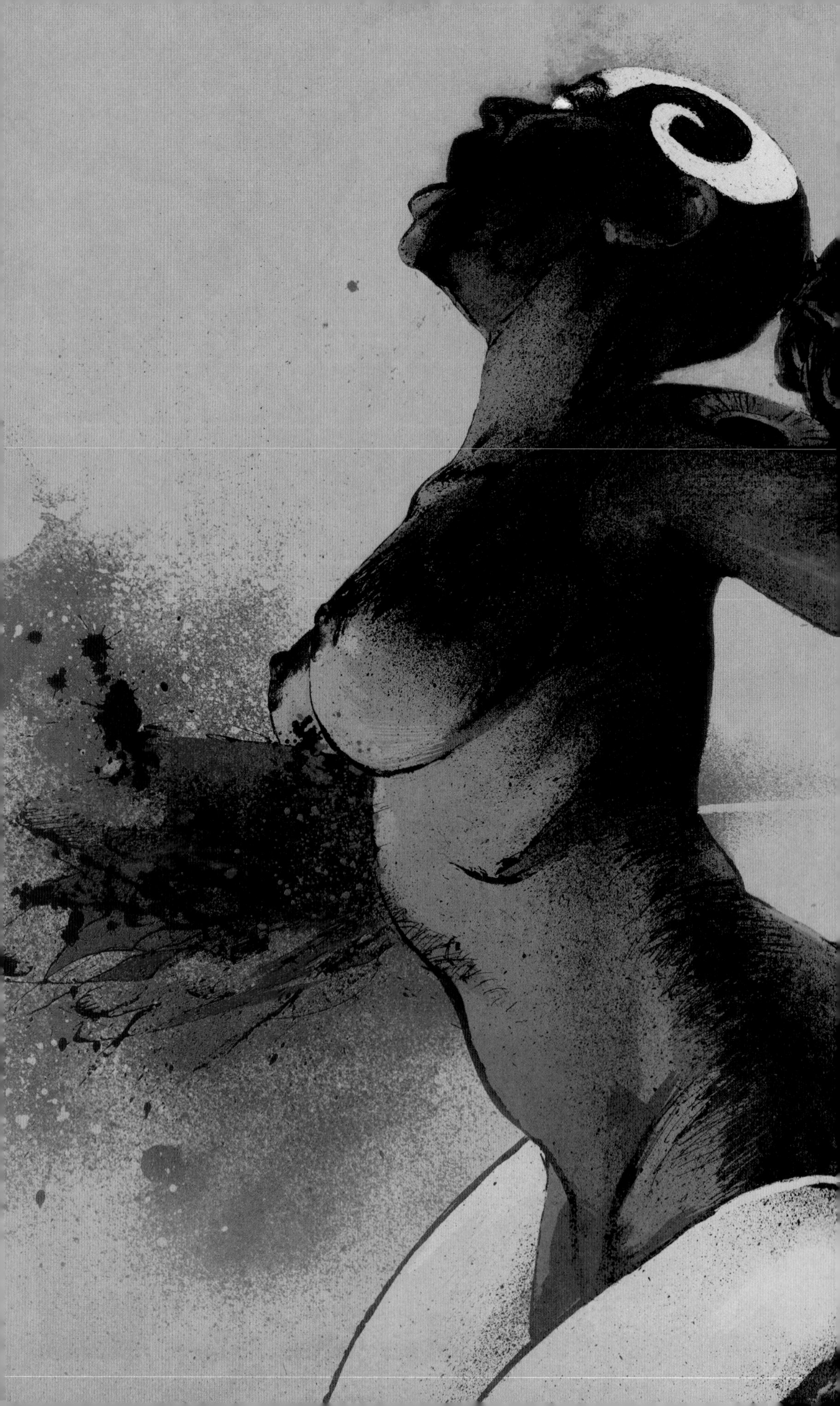

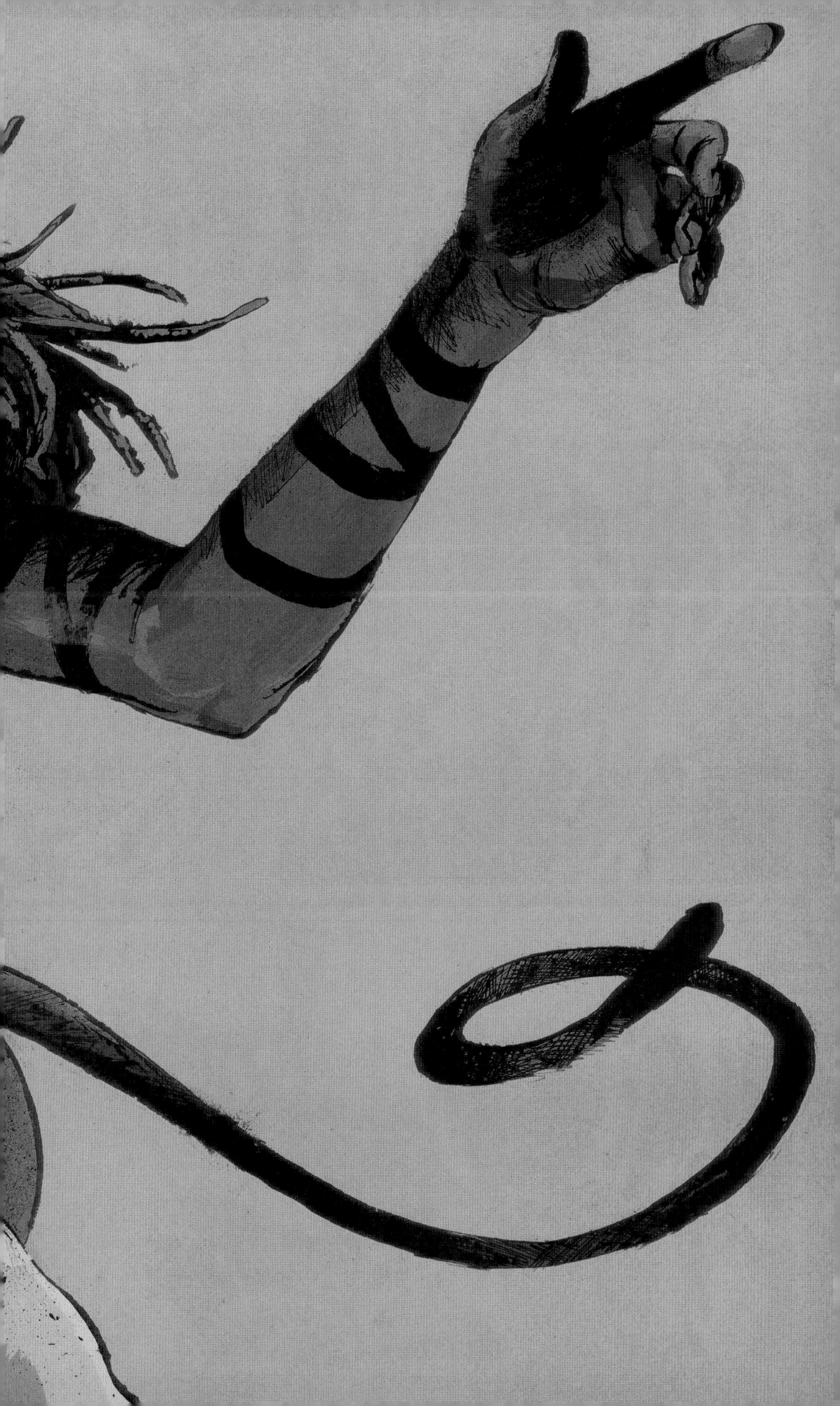

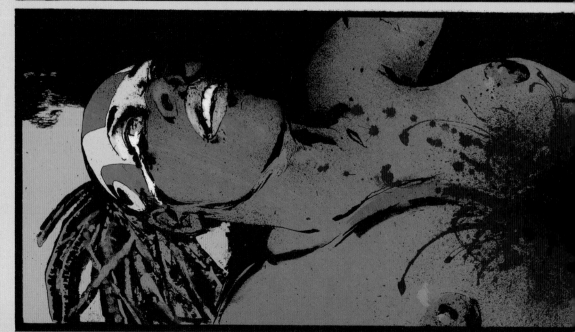

CHAPTER FOUR

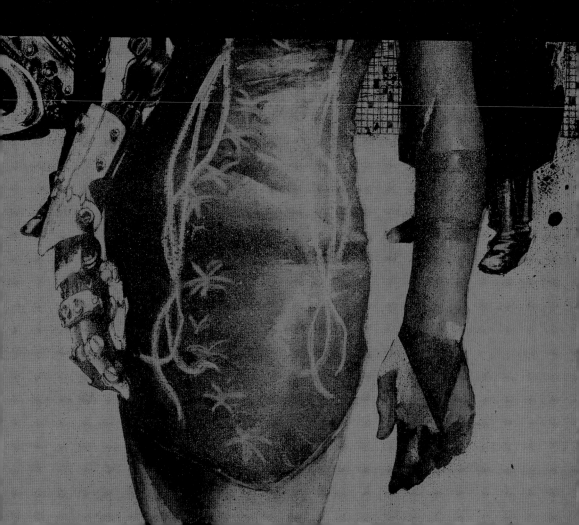

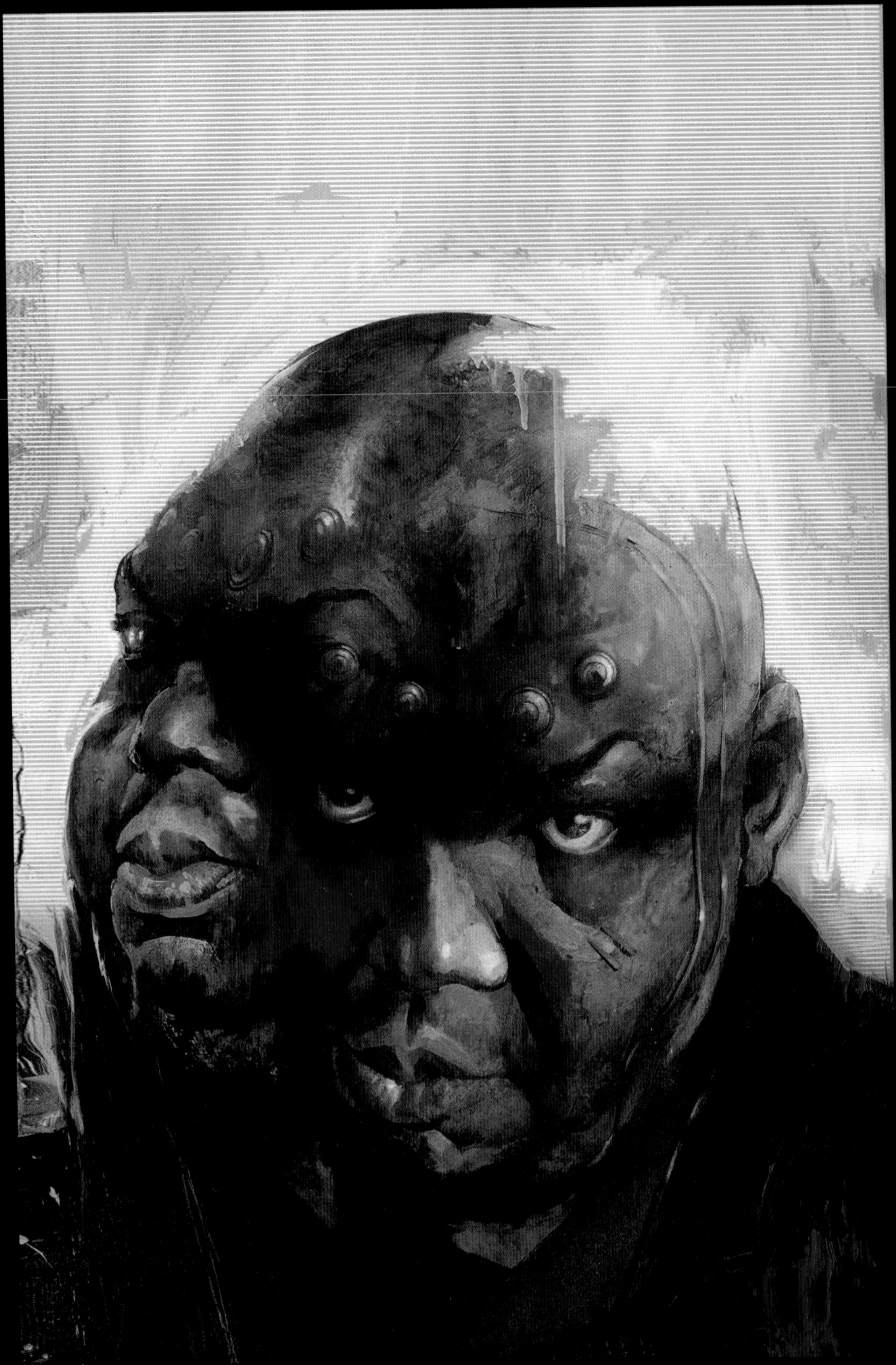

30 x 40 in. ink, acrylic, oil, pastel, spray paint, paper, & digital collage on canvas

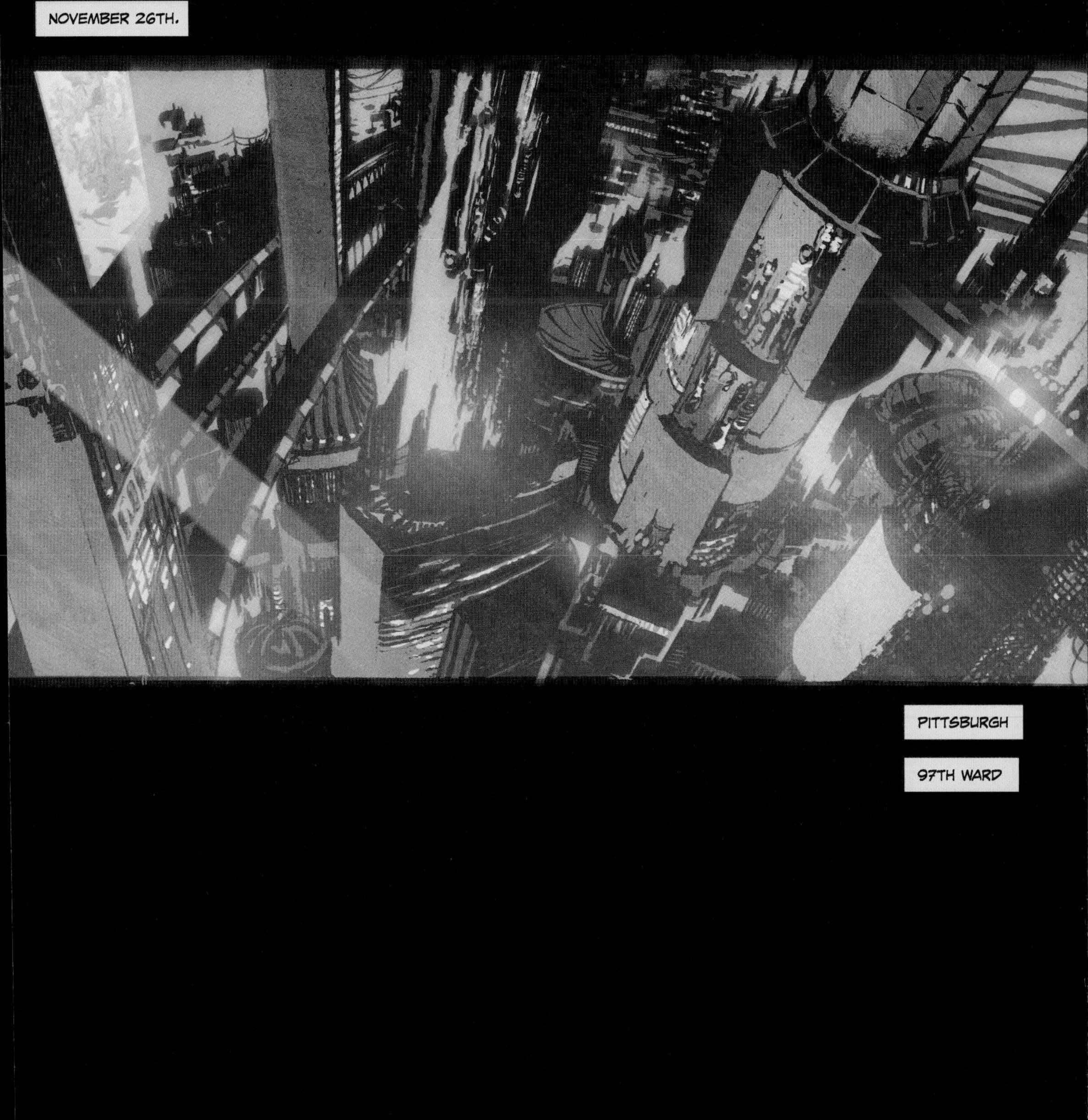
NOVEMBER 26TH.
PITTSBURGH
97TH WARD

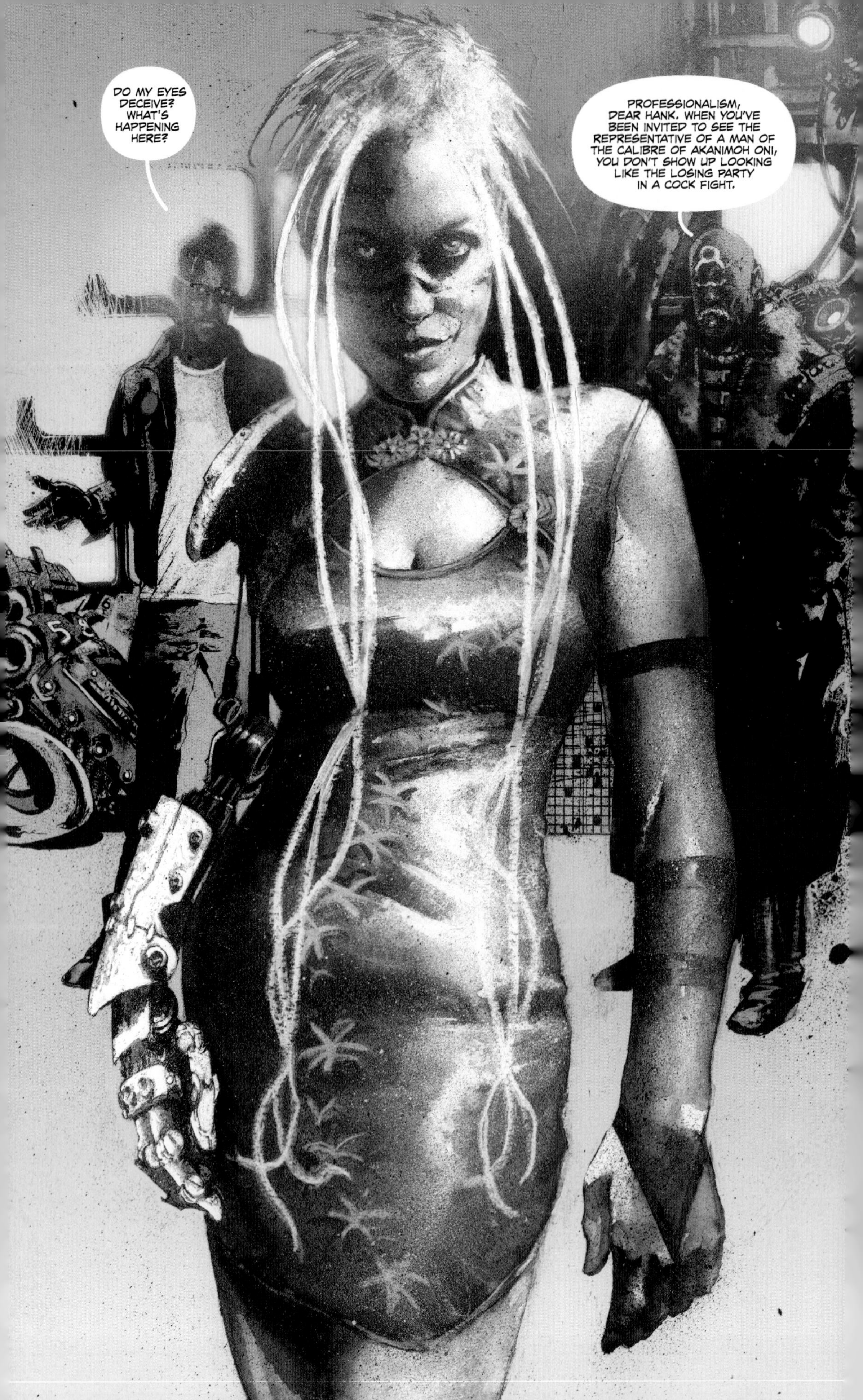
DO MY EYES DECEIVE? WHAT'S HAPPENING HERE?
PROFESSIONALISM, DEAR HANK. WHEN YOU'VE BEEN INVITED TO SEE THE REPRESENTATIVE OF A MAN OF THE CALIBRE OF AKANIMOH ONI, YOU DON'T SHOW UP LOOKING LIKE THE LOSING PARTY IN A COCK FIGHT.

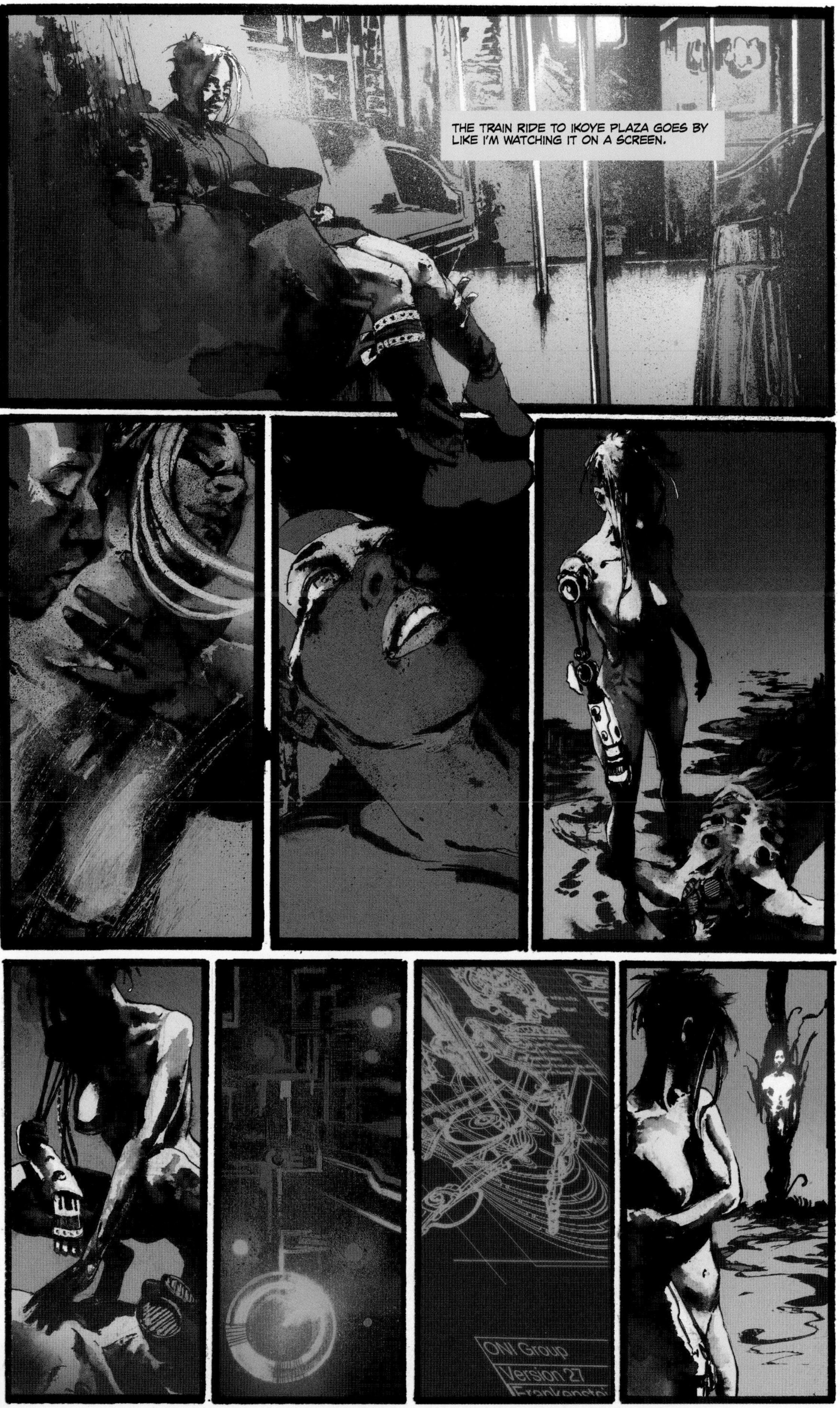
THE TRAIN RIDE TO IKOYE PLAZA GOES BY LIKE I'M WATCHING IT ON A SCREEN.
ONI Group
Version 27

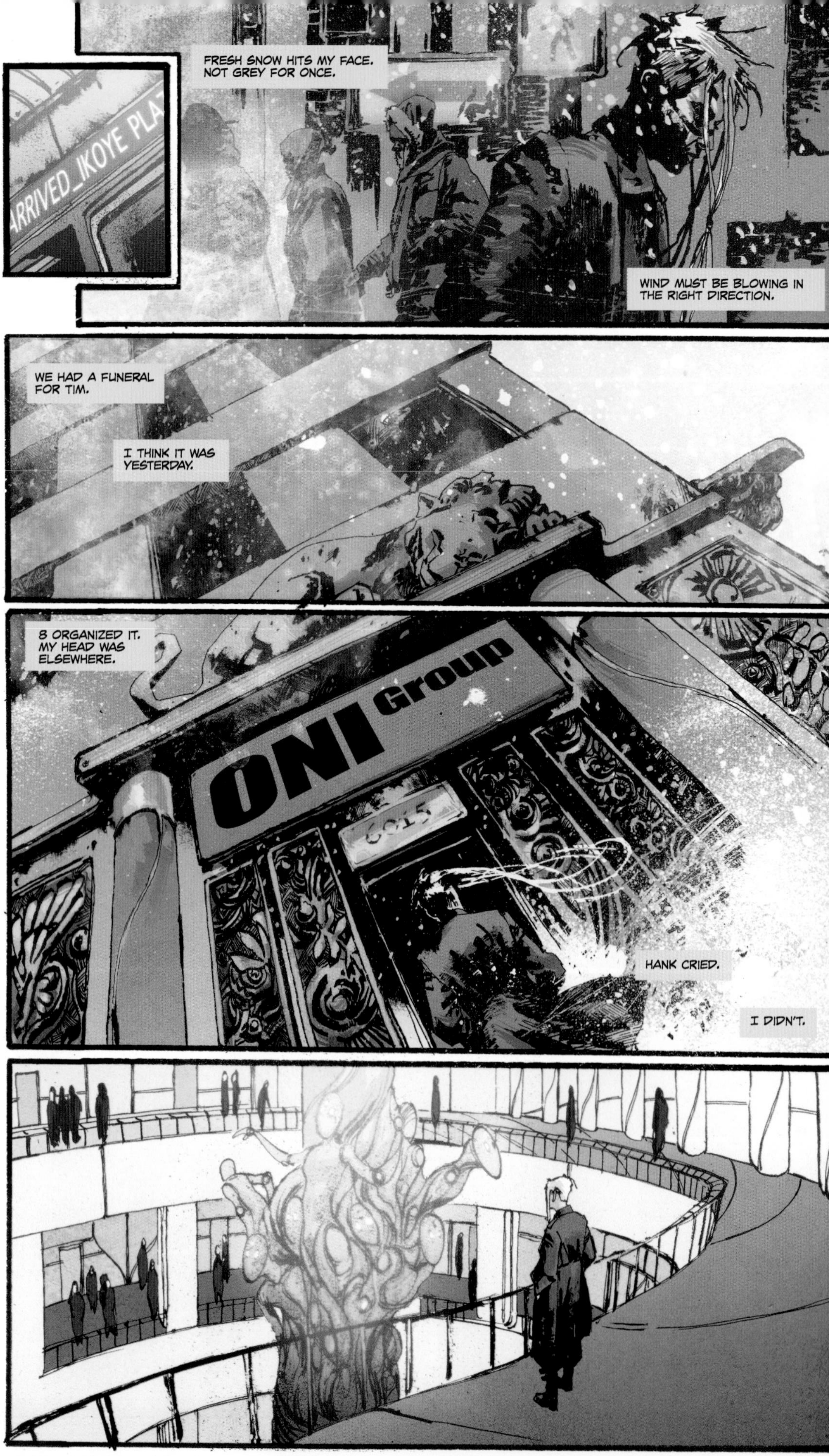
ARRIVED_IKOYE PLAT
FRESH SNOW HITS MY FACE. NOT GREY FOR ONCE.
WIND MUST BE BLOWING IN THE RIGHT DIRECTION.
WE HAD A FUNERAL FOR TIM.
I THINK IT WAS YESTERDAY.
8 ORGANIZED IT. MY HEAD WAS ELSEWHERE.
ONI Group
HANK CRIED.
I DIDN'T.

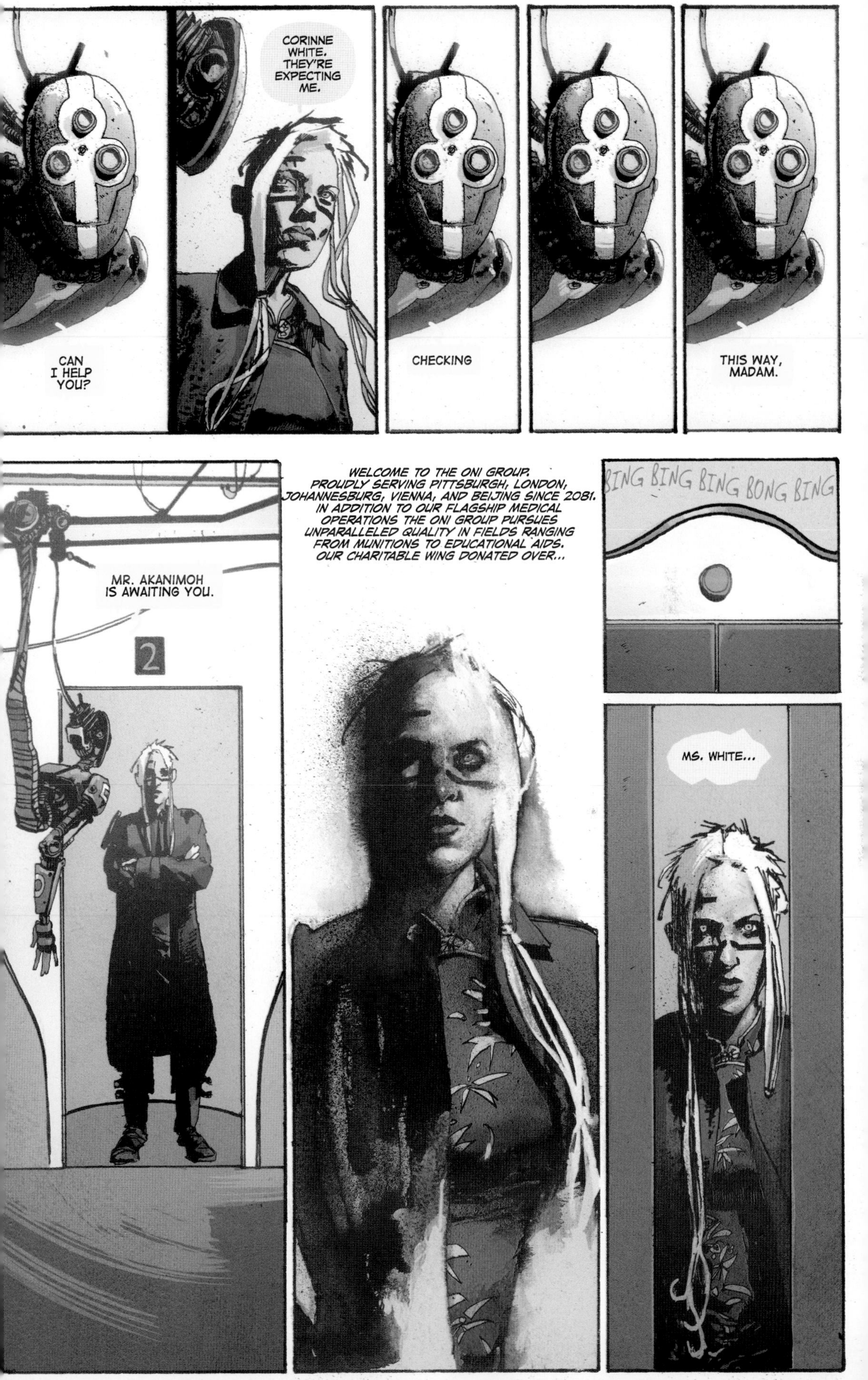
CAN I HELP YOU?
CORINNE WHITE. THEY'RE EXPECTING ME.
CHECKING
THIS WAY, MADAM.
MR. AKANIMOH IS AWAITING YOU.
2
WELCOME TO THE ONI GROUP. PROUDLY SERVING PITTSBURGH, LONDON, JOHANNESBURG, VIENNA, AND BEIJING SINCE 2081. IN ADDITION TO OUR FLAGSHIP MEDICAL OPERATIONS THE ONI GROUP PURSUES UNPARALLELED QUALITY IN FIELDS RANGING FROM MUNITIONS TO EDUCATIONAL AIDS. OUR CHARITABLE WING DONATED OVER...
BING BING BING BONG BING
MS. WHITE...

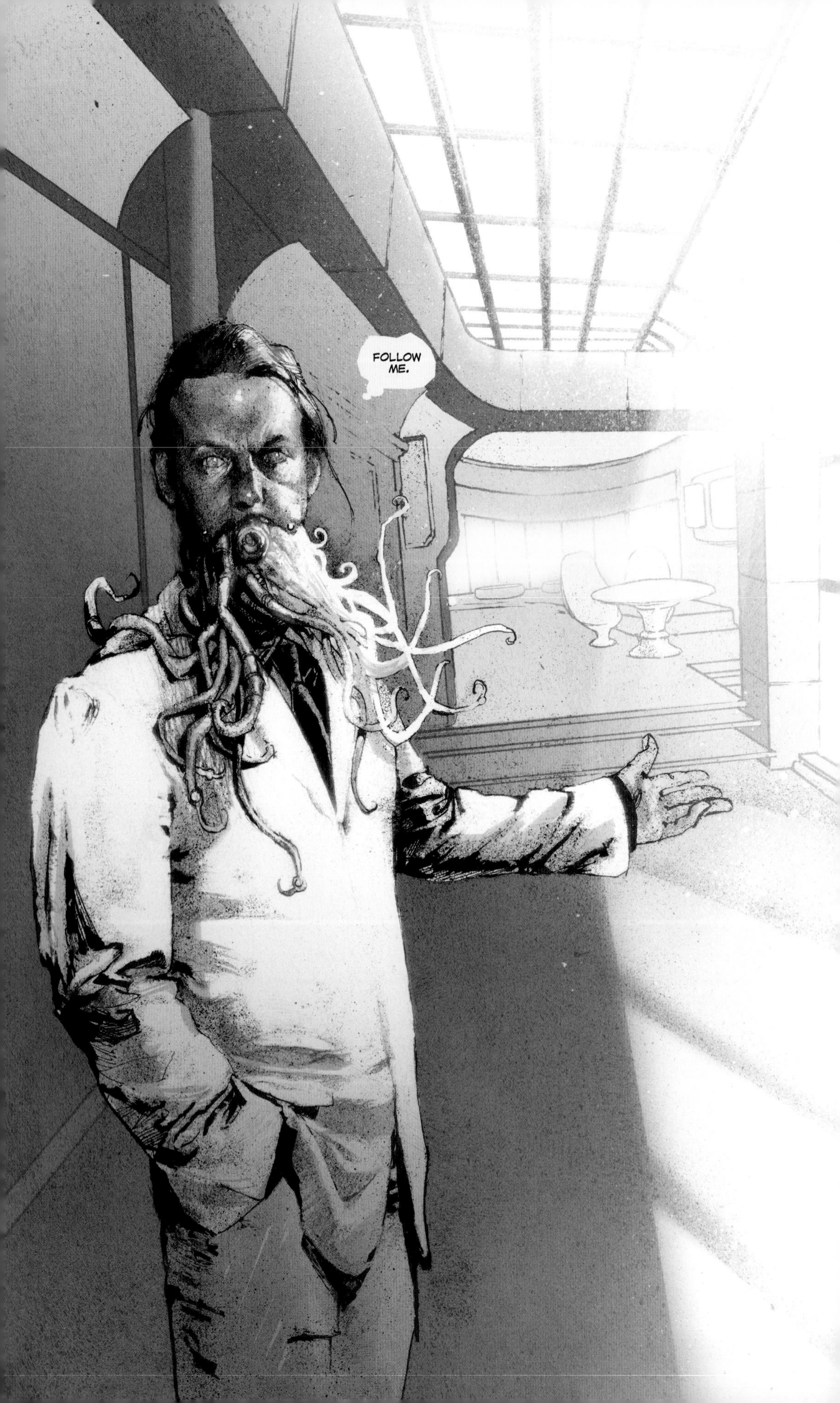
FOLLOW ME.

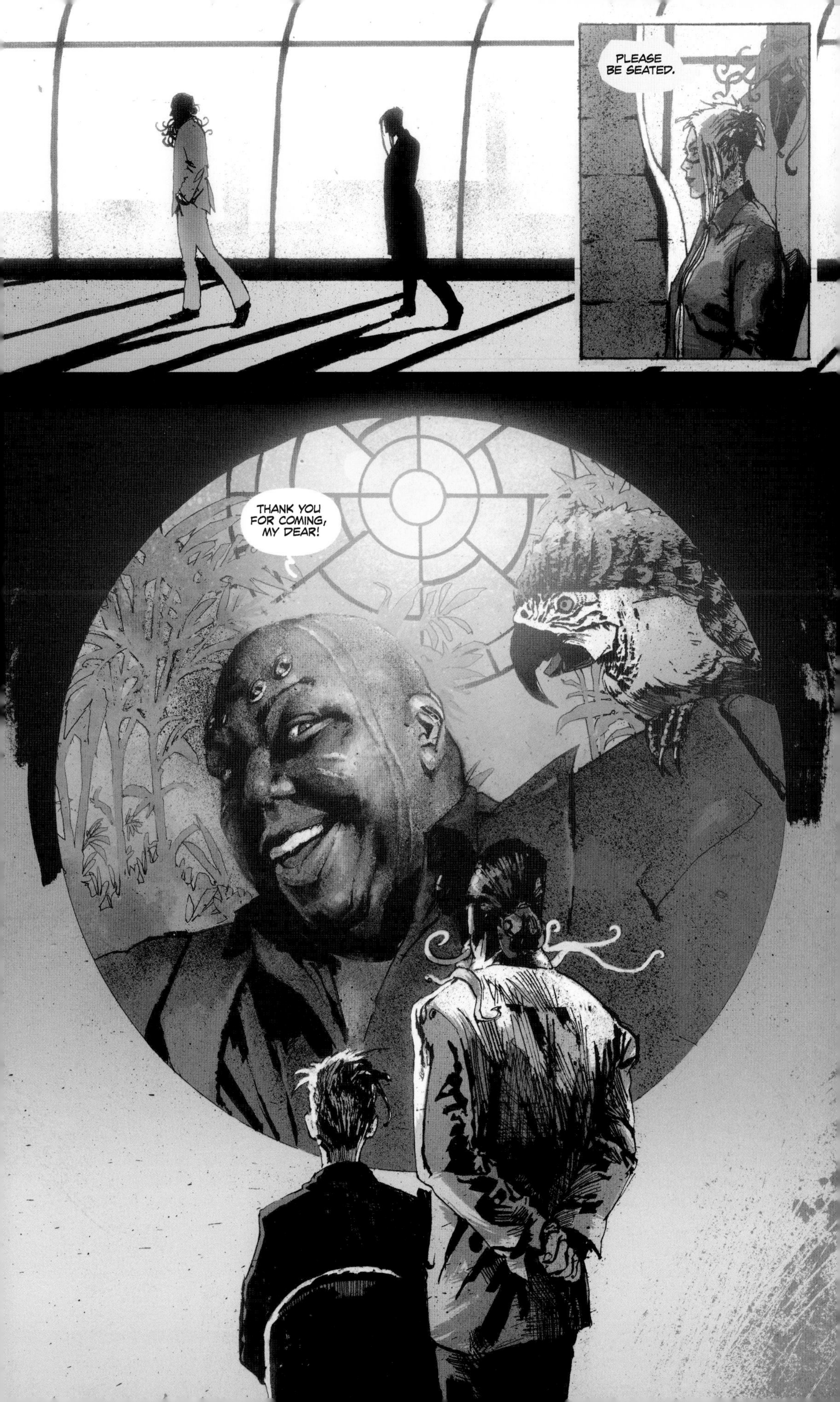
PLEASE BE SEATED.
THANK YOU FOR COMING, MY DEAR!

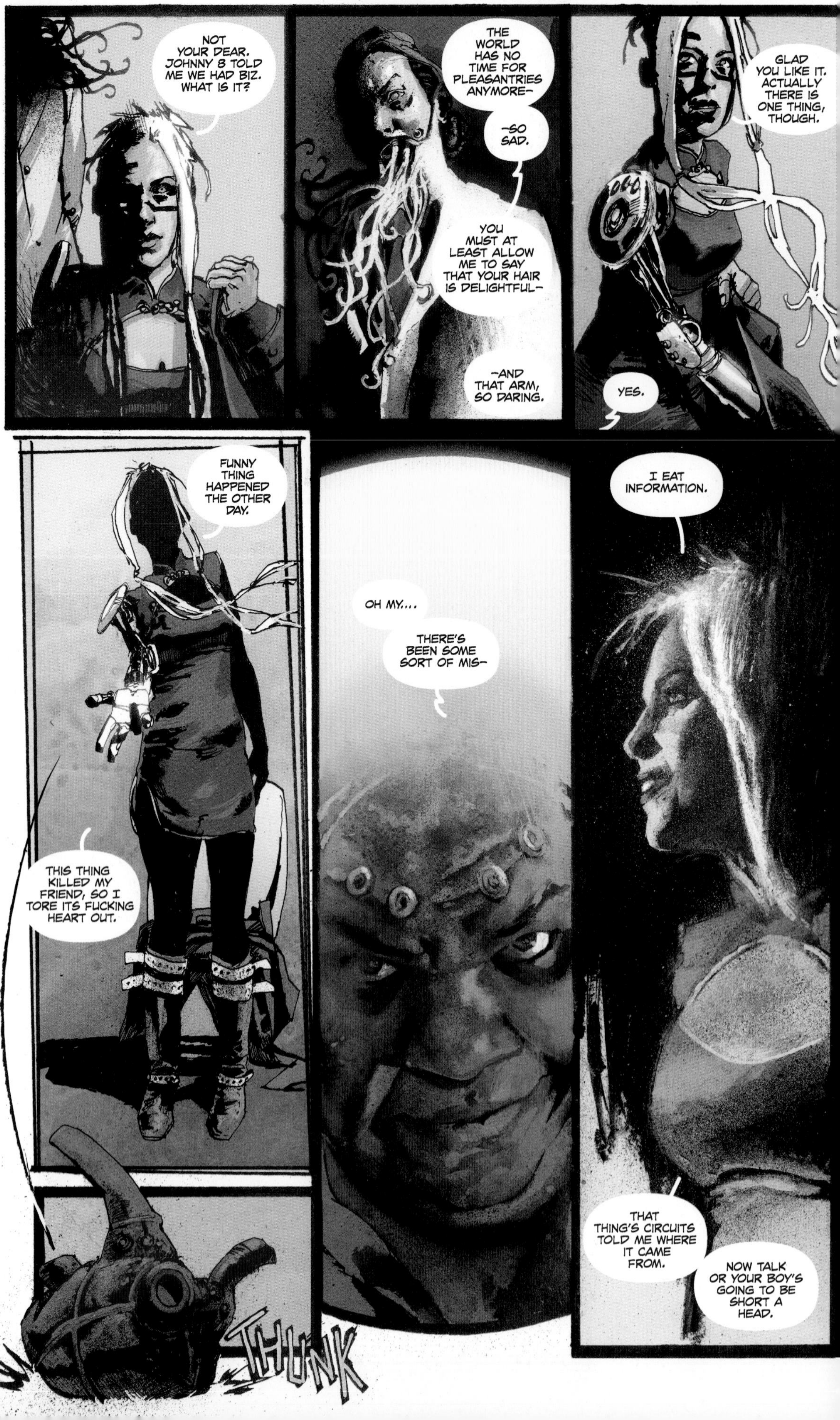
NOT YOUR DEAR. JOHNNY 8 TOLD ME WE HAD BIZ. WHAT IS IT?
THE WORLD HAS NO TIME FOR PLEASANTRIES ANYMORE-
-SO SAD.
YOU MUST AT LEAST ALLOW ME TO SAY THAT YOUR HAIR IS DELIGHTFUL-
-AND THAT ARM, SO DARING.
GLAD YOU LIKE IT. ACTUALLY THERE IS ONE THING, THOUGH.
YES.
FUNNY THING HAPPENED THE OTHER DAY.
THIS THING KILLED MY FRIEND, SO I TORE ITS FUCKING HEART OUT.
THUNK
OH MY....
THERE'S BEEN SOME SORT OF MIS-
I EAT INFORMATION.
THAT THING'S CIRCUITS TOLD ME WHERE IT CAME FROM.
NOW TALK OR YOUR BOY'S GOING TO BE SHORT A HEAD.

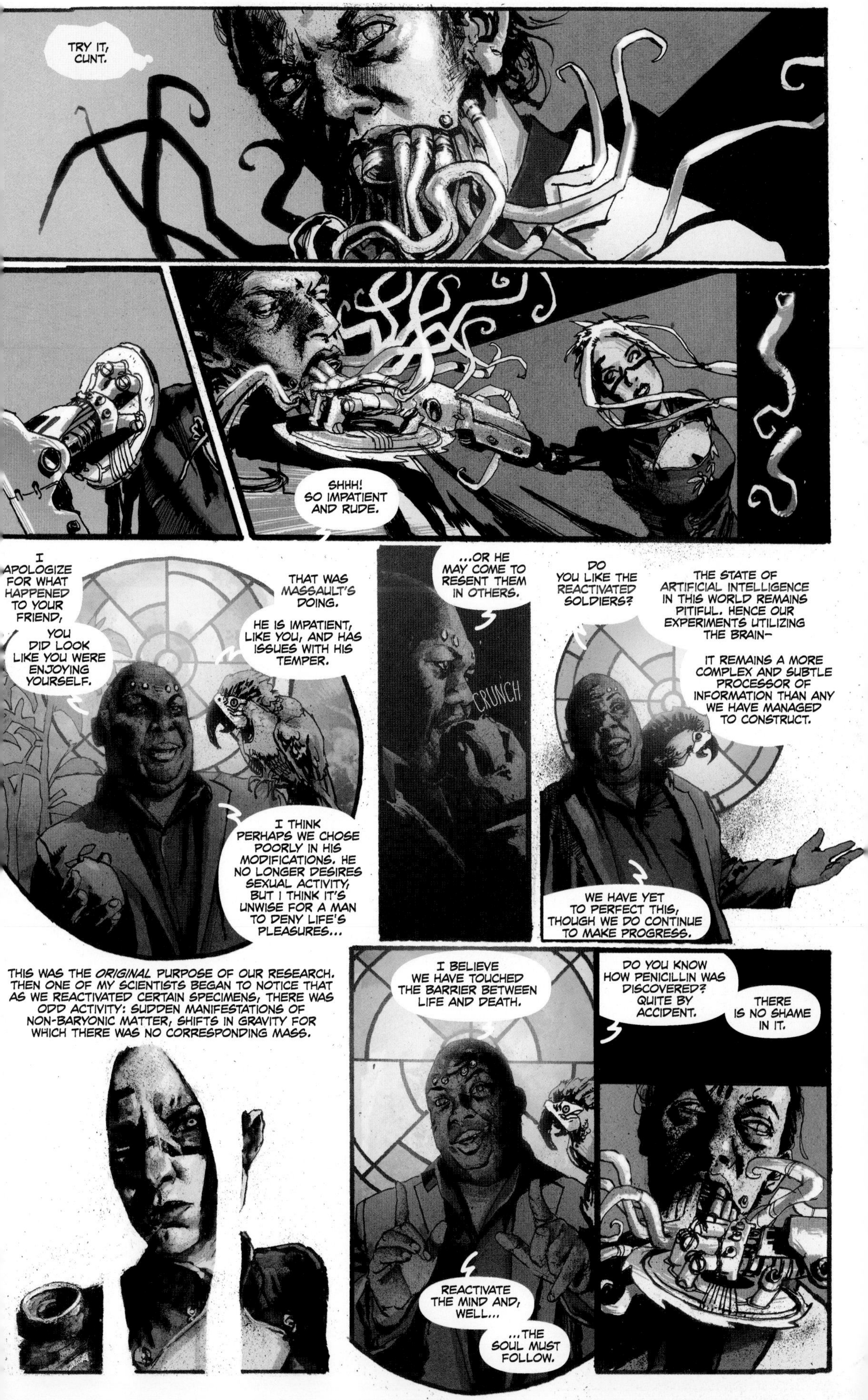
TRY IT, CUNT.
SHHH! SO IMPATIENT AND RUDE.
I APOLOGIZE FOR WHAT HAPPENED TO YOUR FRIEND,
YOU DID LOOK LIKE YOU WERE ENJOYING YOURSELF.
THAT WAS MASSAULT'S DOING.
HE IS IMPATIENT, LIKE YOU, AND HAS ISSUES WITH HIS TEMPER.
I THINK PERHAPS WE CHOSE POORLY IN HIS MODIFICATIONS. HE NO LONGER DESIRES SEXUAL ACTIVITY, BUT I THINK IT'S UNWISE FOR A MAN TO DENY LIFE'S PLEASURES...
...OR HE MAY COME TO RESENT THEM IN OTHERS.
CRUNCH
DO YOU LIKE THE REACTIVATED SOLDIERS?
THE STATE OF ARTIFICIAL INTELLIGENCE IN THIS WORLD REMAINS PITIFUL. HENCE OUR EXPERIMENTS UTILIZING THE BRAIN–
IT REMAINS A MORE COMPLEX AND SUBTLE PROCESSOR OF INFORMATION THAN ANY WE HAVE MANAGED TO CONSTRUCT.
WE HAVE YET TO PERFECT THIS, THOUGH WE DO CONTINUE TO MAKE PROGRESS.
THIS WAS THE *ORIGINAL* PURPOSE OF OUR RESEARCH. THEN ONE OF MY SCIENTISTS BEGAN TO NOTICE THAT AS WE REACTIVATED CERTAIN SPECIMENS, THERE WAS ODD ACTIVITY: SUDDEN MANIFESTATIONS OF NON-BARYONIC MATTER, SHIFTS IN GRAVITY FOR WHICH THERE WAS NO CORRESPONDING MASS.
I BELIEVE WE HAVE TOUCHED THE BARRIER BETWEEN LIFE AND DEATH.
REACTIVATE THE MIND AND, WELL...
...THE SOUL MUST FOLLOW.
DO YOU KNOW HOW PENICILLIN WAS DISCOVERED? QUITE BY ACCIDENT.
THERE IS NO SHAME IN IT.

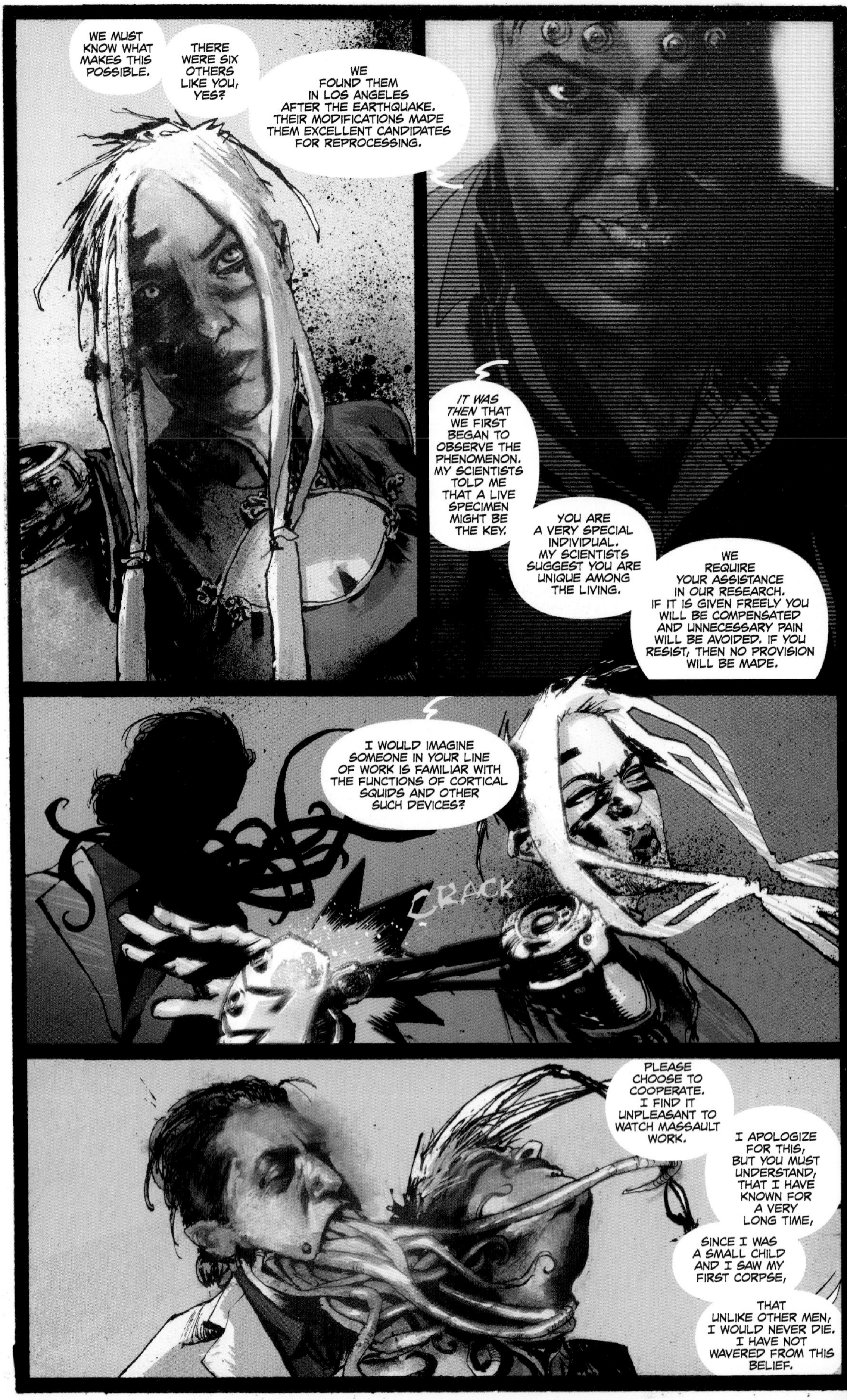
WE MUST KNOW WHAT MAKES THIS POSSIBLE.
THERE WERE SIX OTHERS LIKE YOU, YES?
WE FOUND THEM IN LOS ANGELES AFTER THE EARTHQUAKE. THEIR MODIFICATIONS MADE THEM EXCELLENT CANDIDATES FOR REPROCESSING.
IT WAS THEN THAT WE FIRST BEGAN TO OBSERVE THE PHENOMENON. MY SCIENTISTS TOLD ME THAT A LIVE SPECIMEN MIGHT BE THE KEY.
YOU ARE A VERY SPECIAL INDIVIDUAL. MY SCIENTISTS SUGGEST YOU ARE UNIQUE AMONG THE LIVING.
WE REQUIRE YOUR ASSISTANCE IN OUR RESEARCH. IF IT IS GIVEN FREELY YOU WILL BE COMPENSATED AND UNNECESSARY PAIN WILL BE AVOIDED. IF YOU RESIST, THEN NO PROVISION WILL BE MADE.
I WOULD IMAGINE SOMEONE IN YOUR LINE OF WORK IS FAMILIAR WITH THE FUNCTIONS OF CORTICAL SQUIDS AND OTHER SUCH DEVICES?
CRACK
PLEASE CHOOSE TO COOPERATE. I FIND IT UNPLEASANT TO WATCH MASSAULT WORK.
I APOLOGIZE FOR THIS, BUT YOU MUST UNDERSTAND, THAT I HAVE KNOWN FOR A VERY LONG TIME,
SINCE I WAS A SMALL CHILD AND I SAW MY FIRST CORPSE,
THAT UNLIKE OTHER MEN, I WOULD NEVER DIE. I HAVE NOT WAVERED FROM THIS BELIEF.

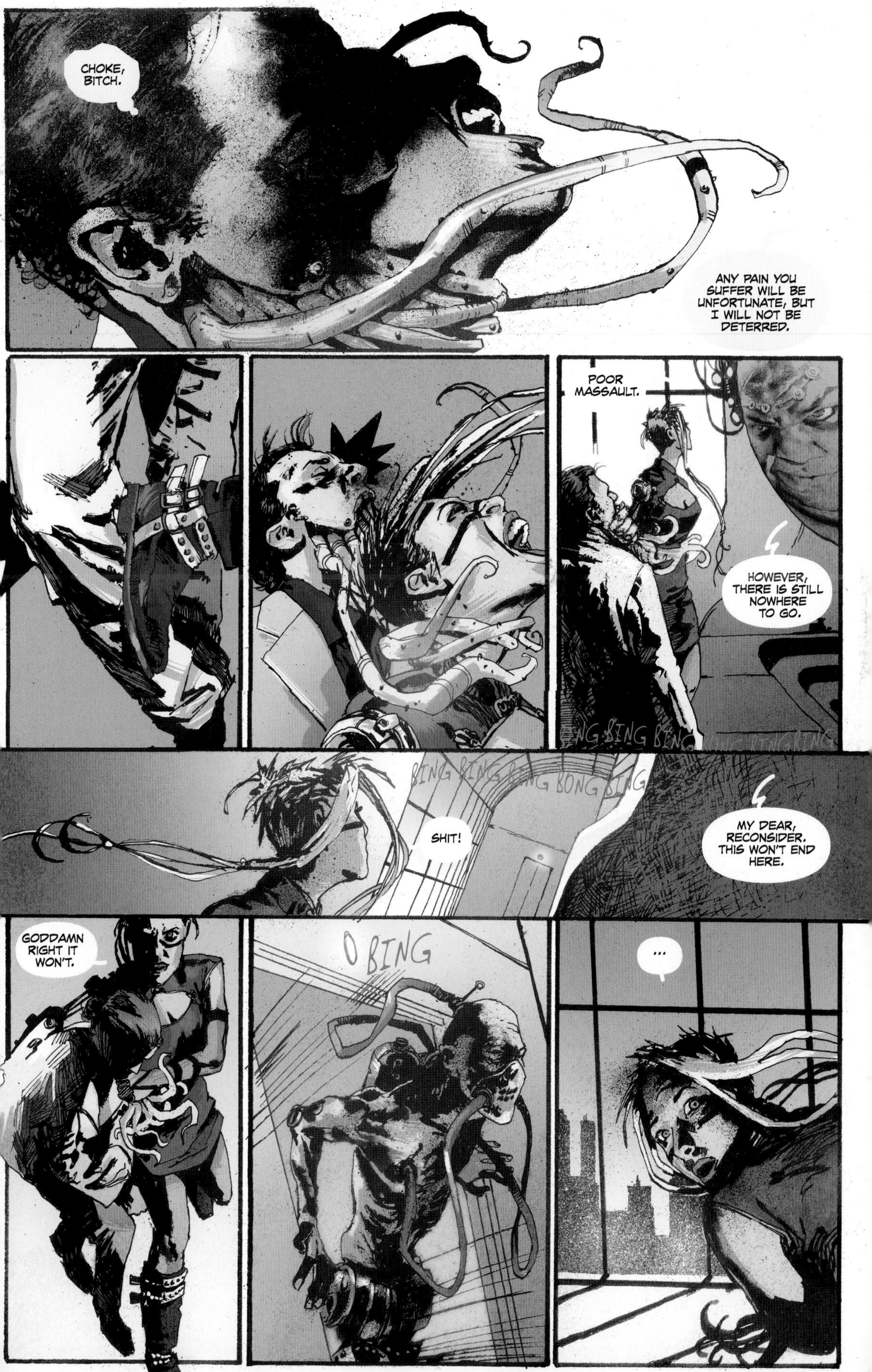
CHOKE, BITCH.
ANY PAIN YOU SUFFER WILL BE UNFORTUNATE, BUT I WILL NOT BE DETERRED.
POOR MASSAULT.
HOWEVER, THERE IS STILL NOWHERE TO GO.
BING BING BING
BING BING BING BONG BING
SHIT!
MY DEAR, RECONSIDER. THIS WON'T END HERE.
GODDAMN RIGHT IT WON'T.
O BING
...

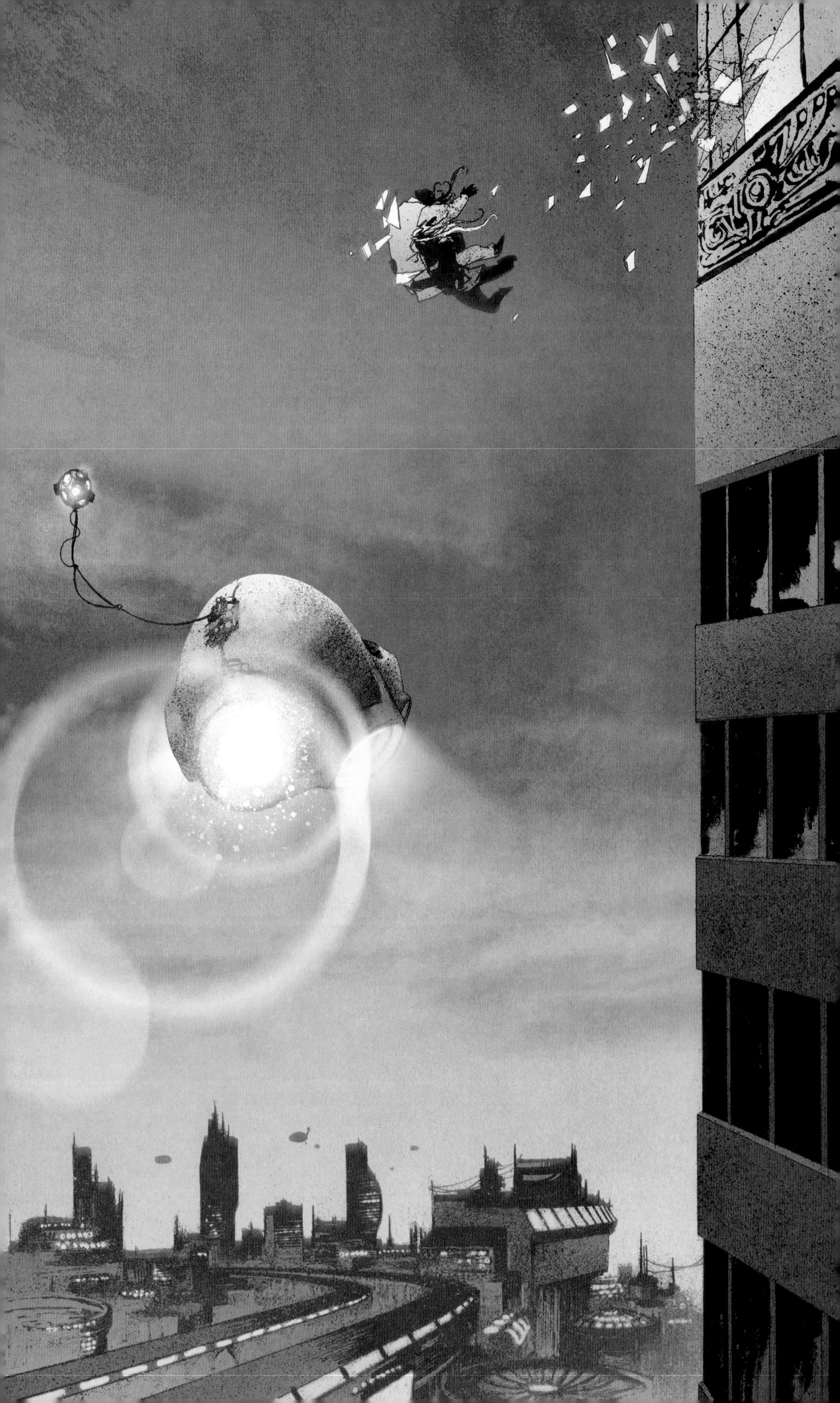

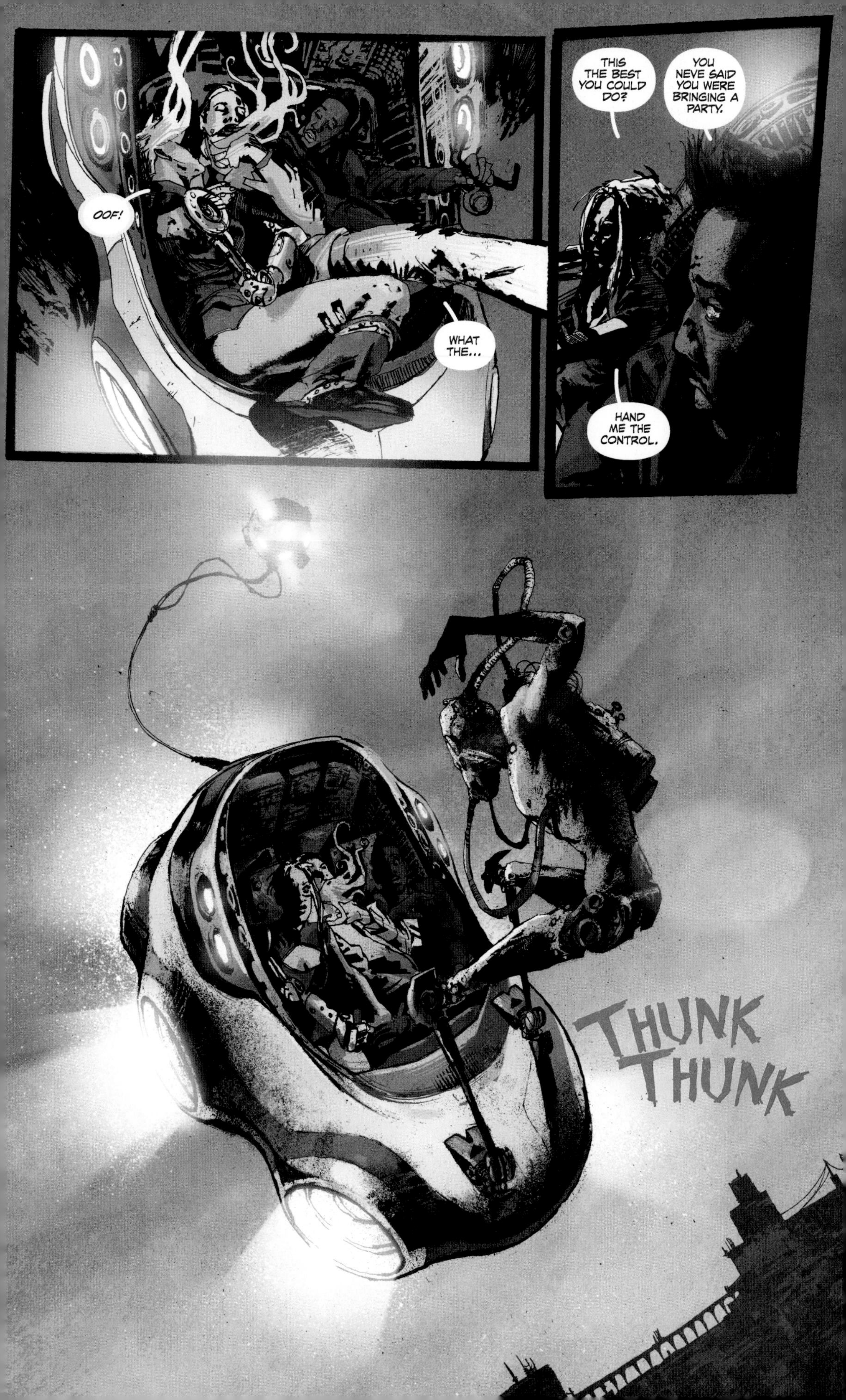
OOF!
WHAT THE...
THIS THE BEST YOU COULD DO?
YOU NEVE SAID YOU WERE BRINGING A PARTY.
HAND ME THE CONTROL.
THUNK THUNK

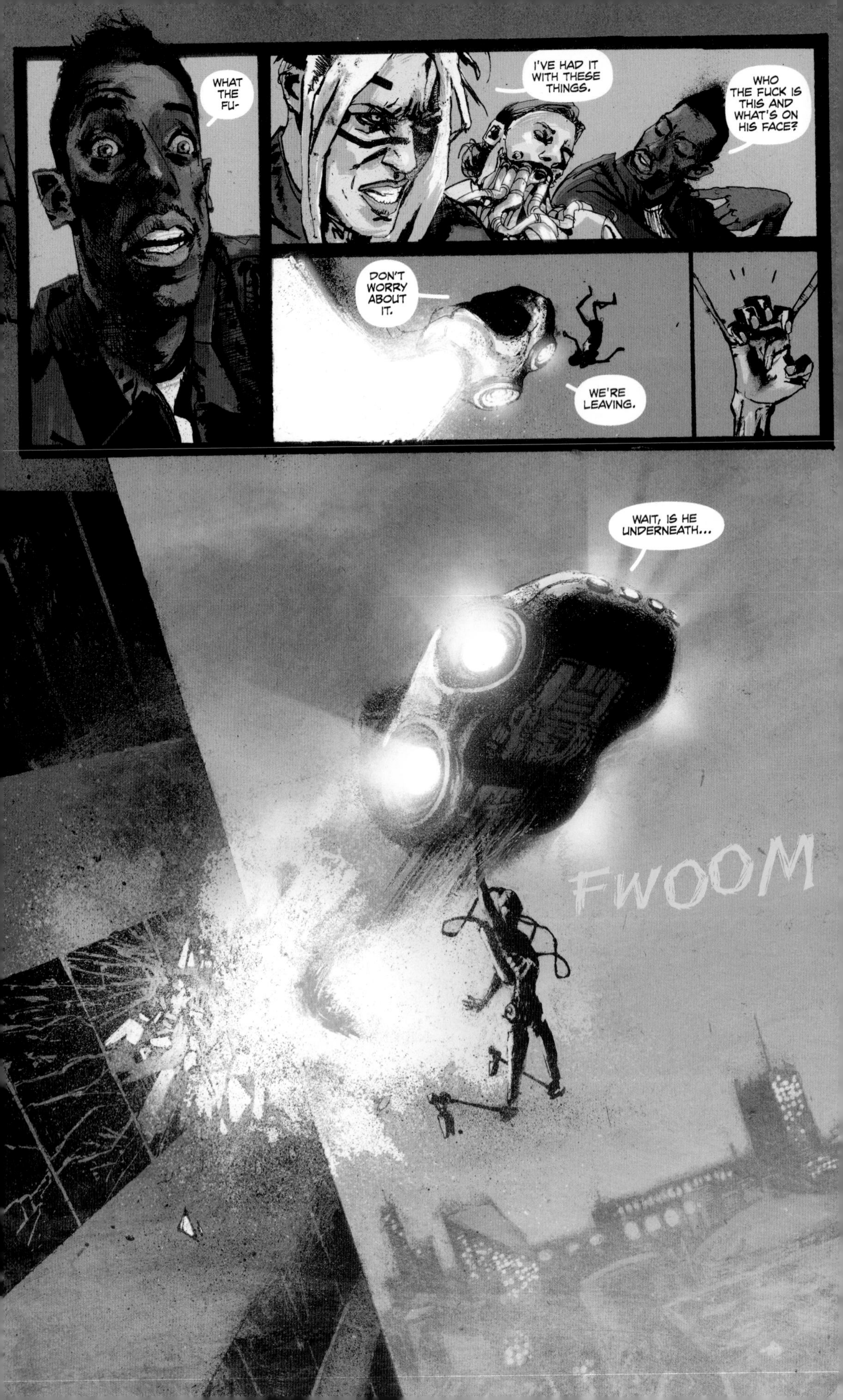
WHAT THE FU-
I'VE HAD IT WITH THESE THINGS.
WHO THE FUCK IS THIS AND WHAT'S ON HIS FACE?
DON'T WORRY ABOUT IT.
WE'RE LEAVING.
WAIT, IS HE UNDERNEATH...
FWOOM

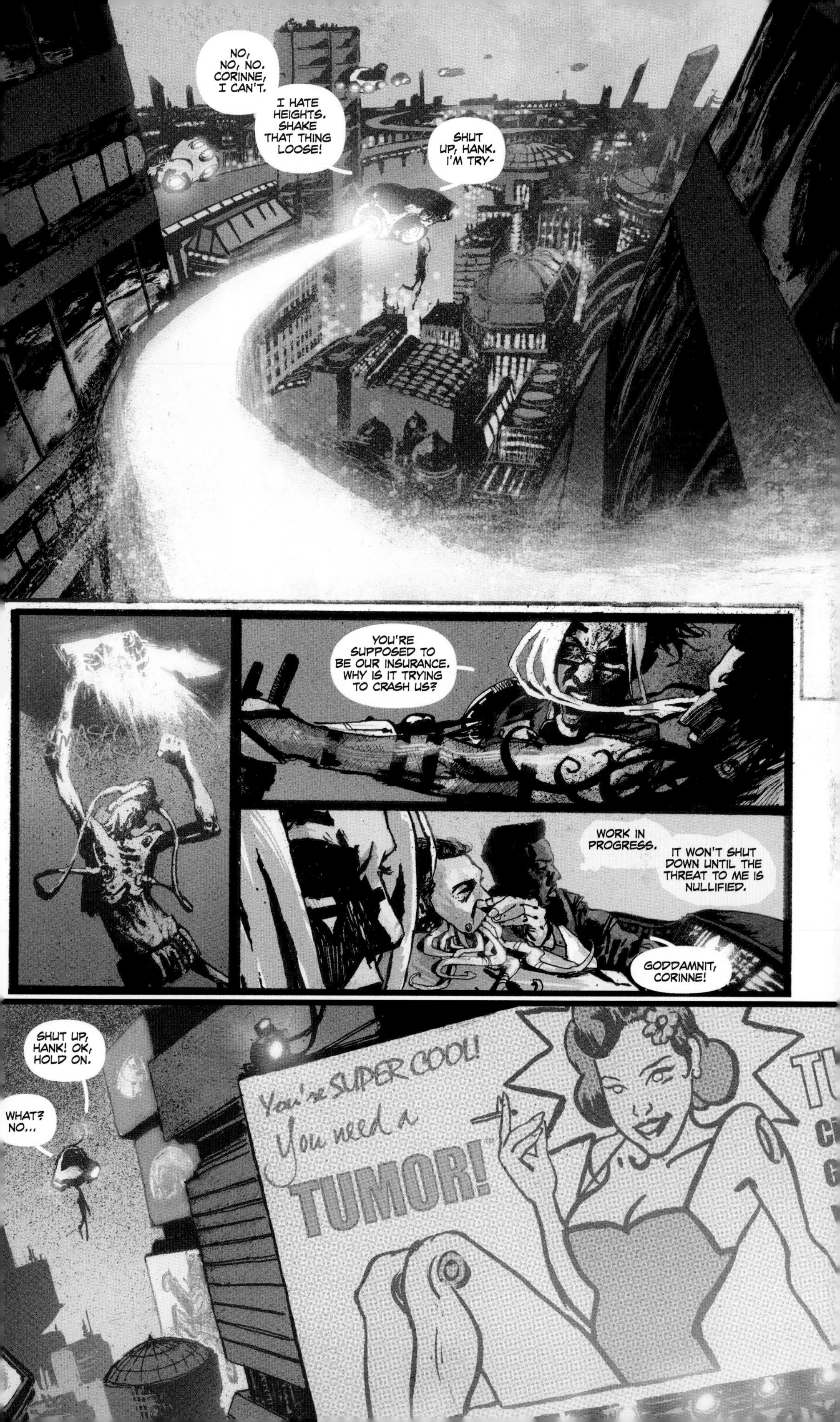
NO, NO, NO. CORINNE, I CAN'T.
I HATE HEIGHTS. SHAKE THAT THING LOOSE!
SHUT UP, HANK. I'M TRY-
SMASH
SMASH
YOU'RE SUPPOSED TO BE OUR INSURANCE. WHY IS IT TRYING TO CRASH US?
WORK IN PROGRESS.
IT WON'T SHUT DOWN UNTIL THE THREAT TO ME IS NULLIFIED.
GODDAMNIT, CORINNE!
SHUT UP, HANK! OK, HOLD ON.
WHAT? NO...
You're SUPER COOL! You need a TUMOR!

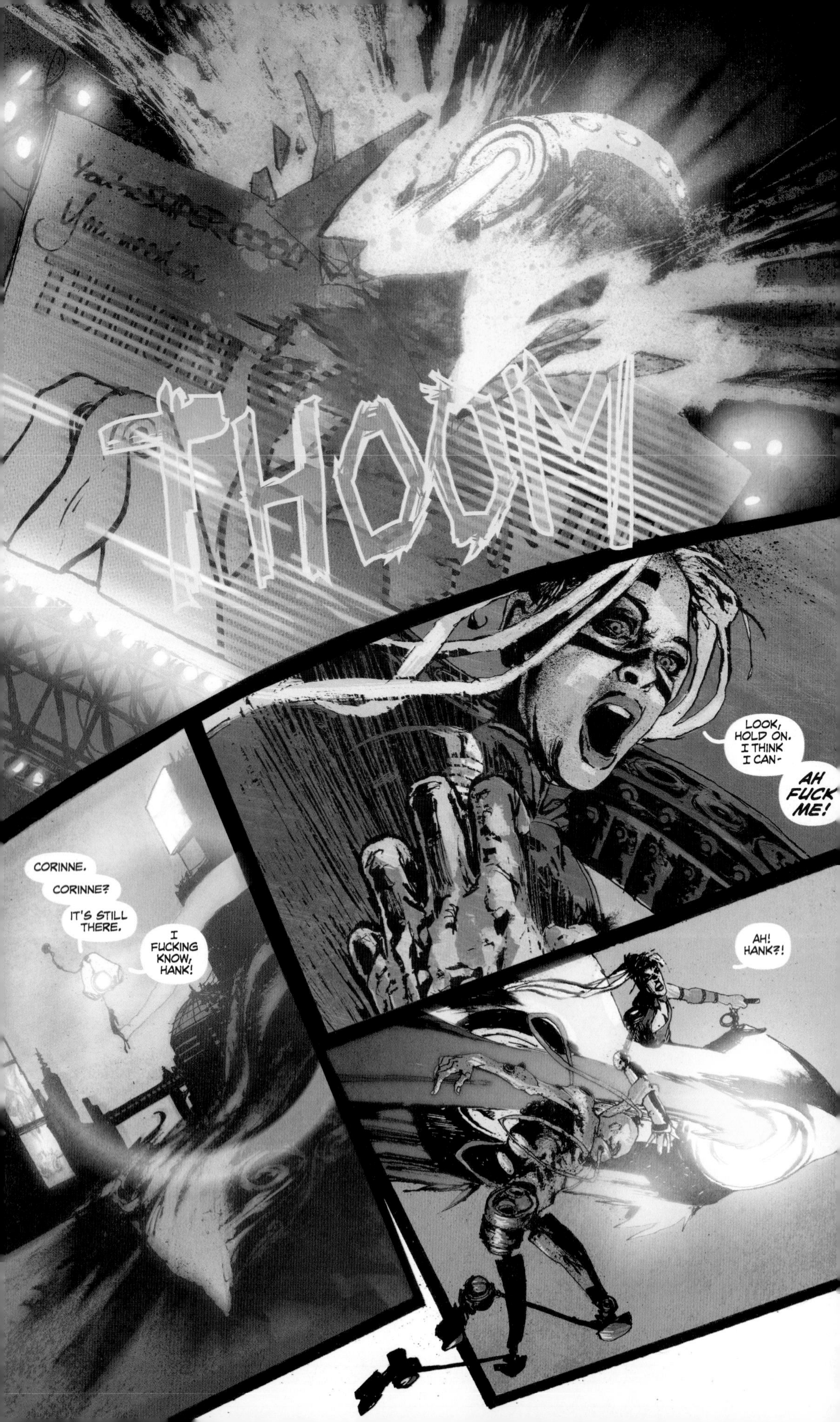
THOOM
LOOK, HOLD ON. I THINK I CAN-
AH FUCK ME!
CORINNE.
CORINNE?
IT'S STILL THERE.
I FUCKING KNOW, HANK!
AH! HANK?!

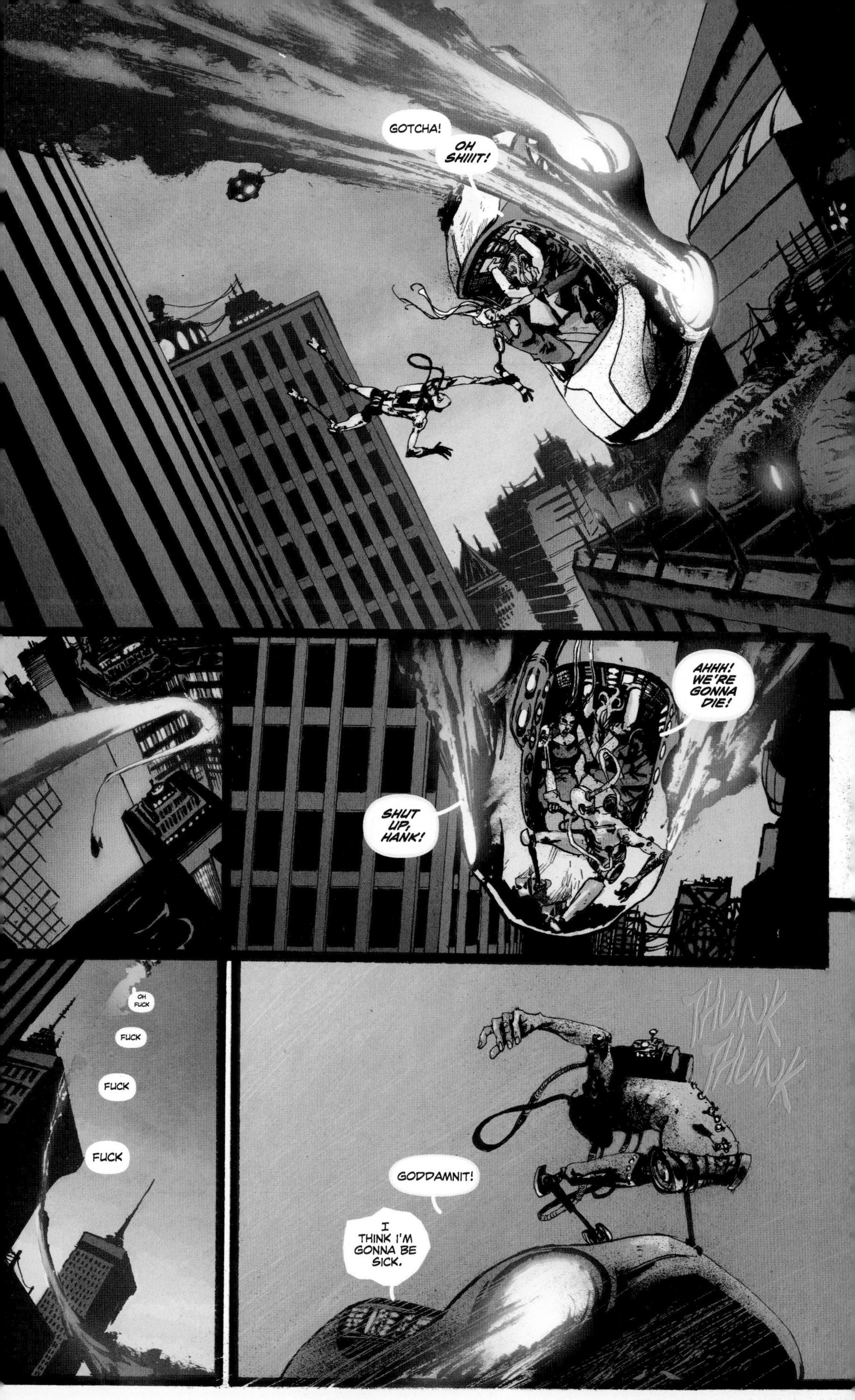
GOTCHA!
OH SHIIIT!
AHHH! WE'RE GONNA DIE!
SHUT UP, HANK!
OH FUCK
FUCK
FUCK
FUCK
THUNK THUNK
GODDAMNIT!
I THINK I'M GONNA BE SICK.

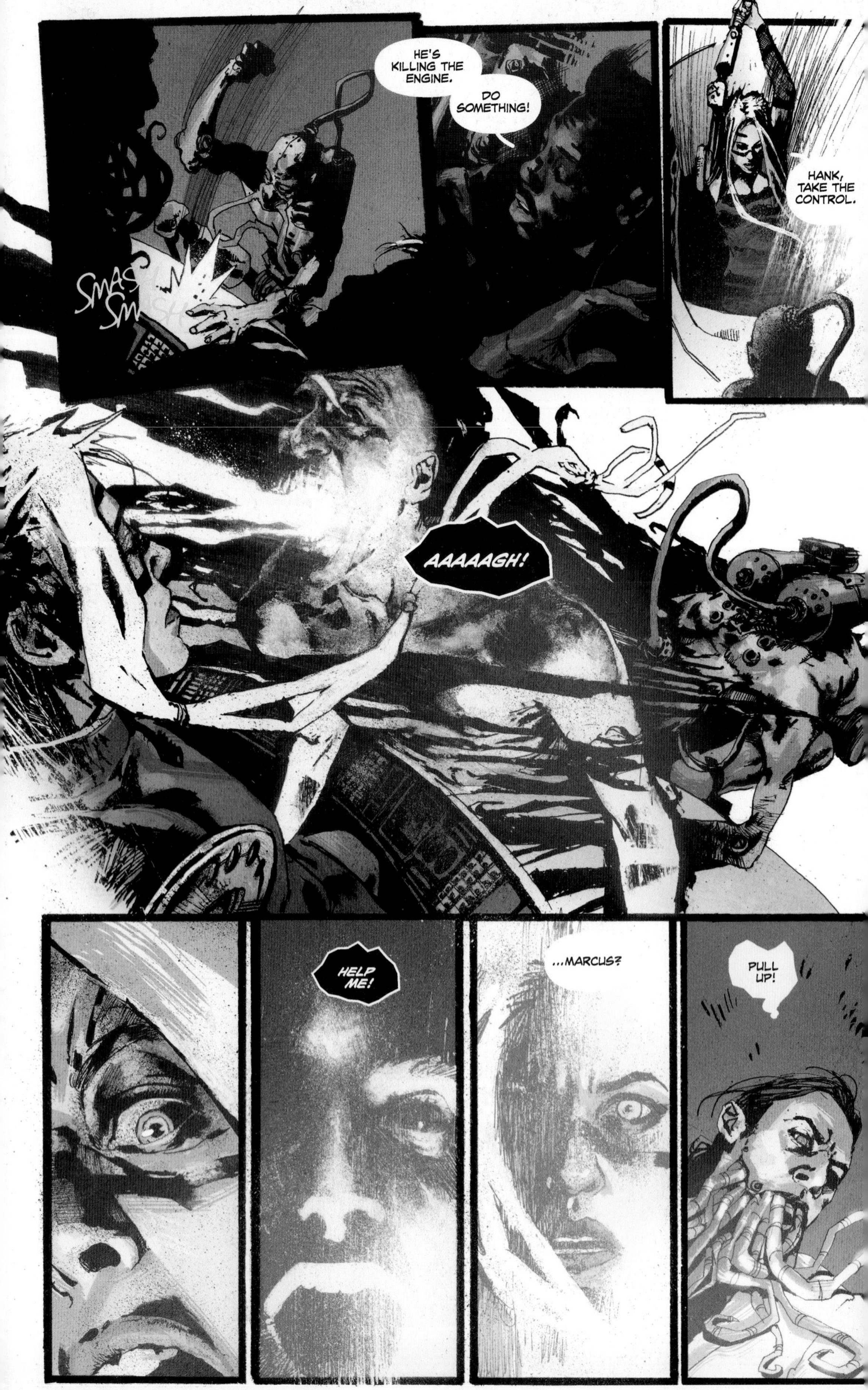

SMASH
SMASH
HE'S KILLING THE ENGINE.
DO SOMETHING!
HANK, TAKE THE CONTROL.
AAAAAGH!
HELP ME!
...MARCUS?
PULL UP!

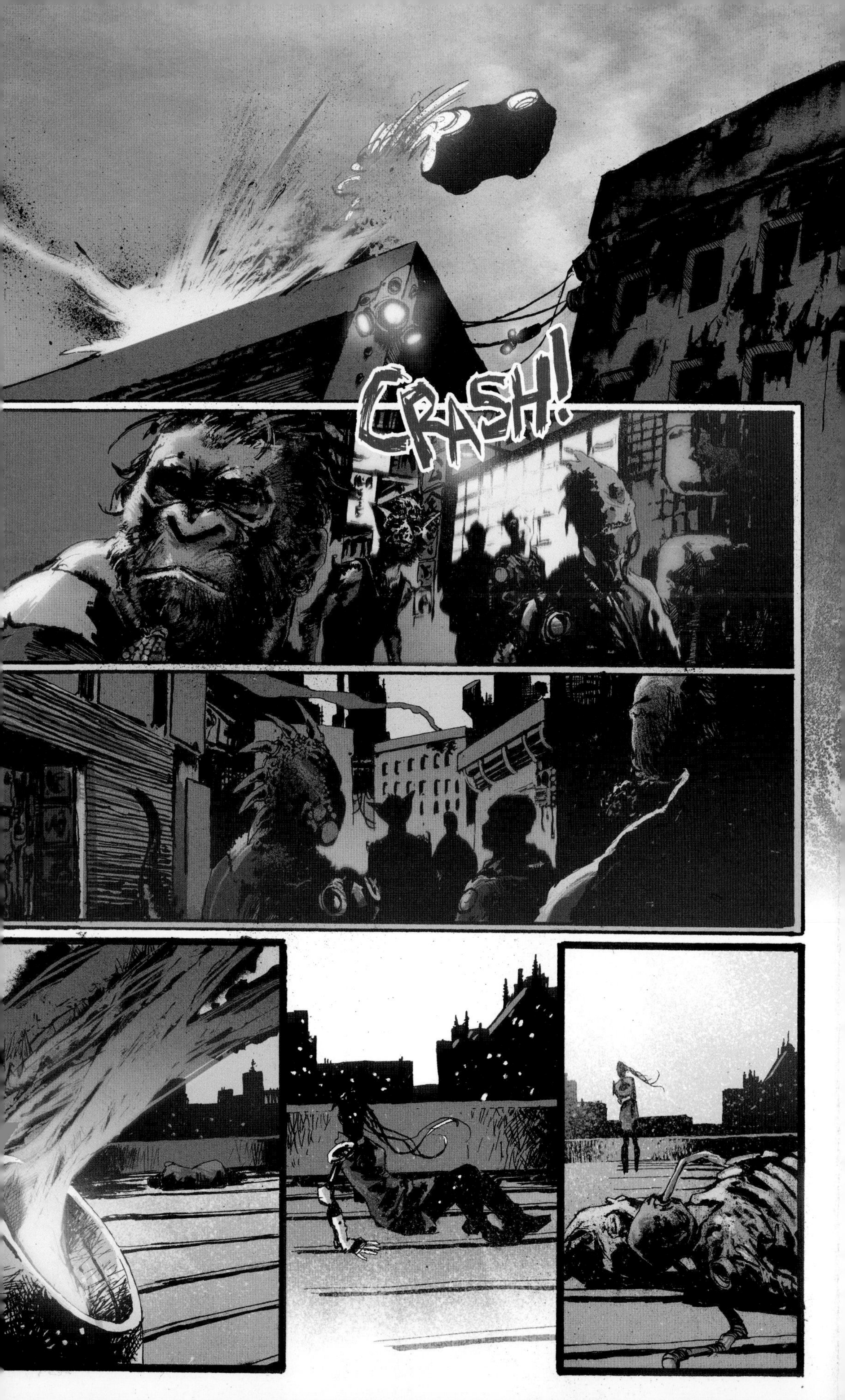
CRASH!

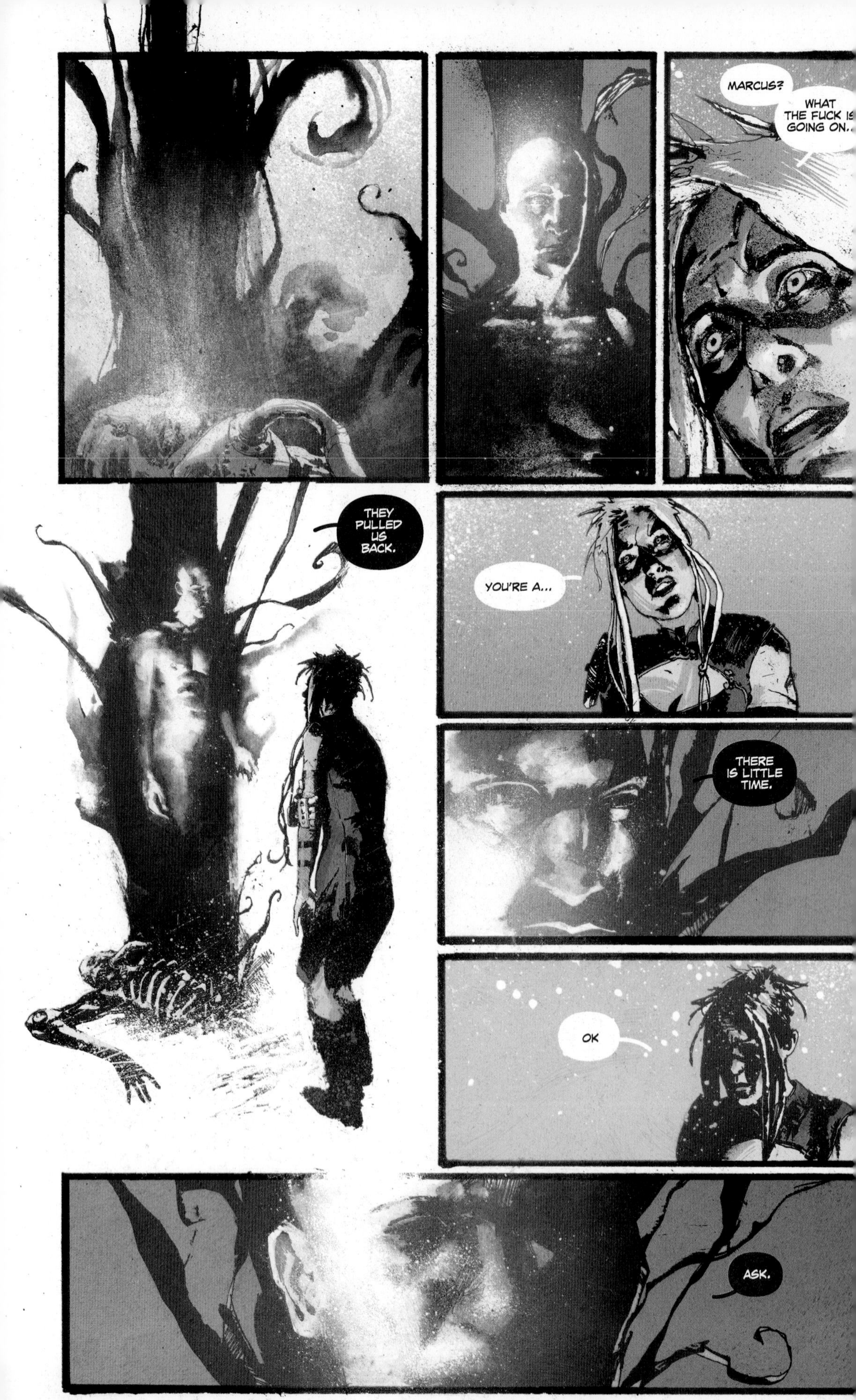
MARCUS?
WHAT THE FUCK IS GOING ON...
THEY PULLED US BACK.
YOU'RE A...
THERE IS LITTLE TIME.
OK
ASK.

JESUS... OK...BISHOP?

HE'S HERE.

...HOW?

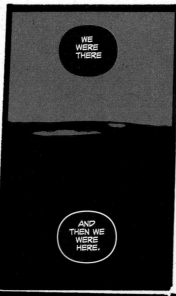

WE WERE THERE

AND THEN WE WERE HERE.

OUR BODIES HAD NOT FORGOTTEN US.

BUT THEY WERE ROTTEN.

"WAS THAT YOU, ON THE ROOF?"

"WE TRIED TO REACH YOU. YOU WERE AFRAID."

"YOU SLIPPED AND FELL UNCONSCIOUS AND DREAMED OF BISHOP AGAIN. SEVERING OUR CONNECTION."

"THE SECOND TIME WAS MORE SUCCESSFUL."

DOES...

DOES IT HURT?

THEY MOVE US LIKE PUPPETS, WE ARE PRISONERS IN OUR BODIES.

IT IS VERY COLD HERE.

THESE THINGS HURT.

WHY CAN I SEE YOU?

WE WERE AND ARE LINKED TO ONE ANOTHER.

THE SEVEN OF US WERE MADE TO ABSORB ALL TYPES OF INFORMATION. EVERYTHING IS INFORMATION CORINNE.

DO YOU UNDERSTAND?

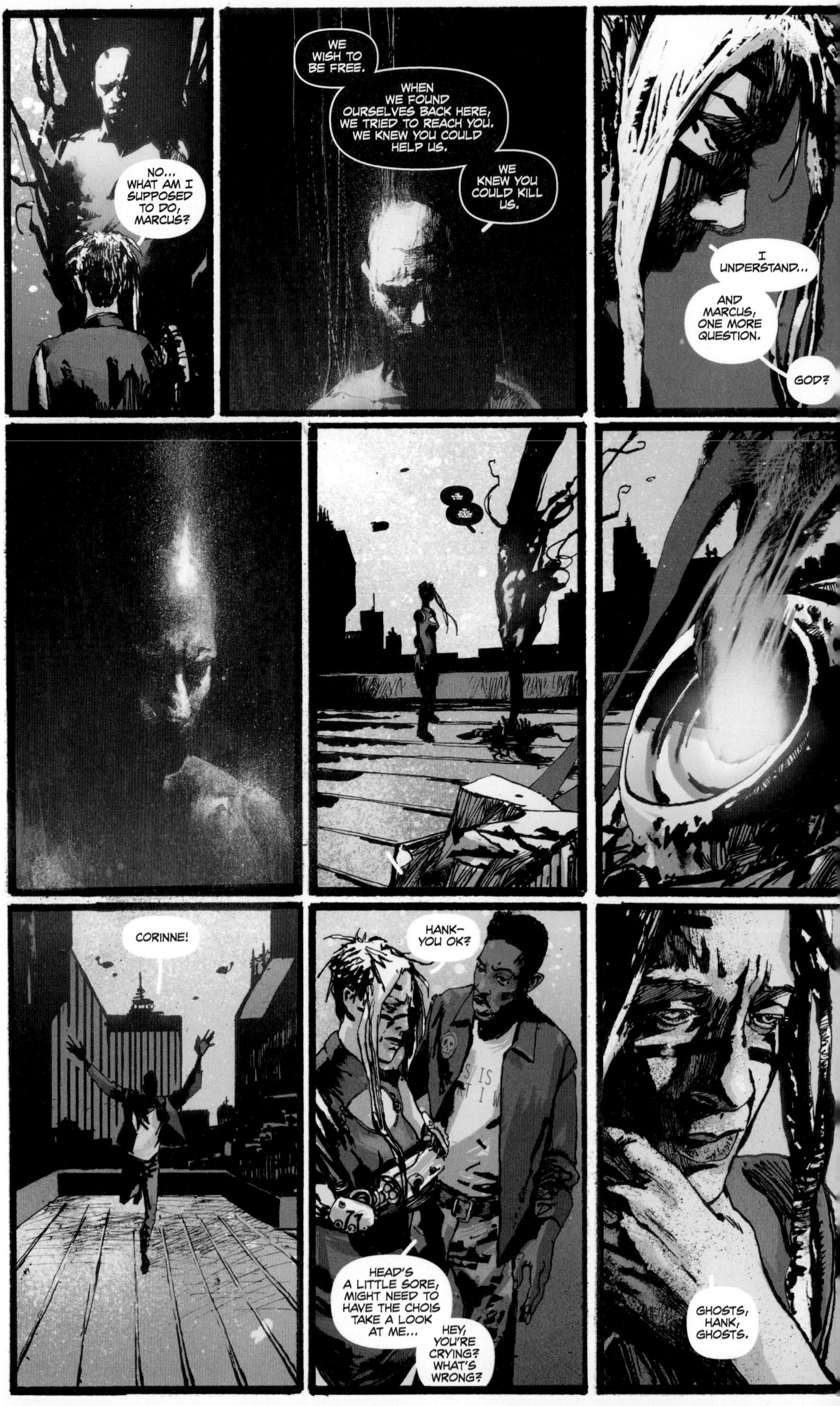
NO... WHAT AM I SUPPOSED TO DO, MARCUS?
WE WISH TO BE FREE.
WHEN WE FOUND OURSELVES BACK HERE, WE TRIED TO REACH YOU. WE KNEW YOU COULD HELP US.
WE KNEW YOU COULD KILL US.
I UNDERSTAND...
AND MARCUS, ONE MORE QUESTION.
GOD?
CORINNE!
HANK-- YOU OK?
HEAD'S A LITTLE SORE, MIGHT NEED TO HAVE THE CHOIS TAKE A LOOK AT ME...
HEY, YOU'RE CRYING? WHAT'S WRONG?
GHOSTS, HANK, GHOSTS.

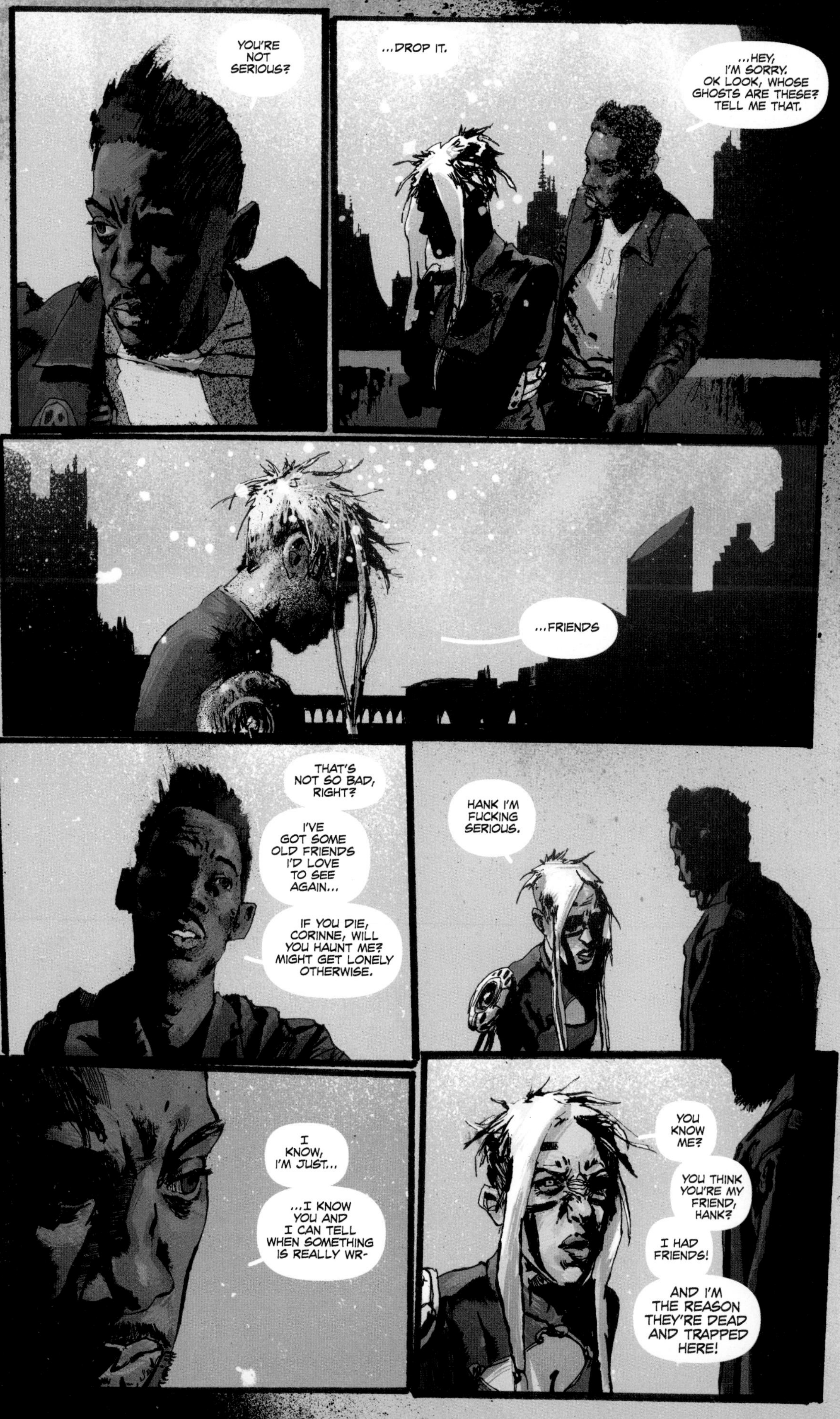
YOU'RE NOT SERIOUS?
...DROP IT.
...HEY, I'M SORRY. OK LOOK, WHOSE GHOSTS ARE THESE? TELL ME THAT.
...FRIENDS
THAT'S NOT SO BAD, RIGHT?
I'VE GOT SOME OLD FRIENDS I'D LOVE TO SEE AGAIN...
IF YOU DIE, CORINNE, WILL YOU HAUNT ME? MIGHT GET LONELY OTHERWISE.
HANK I'M FUCKING SERIOUS.
I KNOW, I'M JUST...
...I KNOW YOU AND I CAN TELL WHEN SOMETHING IS REALLY WR-
YOU KNOW ME?
YOU THINK YOU'RE MY FRIEND, HANK?
I HAD FRIENDS!
AND I'M THE REASON THEY'RE DEAD AND TRAPPED HERE!

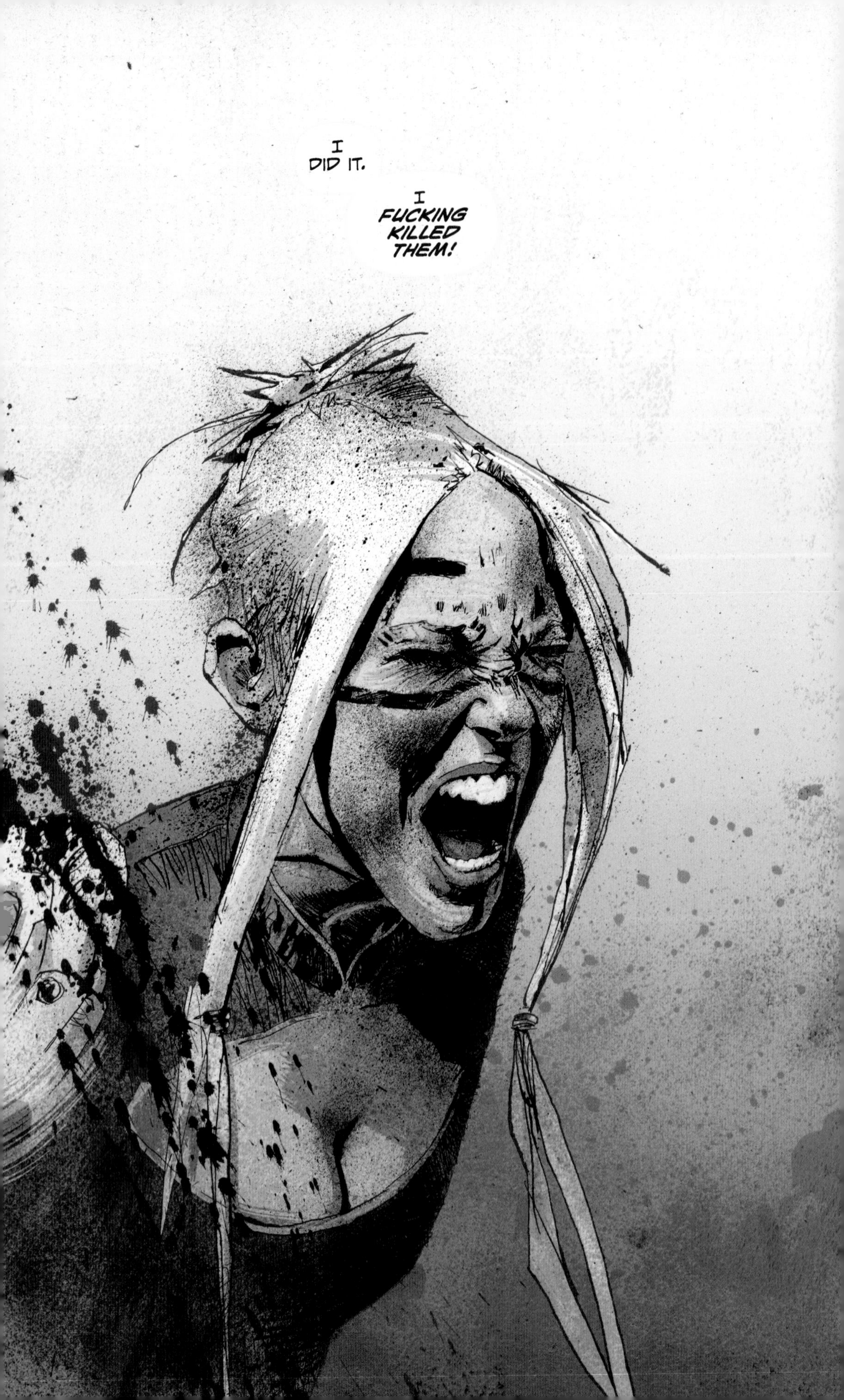
I DID IT.
I FUCKING KILLED THEM!

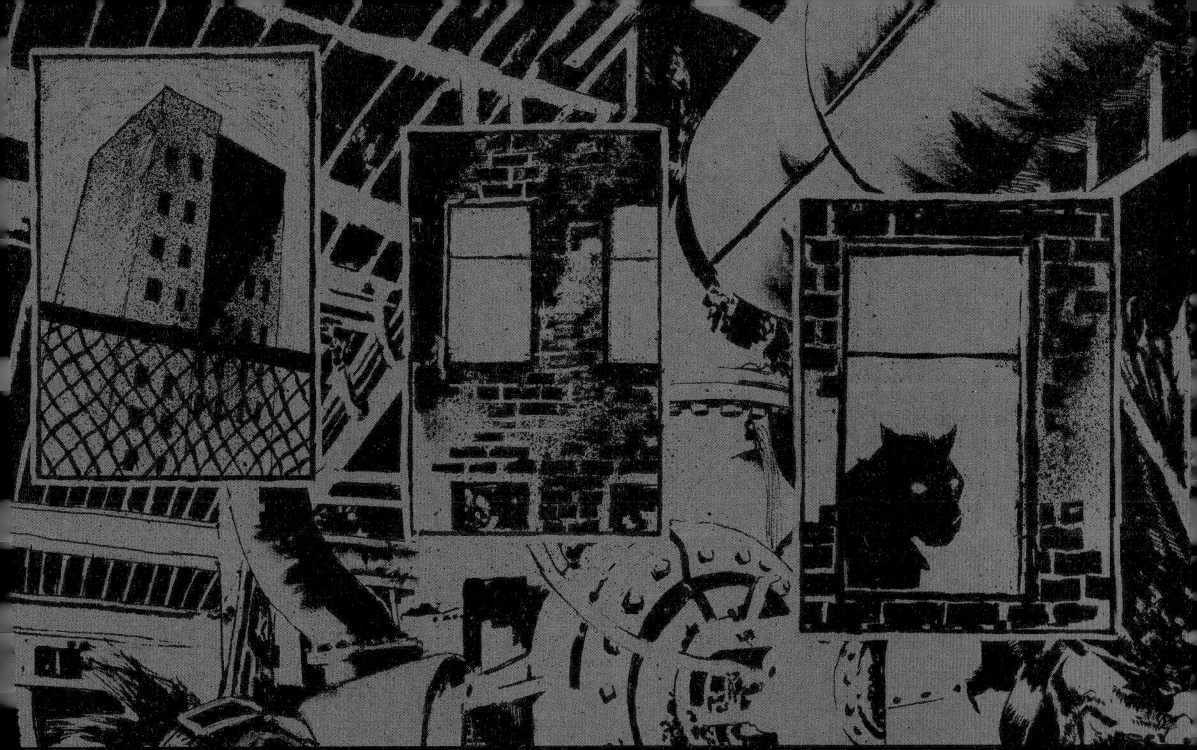

CHAPTER FIVE

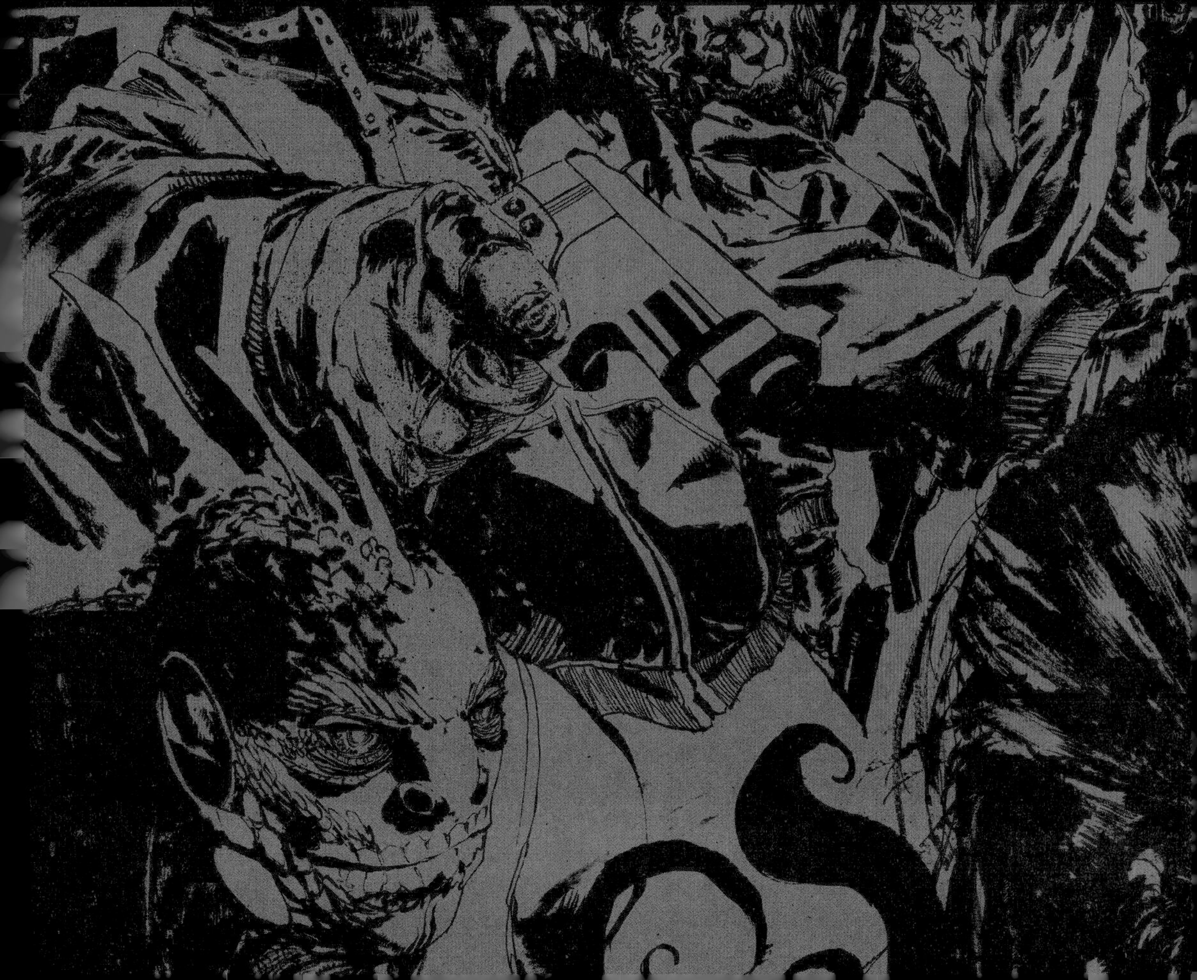

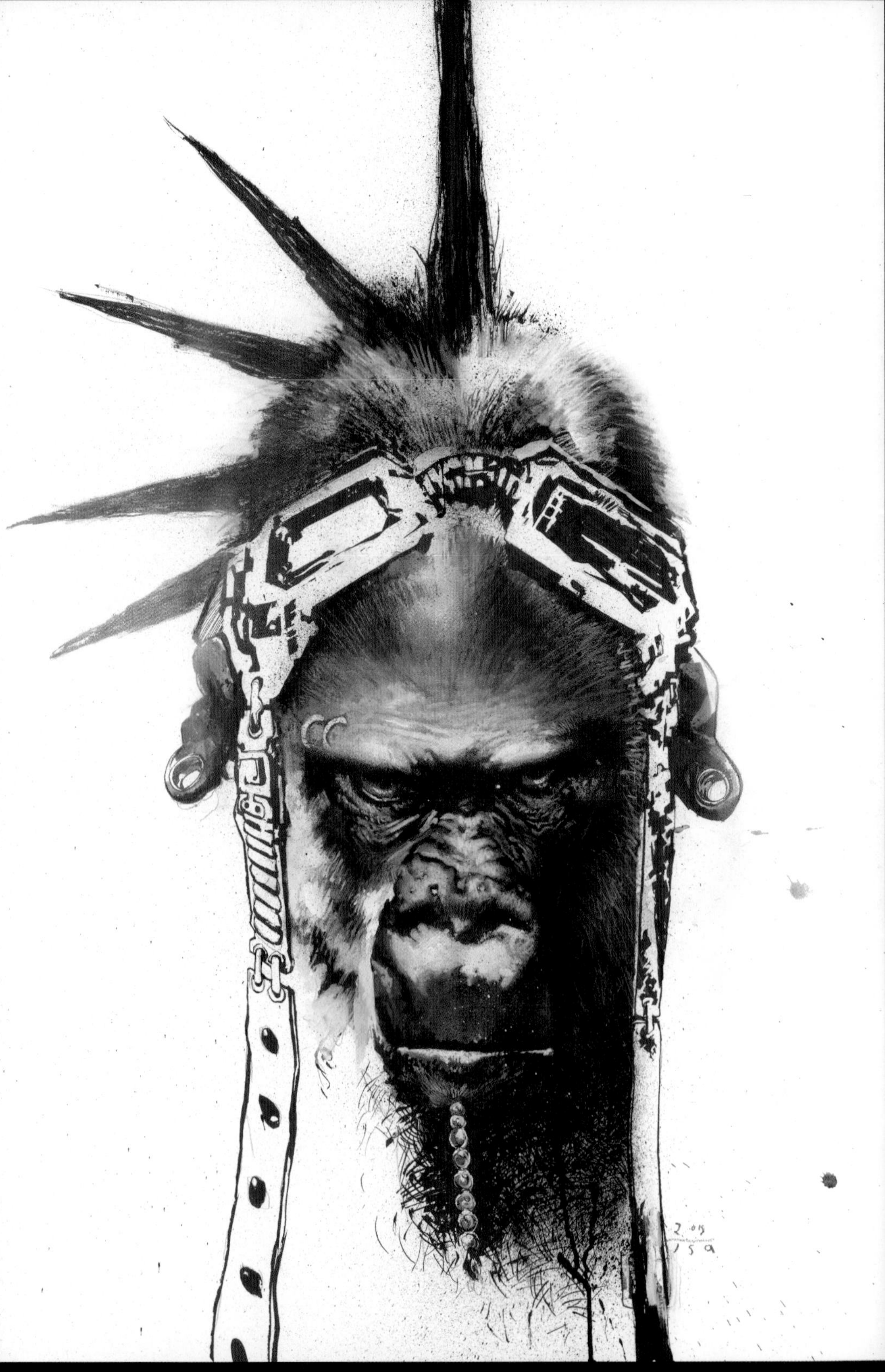

30 x 44 in. ink, acrylic, pastel, spray paint on paper

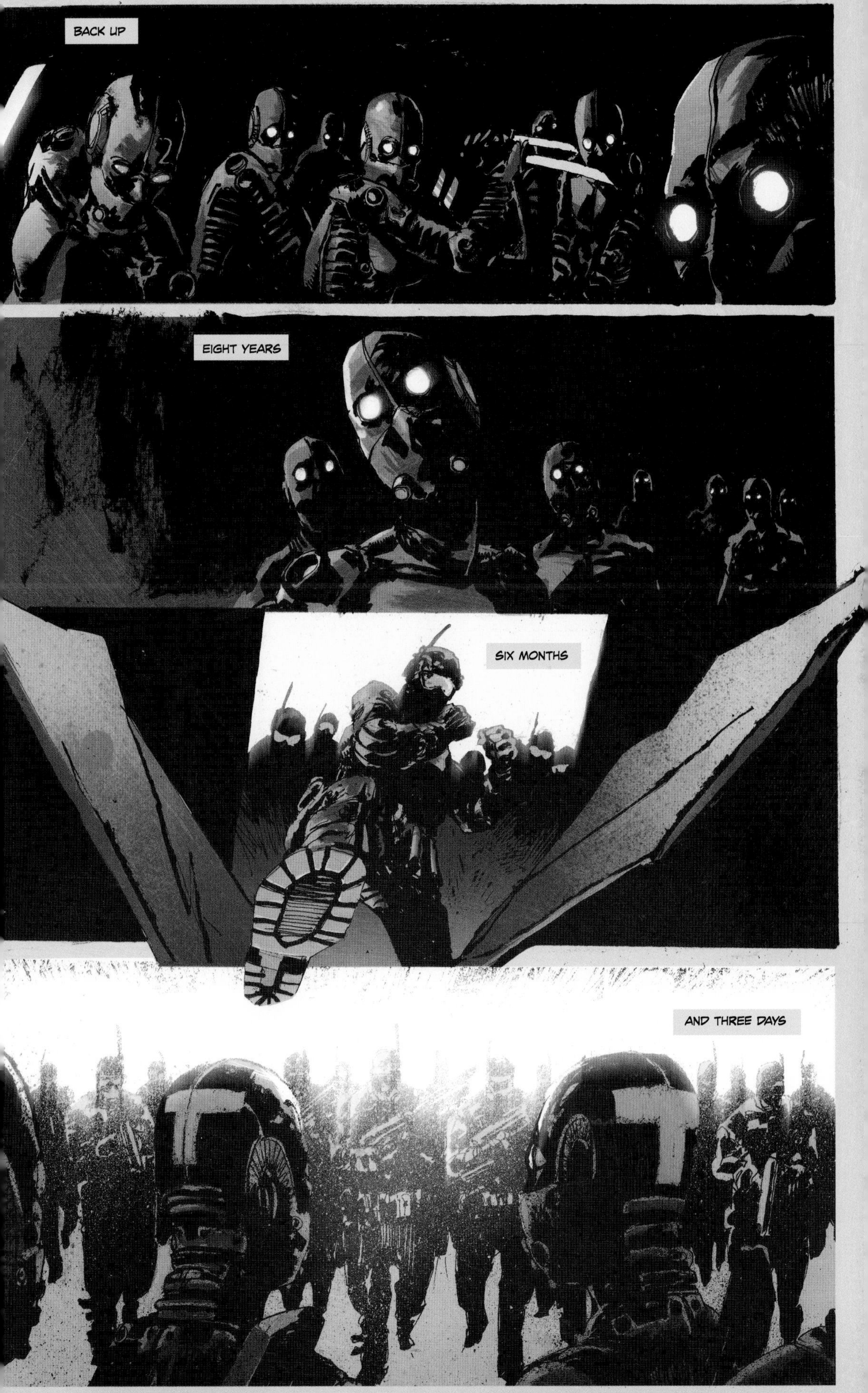
BACK UP
EIGHT YEARS
SIX MONTHS
AND THREE DAYS

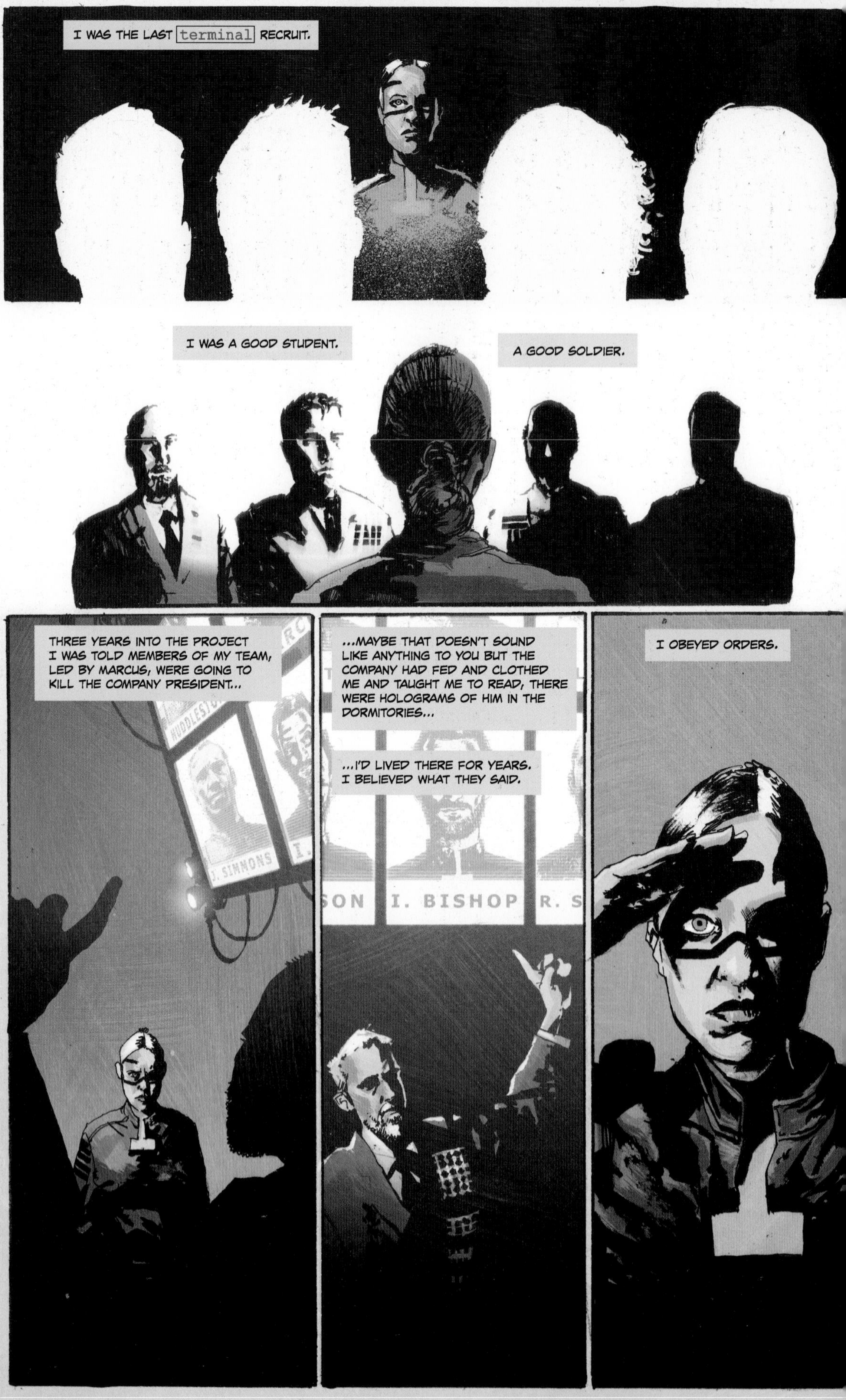
I WAS THE LAST terminal RECRUIT.
I WAS A GOOD STUDENT.
A GOOD SOLDIER.
THREE YEARS INTO THE PROJECT I WAS TOLD MEMBERS OF MY TEAM, LED BY MARCUS, WERE GOING TO KILL THE COMPANY PRESIDENT...
HUDDLES
J. SIMMONS
...MAYBE THAT DOESN'T SOUND LIKE ANYTHING TO YOU BUT THE COMPANY HAD FED AND CLOTHED ME AND TAUGHT ME TO READ; THERE WERE HOLOGRAMS OF HIM IN THE DORMITORIES...
...I'D LIVED THERE FOR YEARS. I BELIEVED WHAT THEY SAID.
SON I. BISHOP R. S
I OBEYED ORDERS.

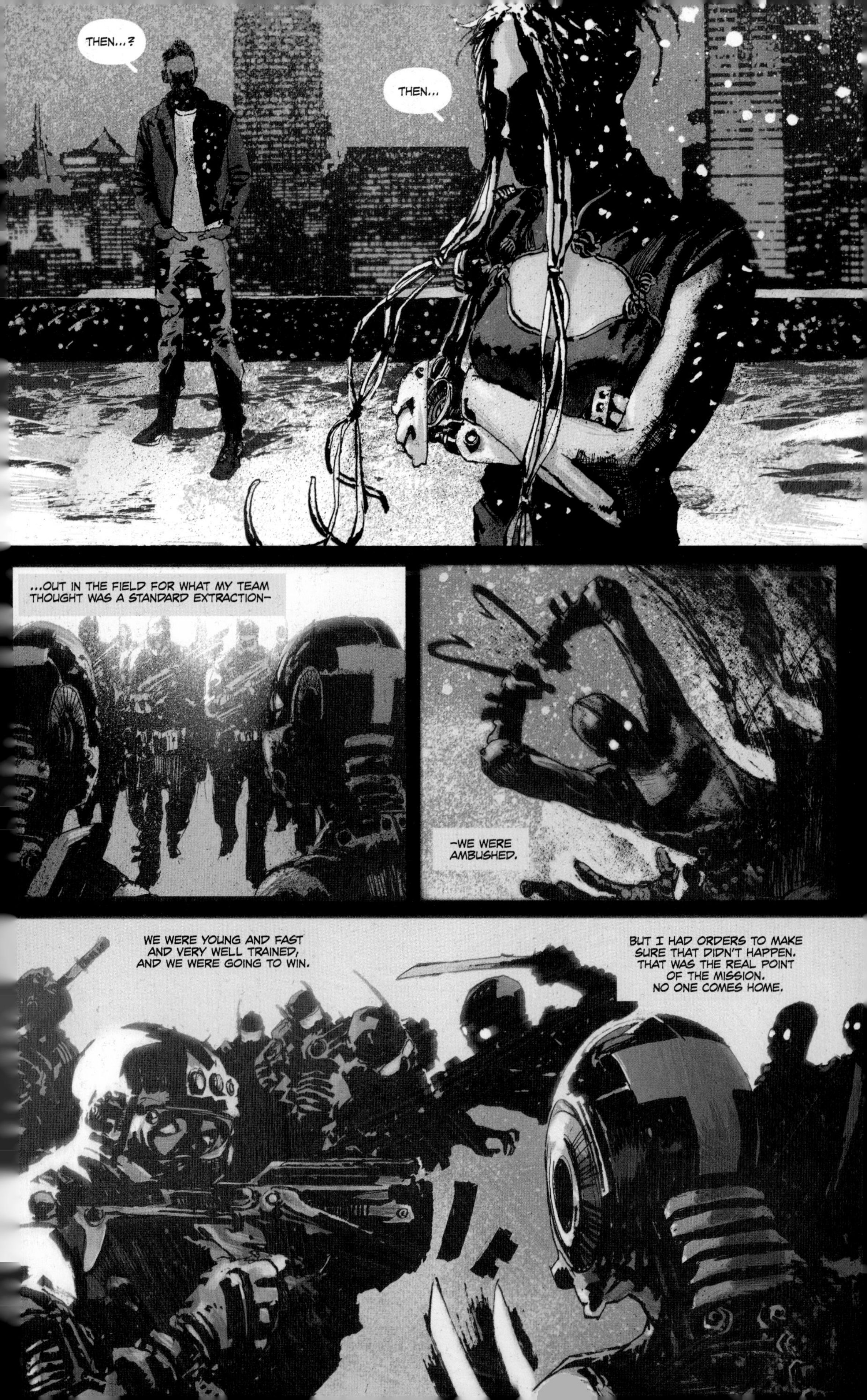
THEN...?
THEN...
...OUT IN THE FIELD FOR WHAT MY TEAM THOUGHT WAS A STANDARD EXTRACTION-
-WE WERE AMBUSHED.
WE WERE YOUNG AND FAST AND VERY WELL TRAINED, AND WE WERE GOING TO WIN.
BUT I HAD ORDERS TO MAKE SURE THAT DIDN'T HAPPEN. THAT WAS THE REAL POINT OF THE MISSION. NO ONE COMES HOME.

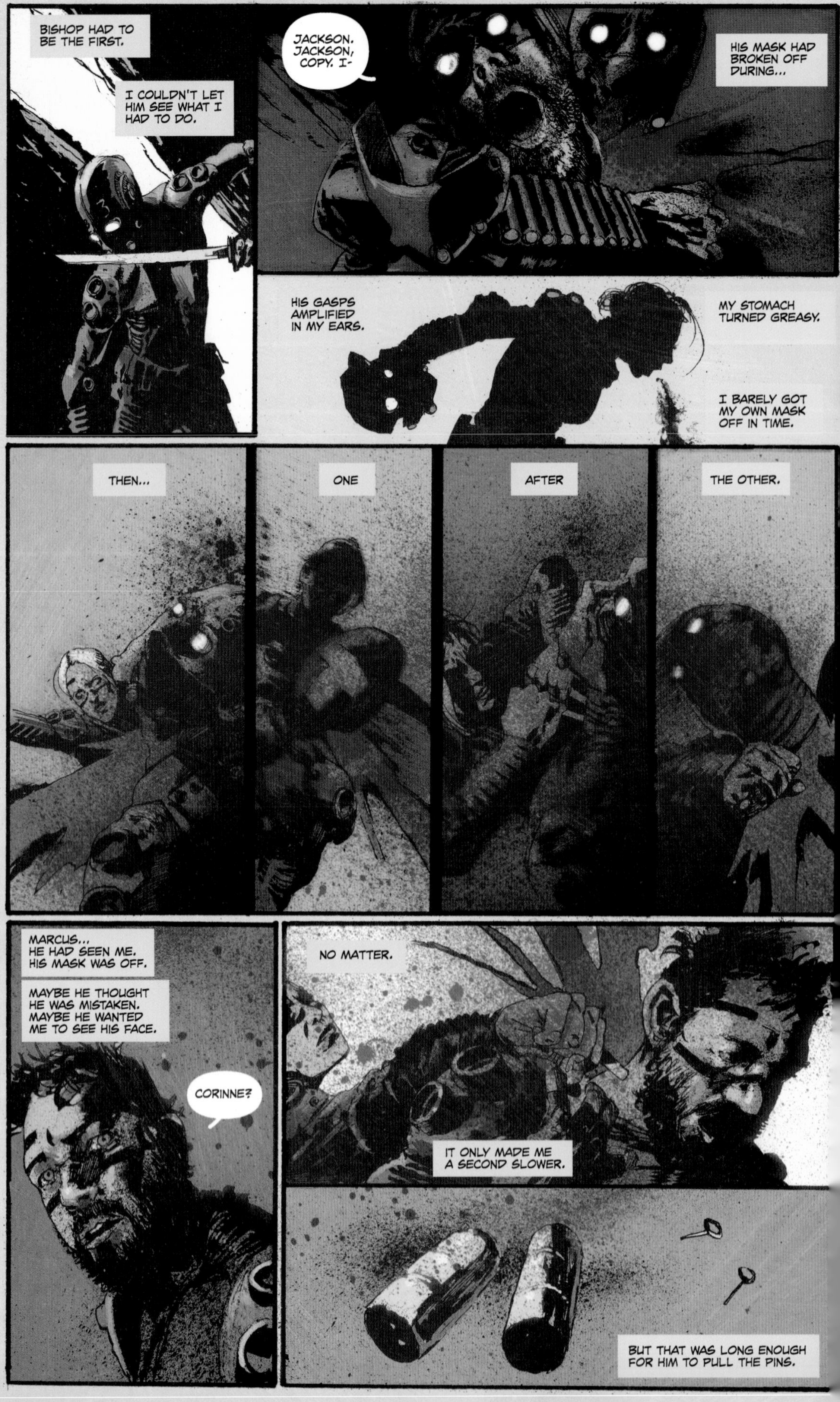
BISHOP HAD TO BE THE FIRST.
I COULDN'T LET HIM SEE WHAT I HAD TO DO.
JACKSON. JACKSON, COPY. I-
HIS MASK HAD BROKEN OFF DURING...
HIS GASPS AMPLIFIED IN MY EARS.
MY STOMACH TURNED GREASY.
I BARELY GOT MY OWN MASK OFF IN TIME.
THEN...
ONE
AFTER
THE OTHER.
MARCUS... HE HAD SEEN ME. HIS MASK WAS OFF.
MAYBE HE THOUGHT HE WAS MISTAKEN. MAYBE HE WANTED ME TO SEE HIS FACE.
CORINNE?
NO MATTER.
IT ONLY MADE ME A SECOND SLOWER.
BUT THAT WAS LONG ENOUGH FOR HIM TO PULL THE PINS.

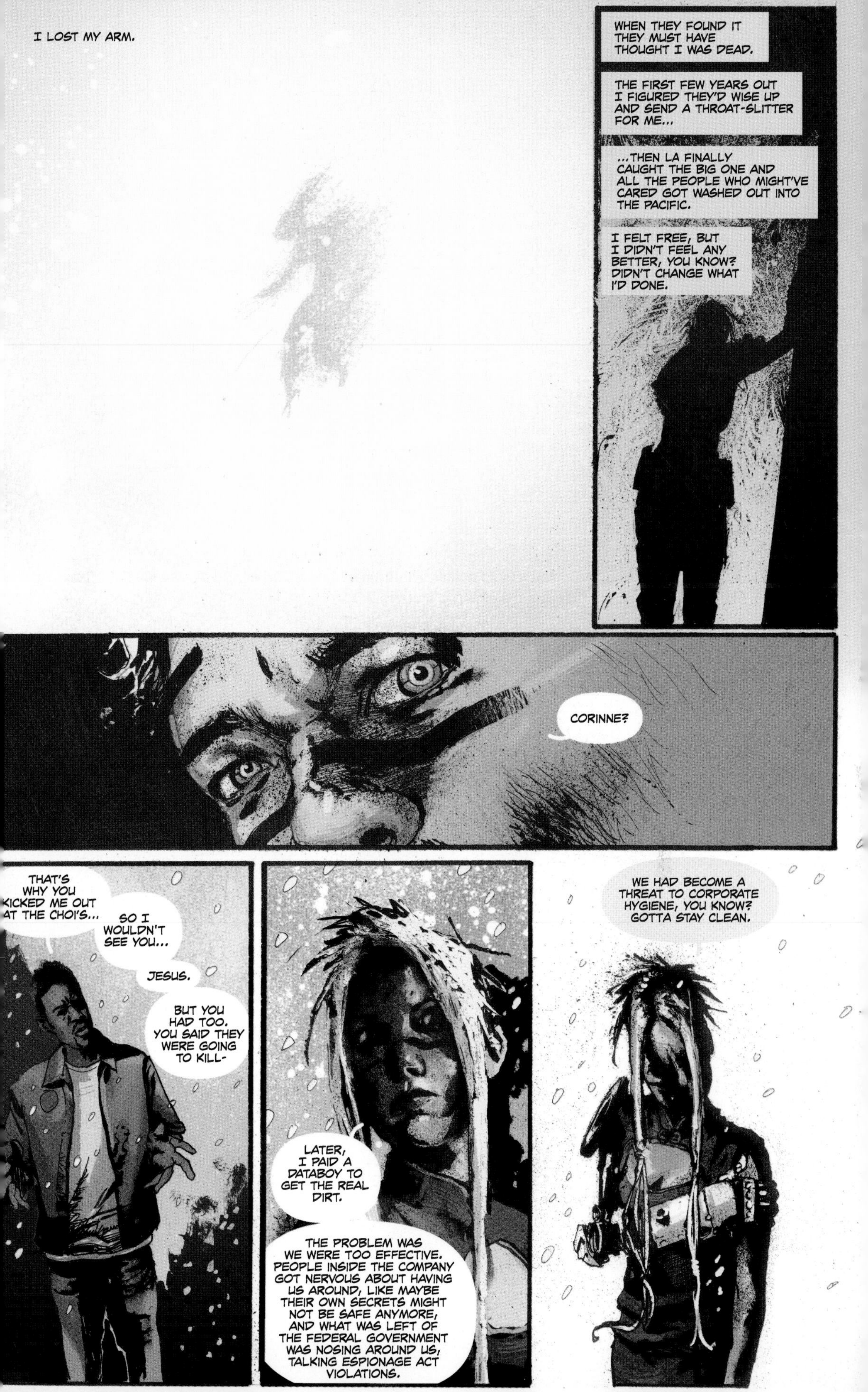

I LOST MY ARM.
WHEN THEY FOUND IT THEY MUST HAVE THOUGHT I WAS DEAD.
THE FIRST FEW YEARS OUT I FIGURED THEY'D WISE UP AND SEND A THROAT-SLITTER FOR ME...
...THEN LA FINALLY CAUGHT THE BIG ONE AND ALL THE PEOPLE WHO MIGHT'VE CARED GOT WASHED OUT INTO THE PACIFIC.
I FELT FREE, BUT I DIDN'T FEEL ANY BETTER, YOU KNOW? DIDN'T CHANGE WHAT I'D DONE.
CORINNE?
THAT'S WHY YOU KICKED ME OUT AT THE CHOI'S...
SO I WOULDN'T SEE YOU...
JESUS.
BUT YOU HAD TOO. YOU SAID THEY WERE GOING TO KILL-
LATER, I PAID A DATABOY TO GET THE REAL DIRT.
THE PROBLEM WAS WE WERE TOO EFFECTIVE. PEOPLE INSIDE THE COMPANY GOT NERVOUS ABOUT HAVING US AROUND, LIKE MAYBE THEIR OWN SECRETS MIGHT NOT BE SAFE ANYMORE, AND WHAT WAS LEFT OF THE FEDERAL GOVERNMENT WAS NOSING AROUND US, TALKING ESPIONAGE ACT VIOLATIONS.
WE HAD BECOME A THREAT TO CORPORATE HYGIENE, YOU KNOW? GOTTA STAY CLEAN.

THIS IS A LONG TIME AGO, RIGHT? WHY WERE YOU CRYING WHEN I WALKED UP?

I AM RELEASED.

YOU ARE NOT FORGIVEN.

NEXT TIME, DON'T KILL YOUR FRIENDS.

I JUST... NOTHING, REALLY.

LET'S GO GET THAT CREEP BEFORE HE WANDERS OFF.

SHIT! GONE.

...OH NO. SEE THOSE TRACKS?

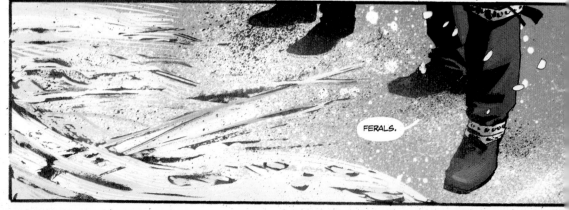

FERALS.

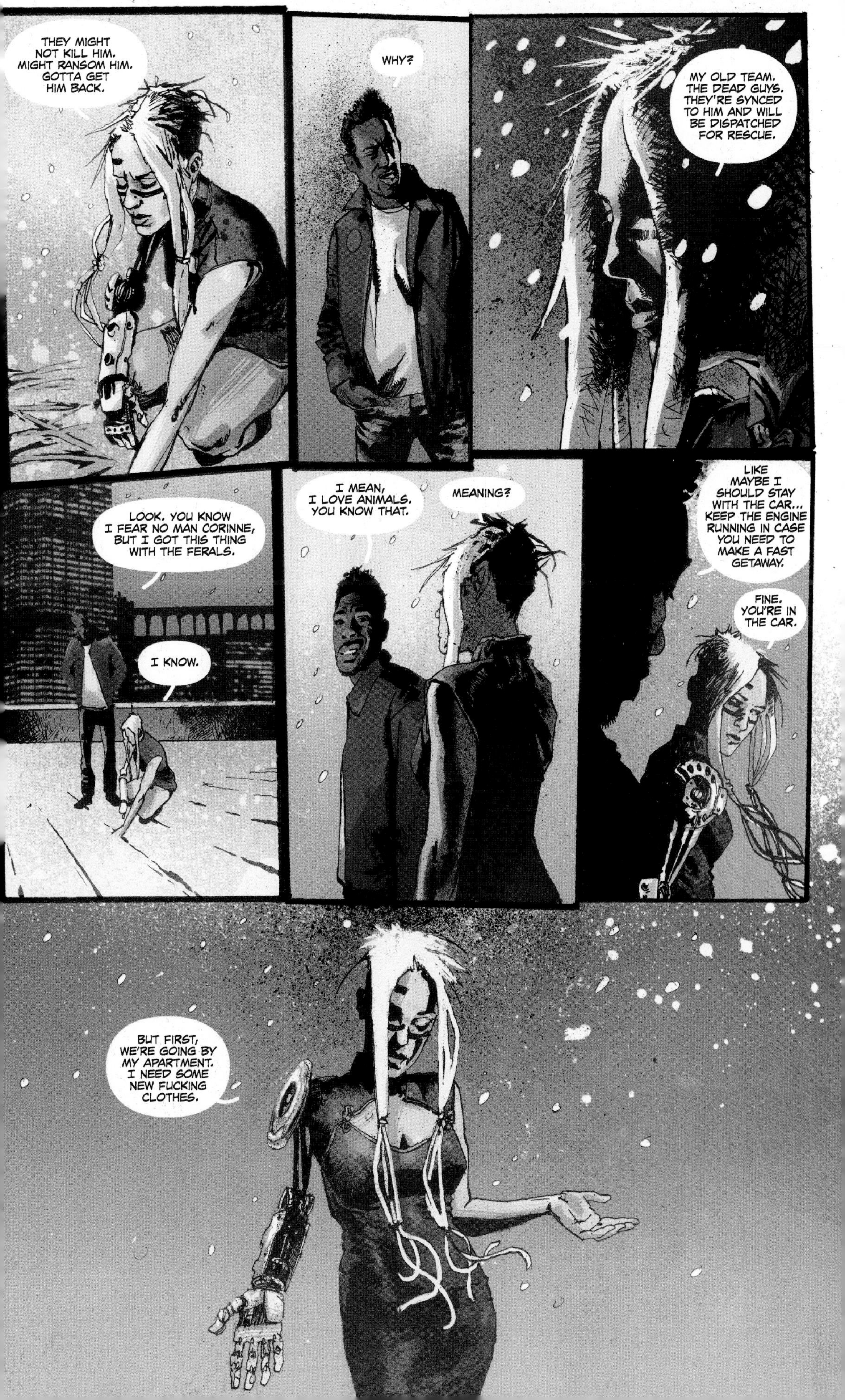
THEY MIGHT NOT KILL HIM. MIGHT RANSOM HIM. GOTTA GET HIM BACK.
WHY?
MY OLD TEAM. THE DEAD GUYS. THEY'RE SYNCED TO HIM AND WILL BE DISPATCHED FOR RESCUE.
LOOK. YOU KNOW I FEAR NO MAN CORINNE, BUT I GOT THIS THING WITH THE FERALS.
I KNOW.
I MEAN, I LOVE ANIMALS. YOU KNOW THAT.
MEANING?
LIKE MAYBE I SHOULD STAY WITH THE CAR... KEEP THE ENGINE RUNNING IN CASE YOU NEED TO MAKE A FAST GETAWAY.
FINE. YOU'RE IN THE CAR.
BUT FIRST, WE'RE GOING BY MY APARTMENT. I NEED SOME NEW FUCKING CLOTHES.

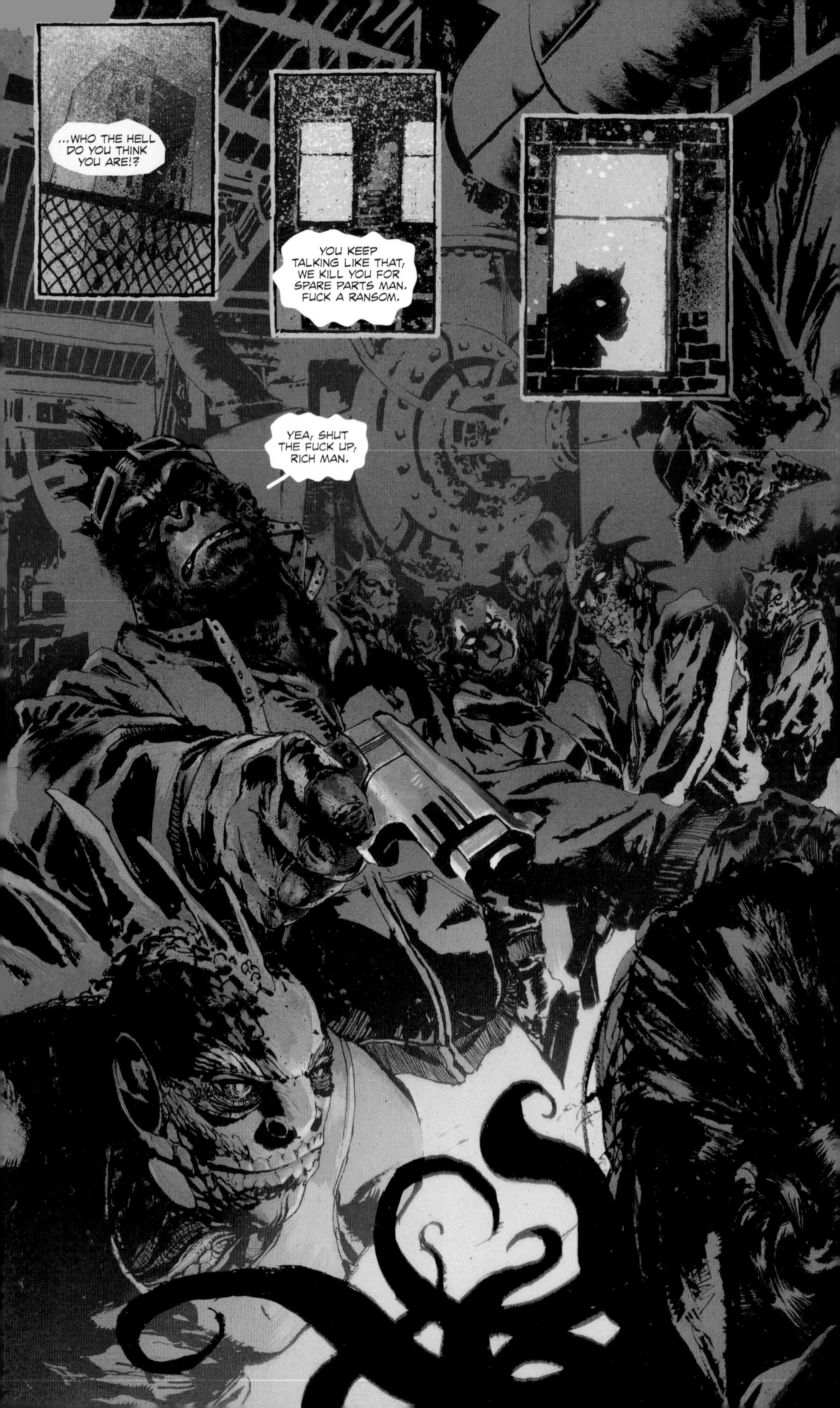
...WHO THE HELL DO YOU THINK YOU ARE!?
YOU KEEP TALKING LIKE THAT, WE KILL YOU FOR SPARE PARTS MAN. FUCK A RANSOM.
YEA, SHUT THE FUCK UP, RICH MAN.

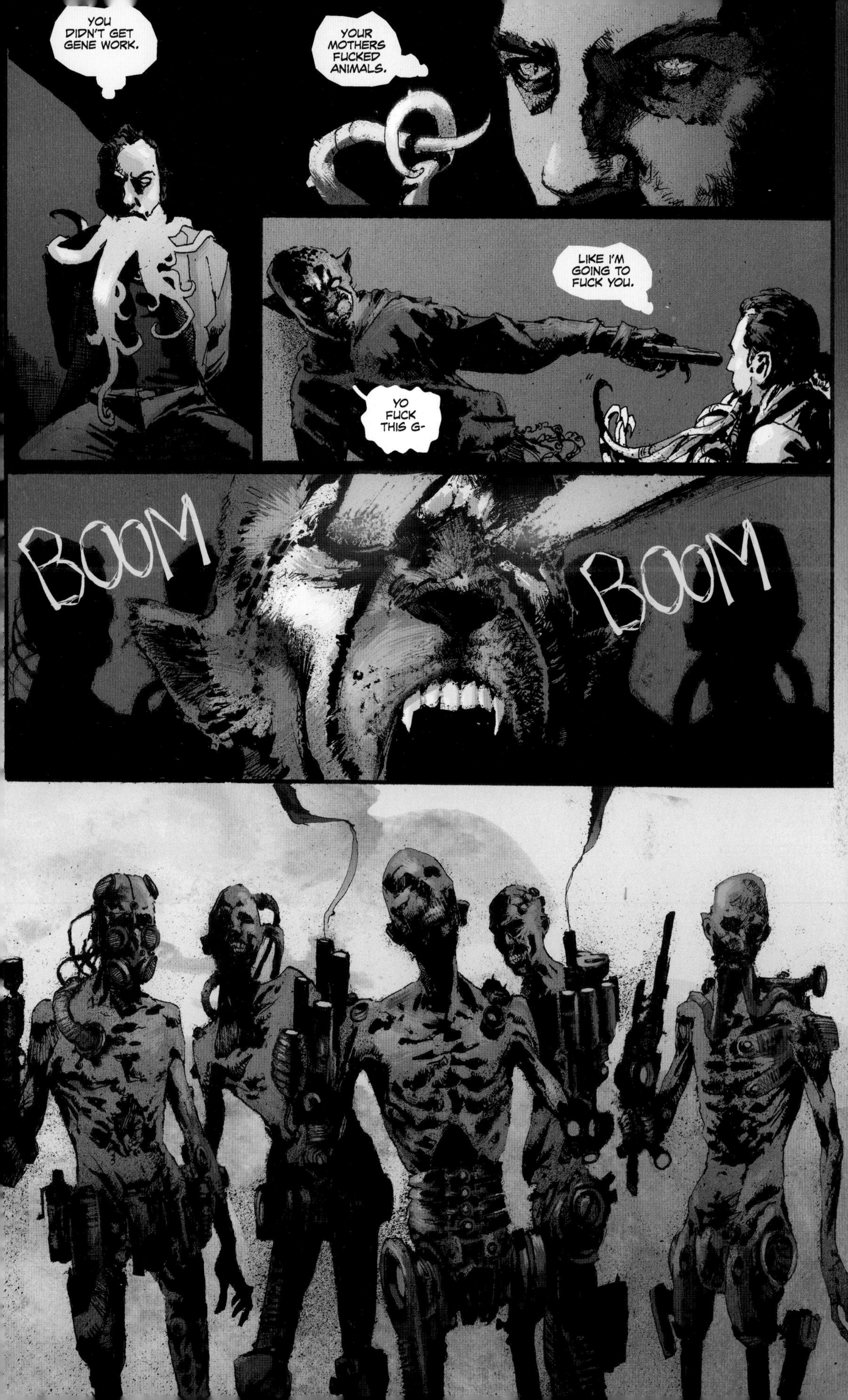
YOU DIDN'T GET GENE WORK.
YOUR MOTHERS FUCKED ANIMALS.
LIKE I'M GOING TO FUCK YOU.
YO FUCK THIS G-
BOOM
BOOM

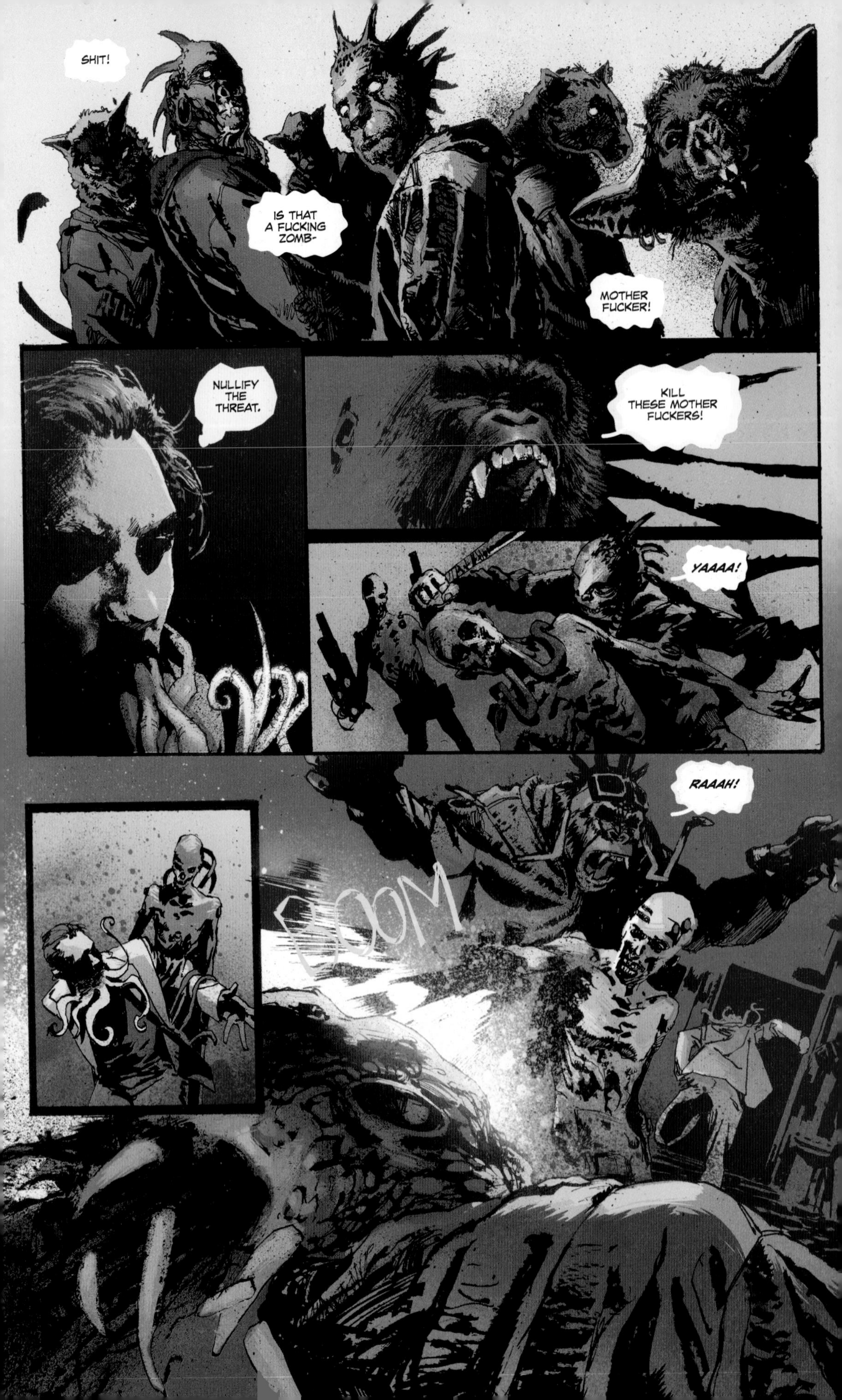
SHIT!
IS THAT A FUCKING ZOMB-
MOTHER FUCKER!
NULLIFY THE THREAT.
KILL THESE MOTHER FUCKERS!
YAAAA!
RAAAH!
BOOOM

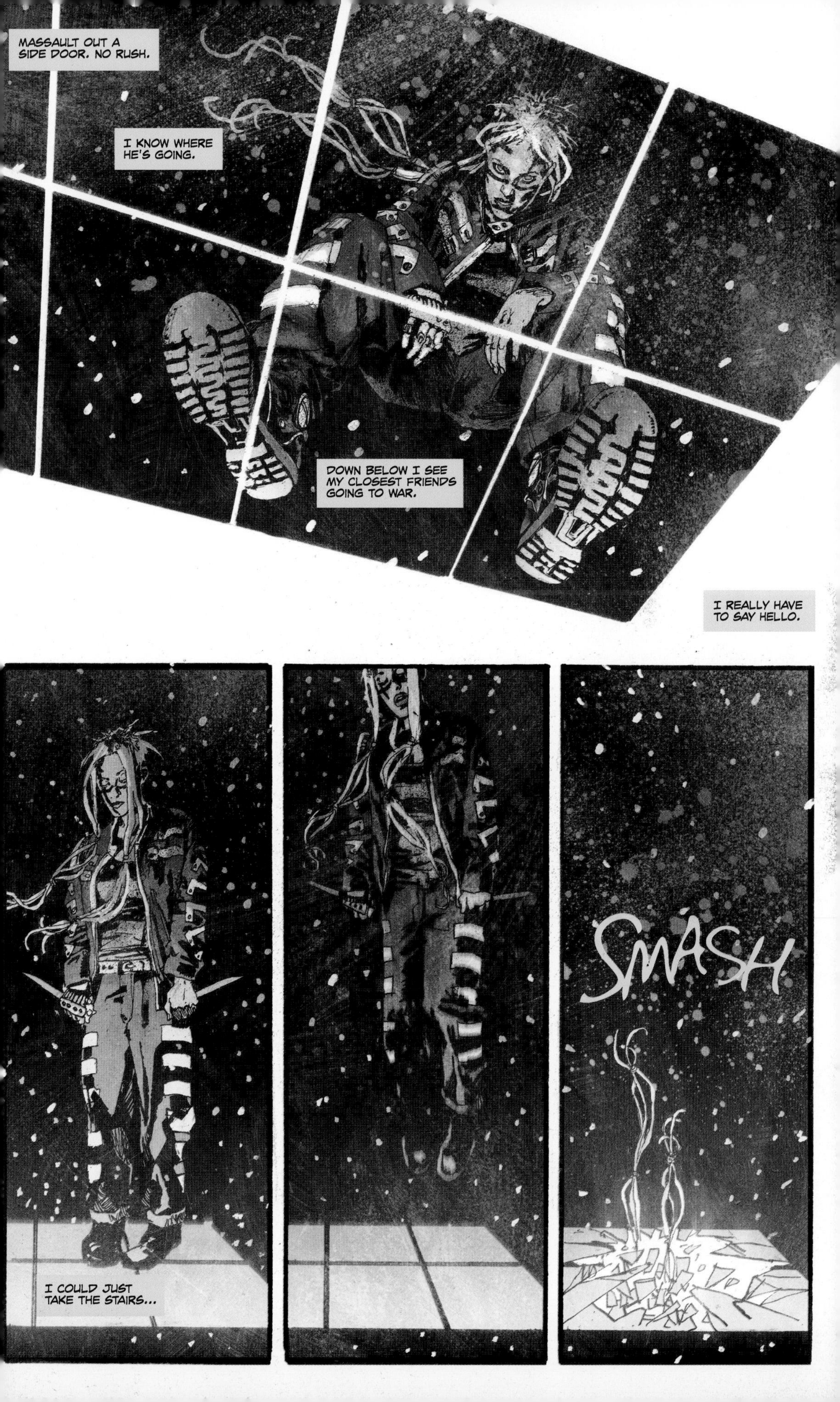
MASSAULT OUT A SIDE DOOR. NO RUSH.
I KNOW WHERE HE'S GOING.
DOWN BELOW I SEE MY CLOSEST FRIENDS GOING TO WAR.
I REALLY HAVE TO SAY HELLO.
I COULD JUST TAKE THE STAIRS...
SMASH

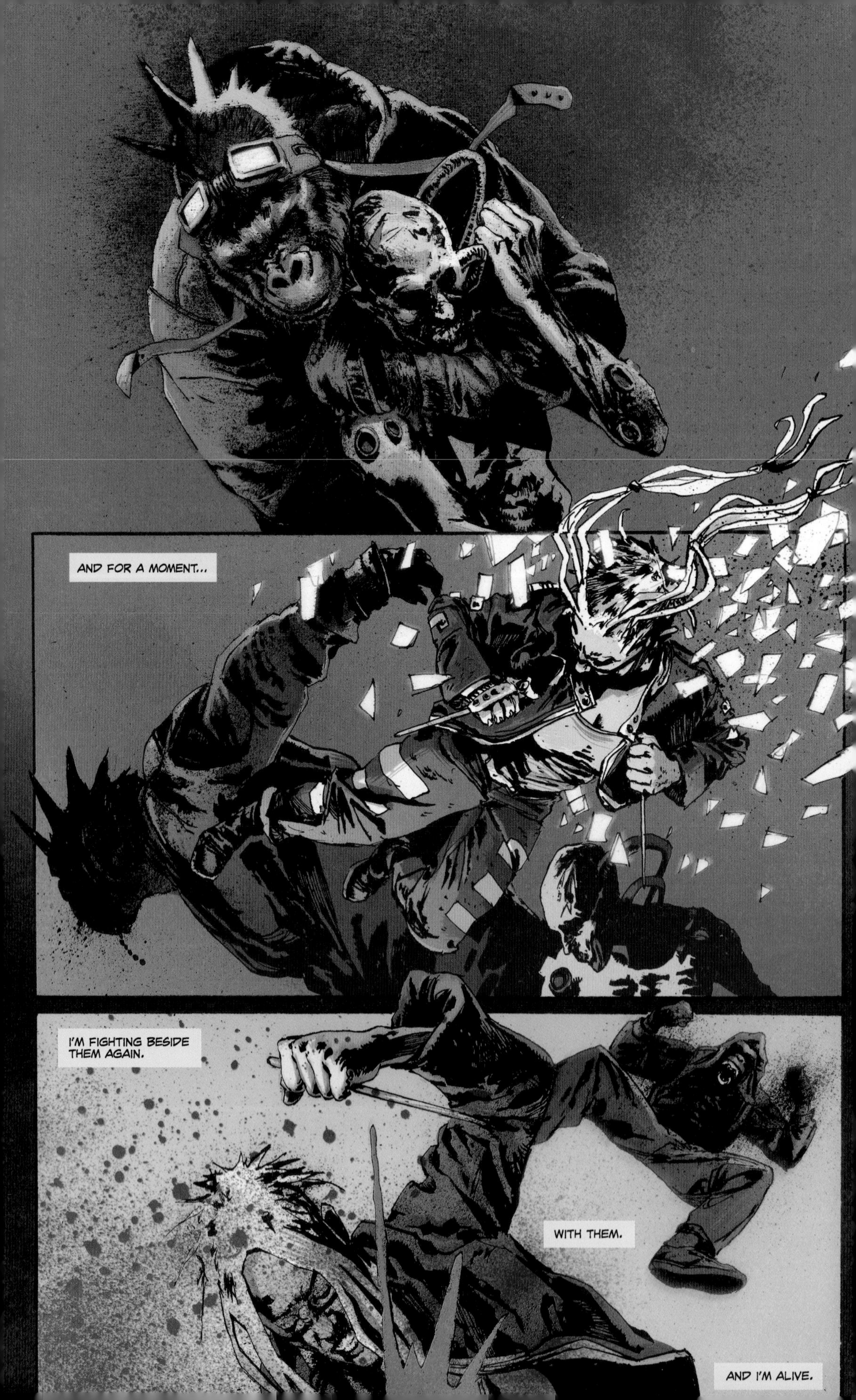
AND FOR A MOMENT...
I'M FIGHTING BESIDE THEM AGAIN.
WITH THEM.
AND I'M ALIVE.

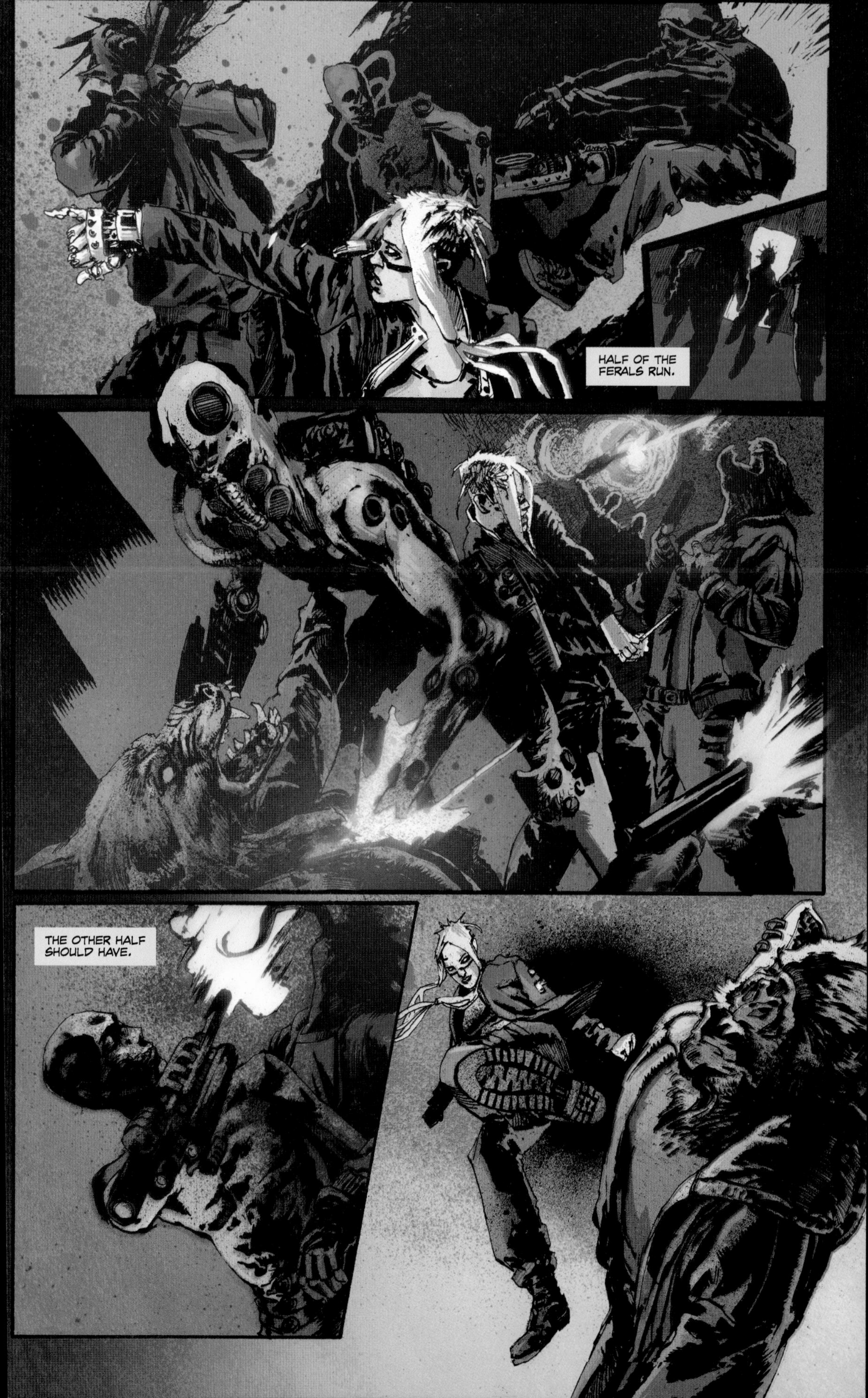
HALF OF THE FERALS RUN.
THE OTHER HALF SHOULD HAVE.

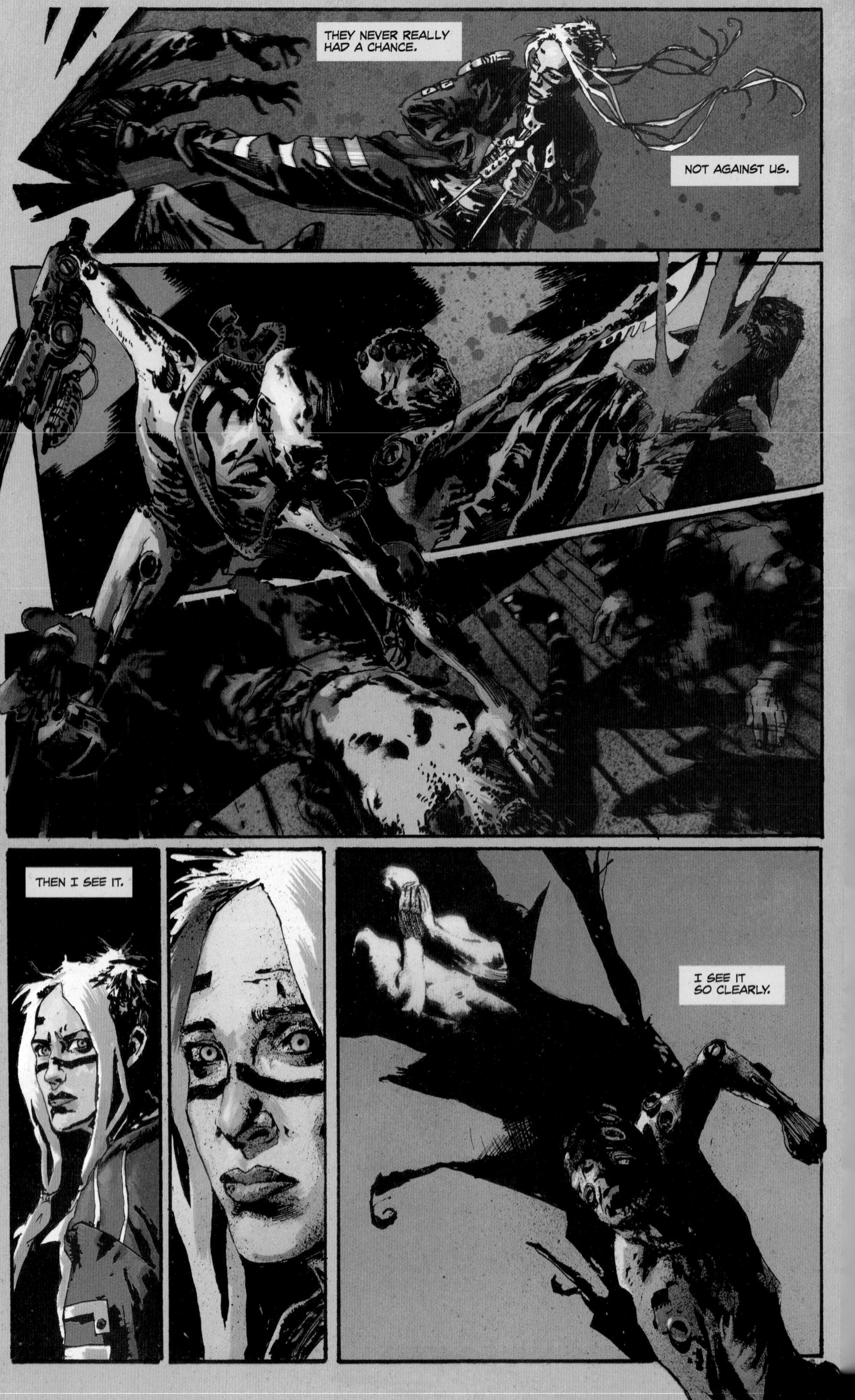
THEY NEVER REALLY HAD A CHANCE.
NOT AGAINST US.
THEN I SEE IT.
I SEE IT SO CLEARLY.

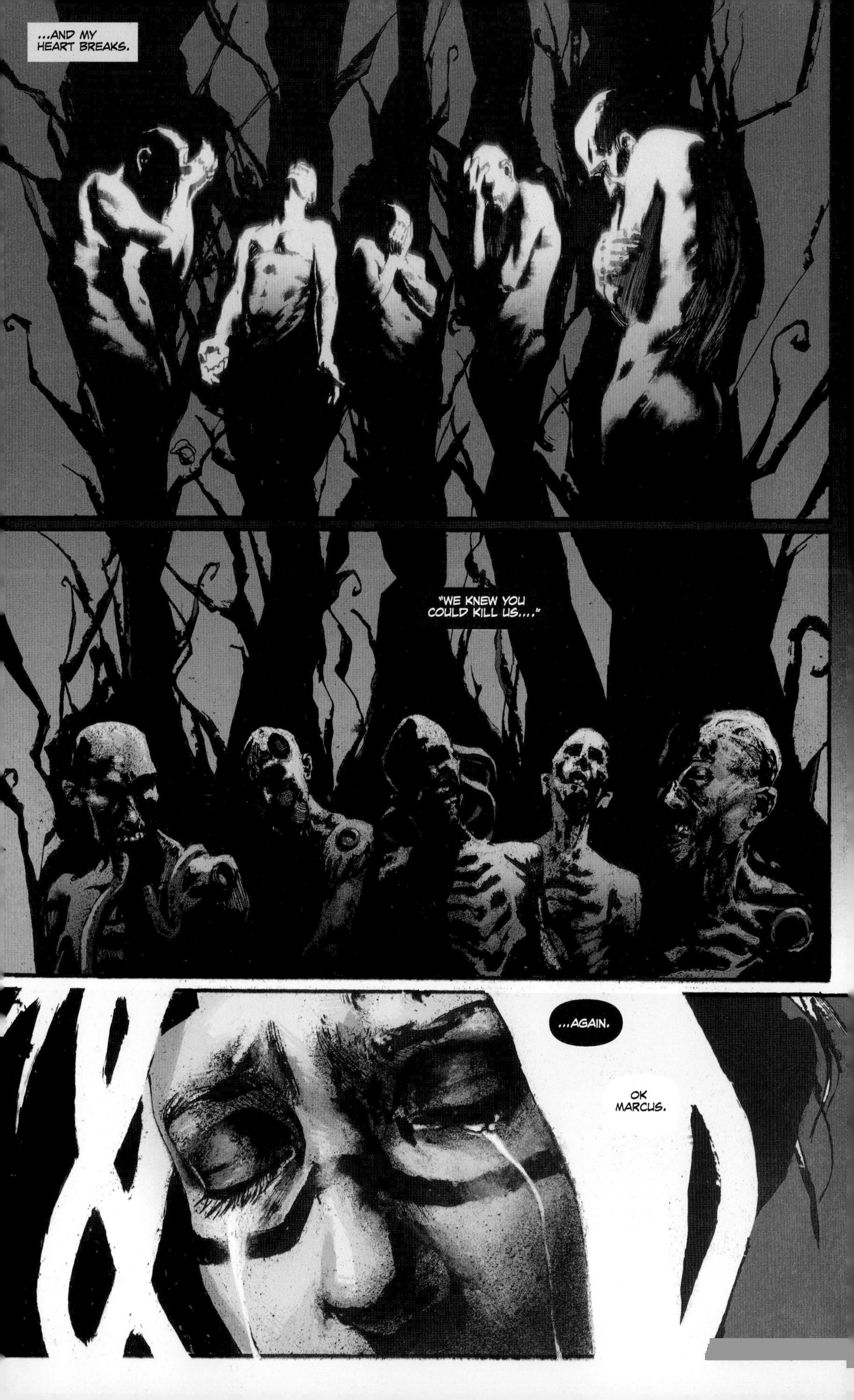
...AND MY HEART BREAKS.
"WE KNEW YOU COULD KILL US...."
...AGAIN.
OK MARCUS.

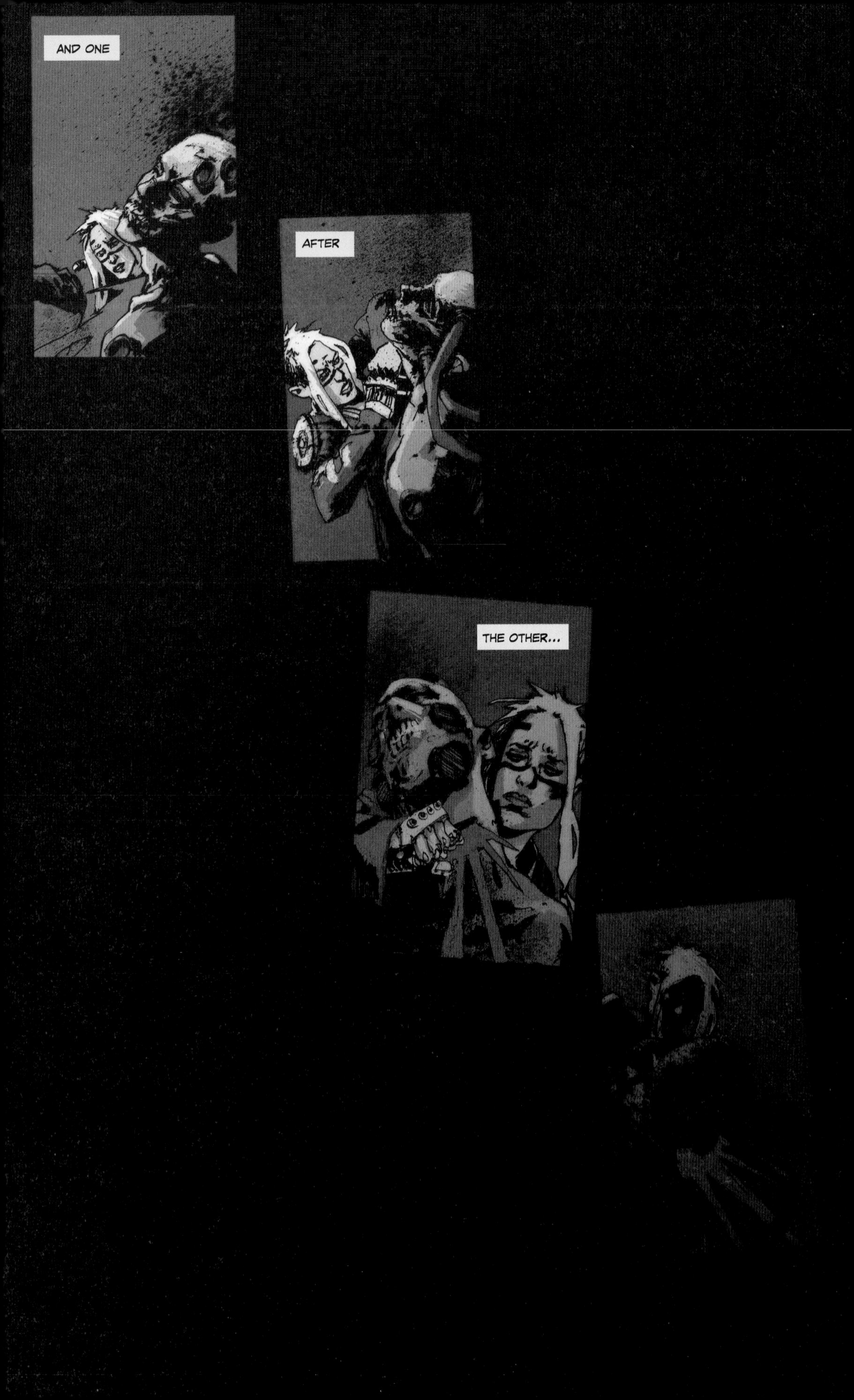
AND ONE
AFTER
THE OTHER...

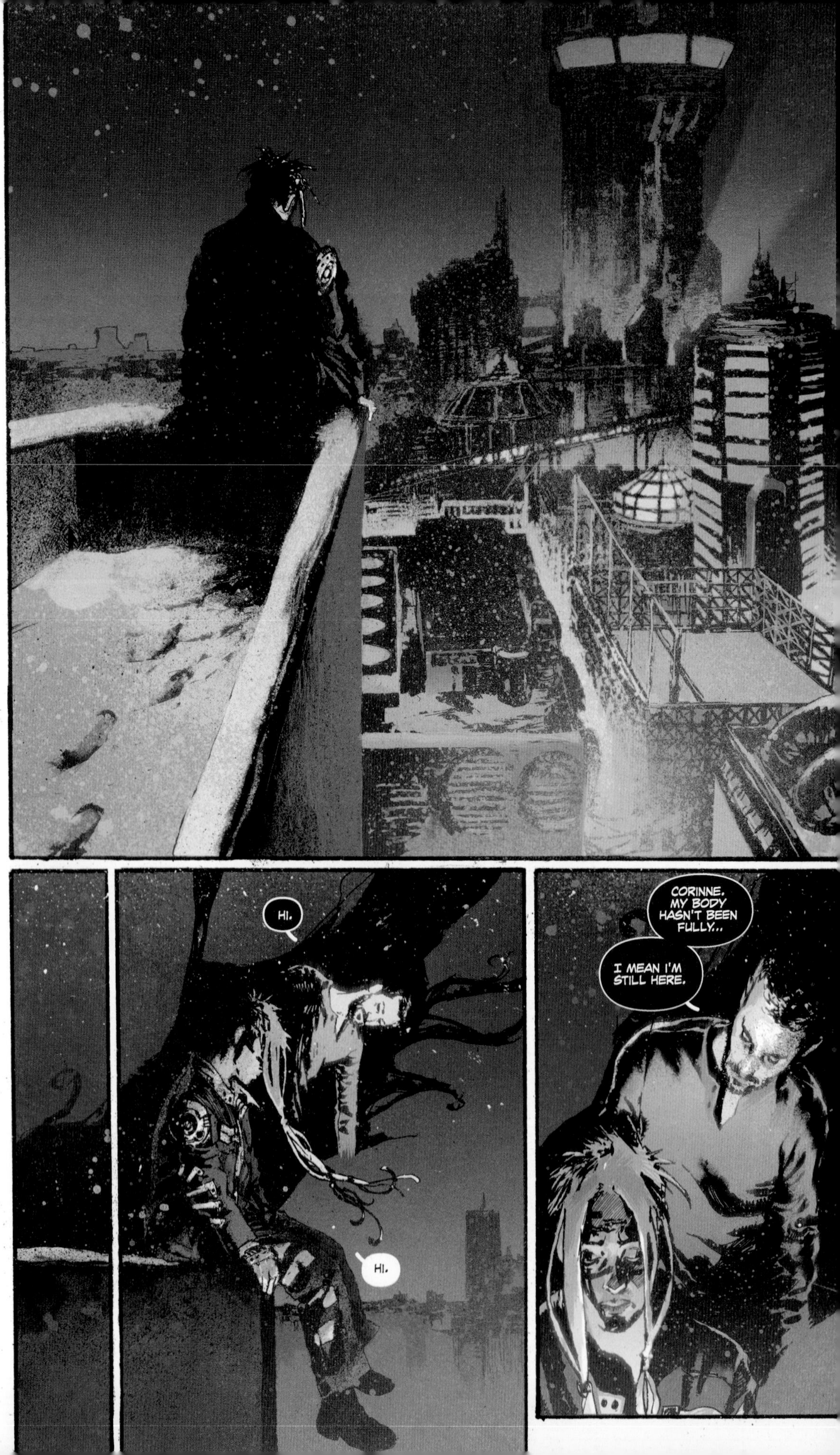
HI.
HI.
CORINNE. MY BODY HASN'T BEEN FULLY...
I MEAN I'M STILL HERE.

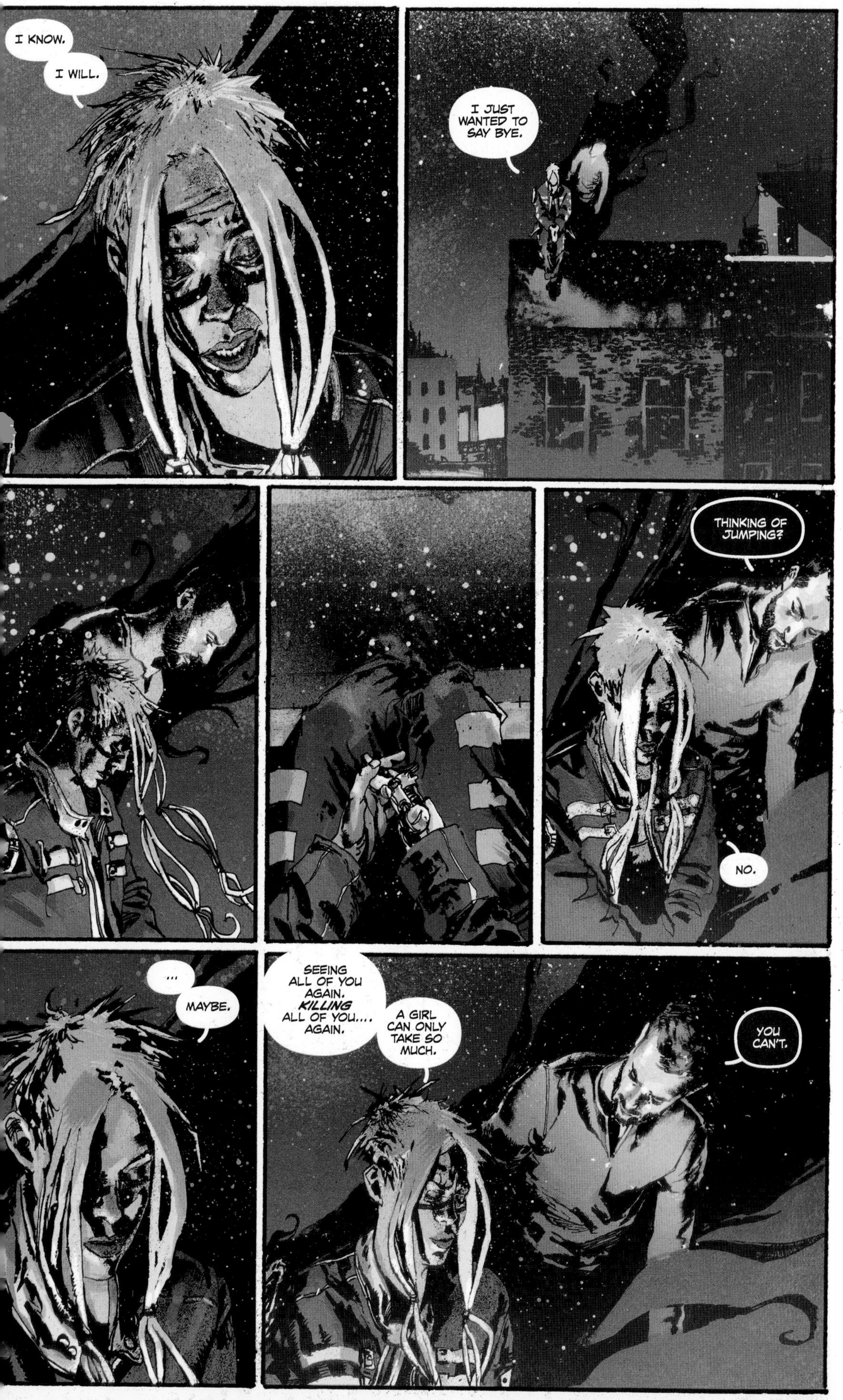
I KNOW.
I WILL.
I JUST WANTED TO SAY BYE.
THINKING OF JUMPING?
NO.
...
MAYBE.
SEEING ALL OF YOU AGAIN. *KILLING* ALL OF YOU.... AGAIN.
A GIRL CAN ONLY TAKE SO MUCH.
YOU CAN'T.

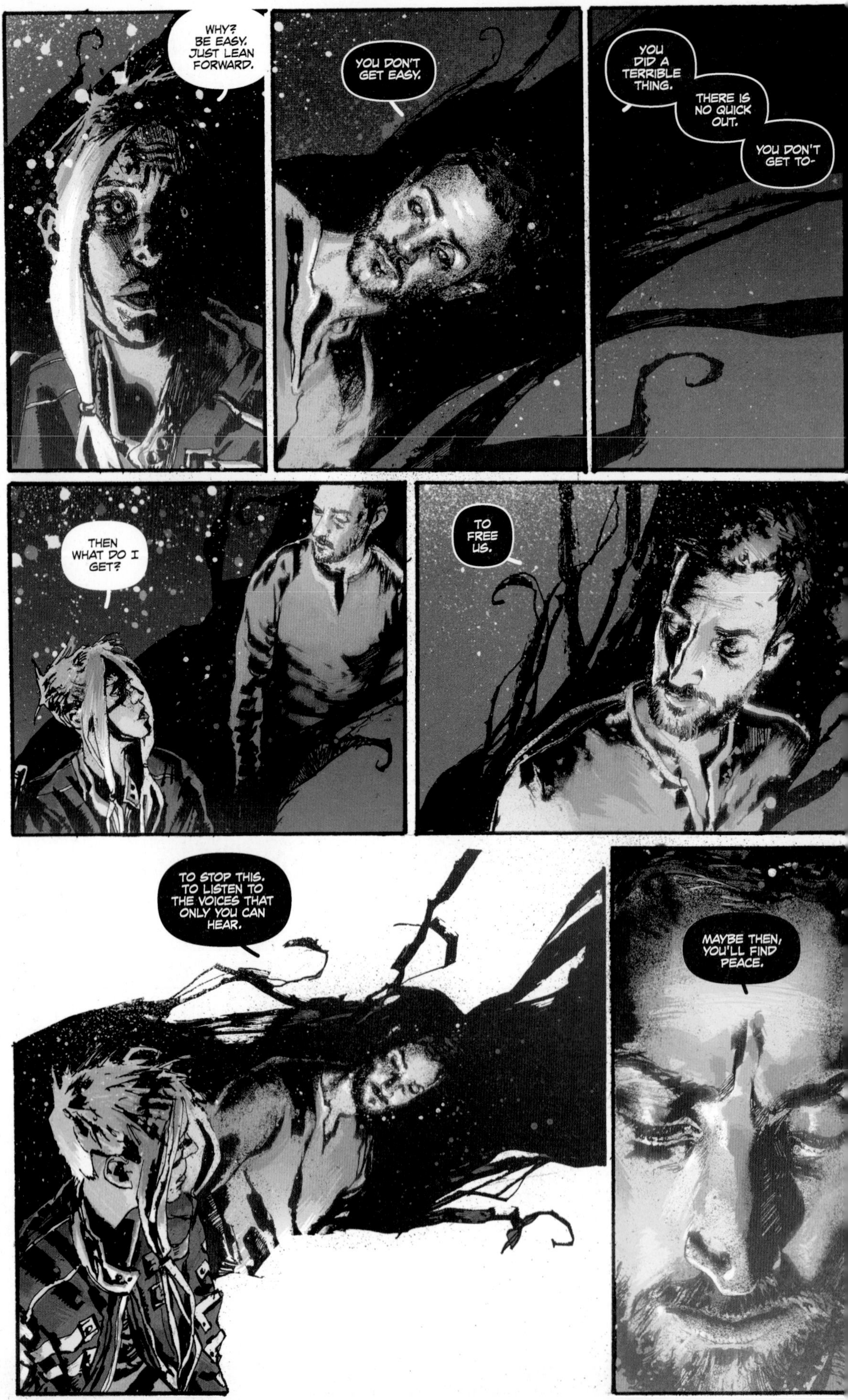
WHY? BE EASY. JUST LEAN FORWARD.
YOU DON'T GET EASY.
YOU DID A TERRIBLE THING.
THERE IS NO QUICK OUT.
YOU DON'T GET TO-
THEN WHAT DO I GET?
TO FREE US.
TO STOP THIS. TO LISTEN TO THE VOICES THAT ONLY YOU CAN HEAR.
MAYBE THEN, YOU'LL FIND PEACE.

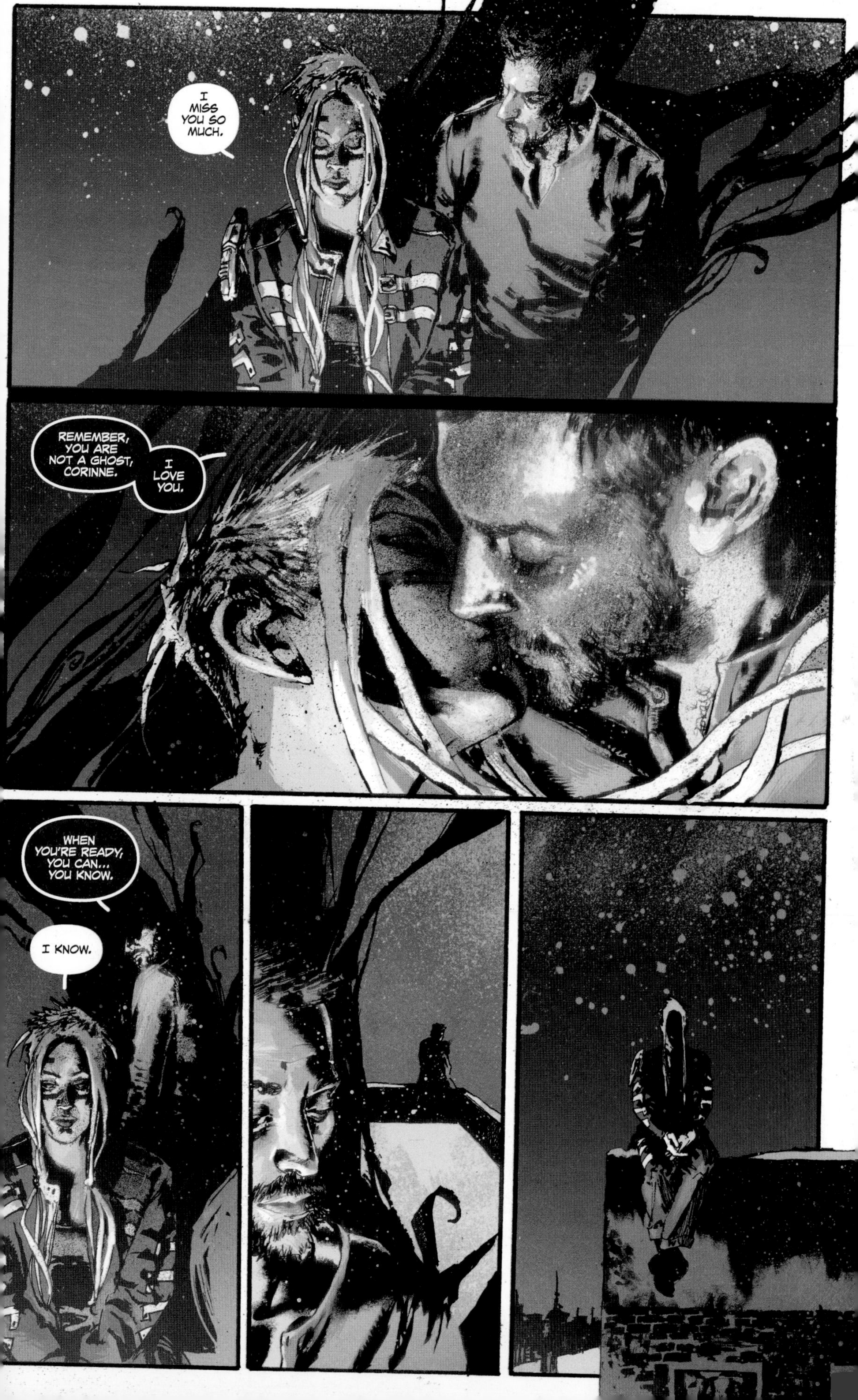
I MISS YOU SO MUCH.
REMEMBER, YOU ARE NOT A GHOST, CORINNE.
I LOVE YOU.
WHEN YOU'RE READY, YOU CAN... YOU KNOW.
I KNOW.

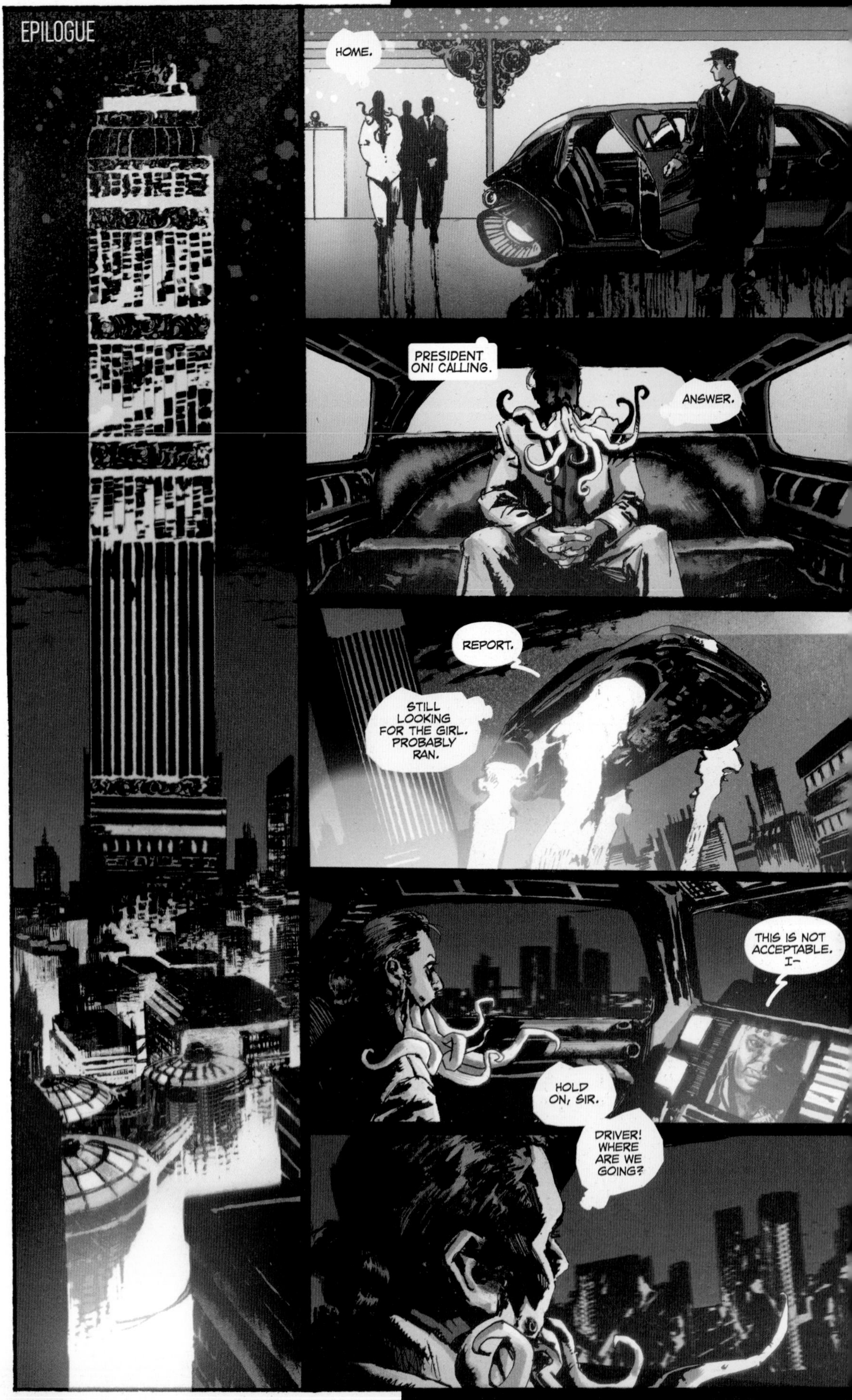
EPILOGUE
HOME.
PRESIDENT ONI CALLING.
ANSWER.
REPORT.
STILL LOOKING FOR THE GIRL. PROBABLY RAN.
THIS IS NOT ACCEPTABLE. I–
HOLD ON, SIR.
DRIVER! WHERE ARE WE GOING?

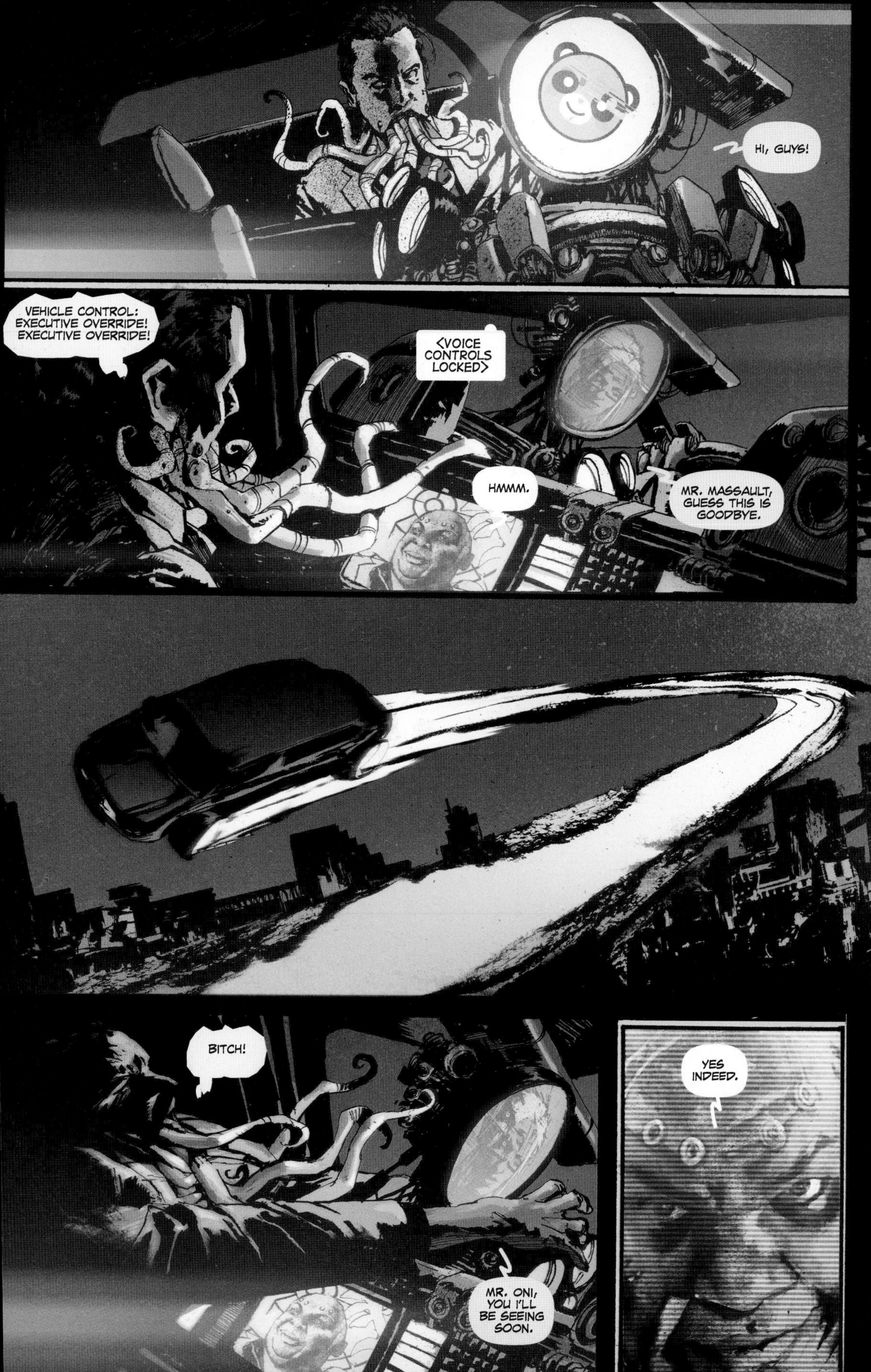

HI, GUYS!
VEHICLE CONTROL: EXECUTIVE OVERRIDE! EXECUTIVE OVERRIDE!
<VOICE CONTROLS LOCKED>
HMMM.
MR. MASSAULT, GUESS THIS IS GOODBYE.
BITCH!
MR. ONI, YOU I'LL BE SEEING SOON.
YES INDEED.

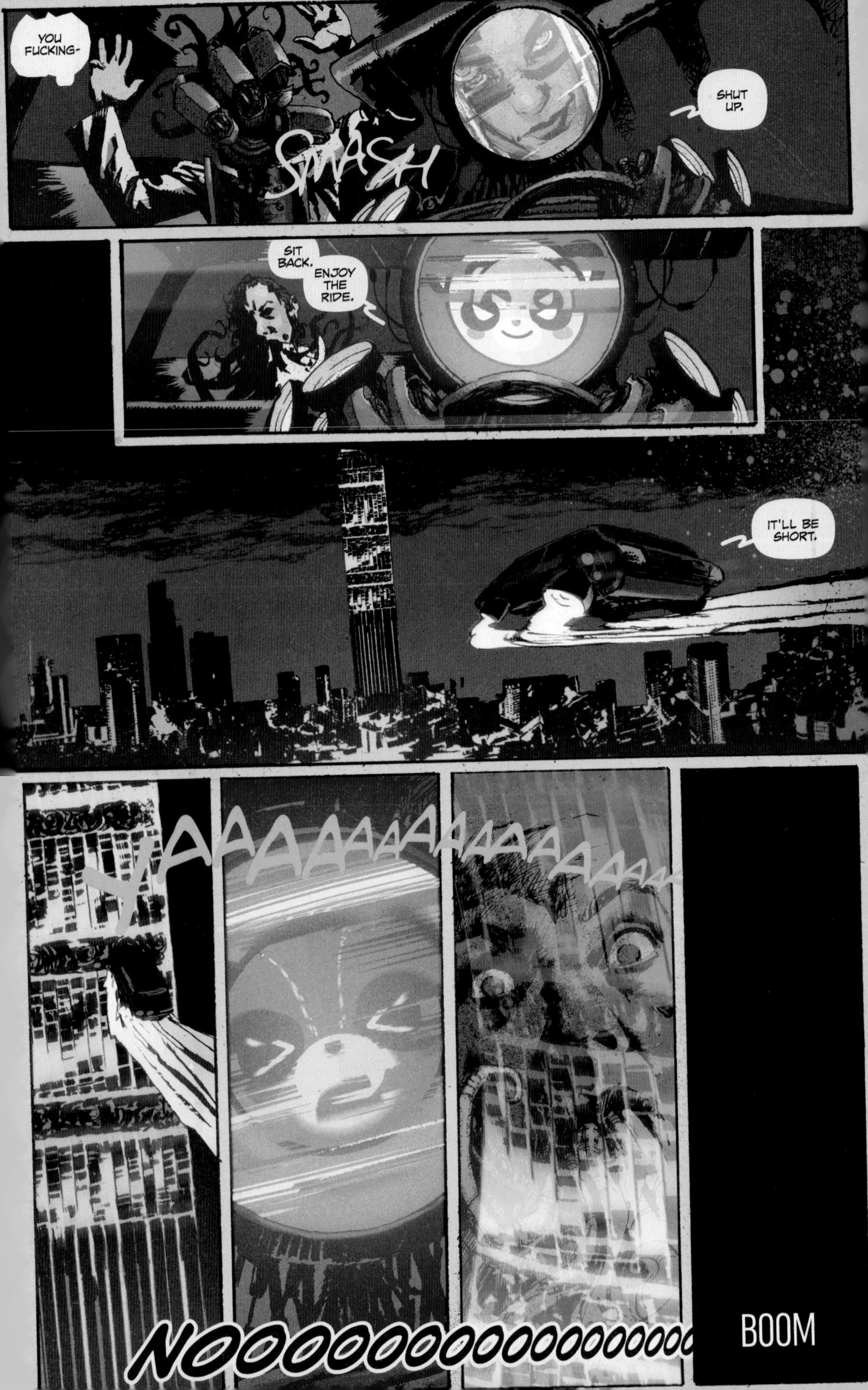
YOU FUCKING-
SMASH
SHUT UP.
SIT BACK.
ENJOY THE RIDE.
IT'LL BE SHORT.
YAAAAAAAAAAAAAAAA
NOOOOOOOOOOOOOOOO
BOOM